SHIN NIHONGO NO KISO II

MAIN TEXTBOOK ROMANIZED EDITION

新日本語の基礎II 本冊 ローマ字版

SHIN NIHONGO NO KISO II

MAIN TEXTBOOK ROMANIZED EDITION

新日本語の基礎II 本冊 ローマ字版

AOTS

THE ASSOCIATION FOR OVERSEAS TECHNICAL SCHOLARSHIP (AOTS)

3A Corporation

Shoei Bldg., 6-3, Sarugaku-cho 2-chome, Chiyoda-ku, Tokyo 101, Japan

First published in Japan by 3A Corporation 1993

ISBN4-906224-86-5 C0081
Printed in Japan

序

財団法人海外技術者研修協会は、1959年に設立されて以来、発展途上諸国の技術研修生の受入れ、研修事業を行ってきた。1993年３月現在、受入研修生数は累計で約５万５千人、対象国150か国に及んでいる。

研修生が、日本で生活し研修を受ける時の最大の悩みは言葉である。日本語が分からなければ、日本になじめないし、日本を知ることも難しい。そして、彼等の究極の目的である工場実習の成果も十分には期待できない。

研修の成果と日本語習得の度合いとは、多くの場合、比例関係にあるというのが、私たちの長年の経験にもとづく結論である。在日期間が比較的短い研修生であっても、私たちが日本語教育を重視してきたのはそのためである。

協会の日本語教育は、企業の実地研修に先立って行われる一般研修の一環として実施されている。一般研修の中心は６週間コースであるが、その中で100時間を日本語学習に充てている。新しい外国語を学ぶには到底十分とは言えないこの100時間で、一定の成果をあげるのは容易なことではない。教授法、カリキュラム、教材等々全般にわたる有機的な研究開発が必要であることは言うまでもない。協会の「日本語の基礎」シリーズは、その長年の積み上げの足跡でもある。

この度、『新日本語の基礎Ⅱ』が完成、発刊することになったが、これは、1989年11月の『新日本語の基礎Ⅰ』に続く、旧版『日本語の基礎Ⅱ』の改訂版である。10年余にわたり好評をいただいてきた旧版だが、時代の流れに対応する語彙等の刷新、各単元の整理と充実、基礎Ⅰから基礎Ⅱの学習に進む際の円滑なつながりなどに一層の改善を試みた。協会その他の教育現場での、試行と検討に十二分の時間をかけたため、発刊が計画より大幅に遅れてしまったことをお詫びしたい。

今後とも、関係者のご助言、ご指導をいただきながら、よりすぐれた日本語教材の開発に努力致したいと考えている。

1993年７月

財団法人　海外技術者研修協会
理事長　山本長昭

改訂にあたって

『日本語の基礎Ⅰ』と『日本語の基礎Ⅱ』はその作成時期において、10年近くの開きがある。そのためⅠからⅡを通してみると、内容的に統一を欠く面が残った。このような内容の是正と共に、これまでの教授法の反省を踏まえて、1985年より、『日本語の基礎Ⅰ・Ⅱ』の全面的改訂に踏み切った。改訂にあたり、留意した点は以下の通りである。

1．まず、基本的で使用頻度の高い日本語の文型、語彙、表現などを再検討し、内容の刷新を図った。更に、文型、例文、会話、練習など、教科書全体の構成を立て直した。

2．『日本語の基礎』の文型練習の積み上げによる文型、語彙の定着の良さという長所を生かしながらも、会話の実際的な運用力が向上するように「練習C」を加えた。

3．研修生及び、技術研修先の会社や工場の方々の協力を仰いで、研修生が来日してから帰国するまでの言語活動を調査した。この中から、研修生が日本語を使用する場面、状況などを選び、「会話」に反映させた。「会話」は簡潔な表現で、しかも実用性が高く、自然な日本語であることに留意した。

4．数課ごとの復習、文法事項のまとめ、関連語彙などを加え、学習者、教授者にも教科書として使いやすくなるように配慮した。

5．日本語学習の初級段階における聞き取り力の養成を重視し、「問題」に聞き取りの内容を多く取り入れた。また、読解力を養う導入として、短い内容の読み物を配した。

『新日本語の基礎Ⅱ』は、上記の意図に基づく初級レベル後期の日本語教科書である。学習時間は約100時間である。２年間の試用期間を置き、検討、補正を重ね、発刊に至った。しかし、まだなお不十分な点があると思われる。多くの方々の御批判、御助言をいただき、より一層の充実を目指したい。

凡　例

Ⅰ．教科書の構成

この教科書は本冊、分冊、及びカセットテープより成る。本冊はローマ字版と漢字かなまじり版の２種類がある。分冊は英語、インドネシア語、タイ語、スペイン語、韓国語、中国語がある。他の言語についても、順次完成させていく予定である。

この教科書は日本語を聞く、話すということを中心に構成されている。従って、ひらがな、かたかな、漢字などの文字の読み書きの指導は含んでいない。

Ⅱ．教科書の内容及び使い方

１．本冊

１）本課

『新日本語の基礎Ⅰ』（全25課）に続く第26課から第50課までの構成で、内容は以下のように分けられる。

① 文型

その課で学ぶ基本文型を提出順序に従って掲げてある。

② 例文

基本文型を質問及び答えという対話の形式で表してある。文型が実際にどのように用いられているかを談話の最小単位の形で示したものである。また、その課で扱われた副詞や接続詞などの使い方をできるだけ取り上げた。基本文型に示された以外のその課で学ぶ学習項目も入っている。

③ 会話

会話はセンターで６週間の一般研修を終えた研修生達が研修先へ赴き、日本の生活になじむと共に、日本人との交流を深め、無事技術研修を修了し、帰国するまでの話をまとめてある。各課の学習内容を密着させた形で日常生活によく使用される挨拶などの慣用的表現を加えて作成した。場面と談話の流れをよく理解し、やり取りができるように練習することが望ましい。余裕があれば、分冊の関連語彙表や視聴覚教材などを利用して、この会話を発展させ、会話力の向上に役立たせてほしい。

④ 練習

練習はA，B，Cの三段階に分かれる。練習Aは文法的な構造を理解しやすいように、視覚的効果を考えてレイアウトしてある。基本的な文型を語彙の代入という形で定着を図ると共に、活用形の作り方、後続句への品詞別の接続のし方などを学びやすく配慮してある。

練習Bは様々なドリル形式を用いて、基本文型の定着の強化を図るものである。の印のついた番号は絵チャートを用いる練習を示す。

練習Cは練習A，Bの基礎的な文型練習が円滑に出来るようになった段階で行う短い会話練習ドリルである。文型が実際にどのような場面、状況の中で、その機能を果たすかを学ばせ、発話力を高めるために設けた。教科書のまま読み上げたり、単にリピートするだけではなく、クラスのレベルや状況に合わせて、モデル文の代入肢を変えたり、さらに練習の展開を図るような工夫が望まれる。

⑤ 問題

問題には、聞き取り（マークの箇所）と文法問題とがある。聞き取りはカセットテープを聞いて、短い質問に答える問題と、短い会話のやりとりを聞いて内容の要点を把握する問題とがある。これらの問題は聞き取りの力の強化を図るために設けた。文法問題は、語彙やその課で学んだ文法事項の理解度を確認するものである。読解問題は既習語彙、文型を使って書き下した平易な文を読んで、その内容に関する質問に答えるものが多い。

2）復習

数課ごとに学習事項の要点を再整理するために設けた。

3）まとめ

本冊の終わりに、「助詞」、「フォームの使い方」、「動詞・形容詞のいろいろな使い方」、「自動詞と他動詞」、「副詞・副詞的表現」及び「接続のいろいろ」として文法事項をまとめ、例文を掲げた。

4）索引

各課の新出語彙・表現などを、各々の初出課と共に示した。

2．分冊

分冊はPARTⅠからPARTⅢまでの3つの内容に分かれる。

1）PARTⅠ　語彙及び訳

各課の新出語彙とその各国語訳が載せてある。

2）PARTⅡ　関連語彙及び訳

必須語彙ではないが、役に立つと思われる語彙を中心に、12項目に分けてまとめた。

3）PARTⅢ　翻訳

本冊中の文型、例文、会話及びまとめの部分の各国語訳である。

3．表記上の注意

1）表記は原則として、ヘボン式による。

撥音はすべて"n"で表記した。

2）長母音は以下のように表記した。

ā、ii、ū、ei（ē）、ō

例　tokei、onēsan

3）文は分かち書きとした。原則として助詞は離したが、助詞を取り込んで1語と認められる語は分かち書きをしない。

例　nanika、desukara

4）接頭語、接尾語、助数詞のほか、複合語などをハイフンでつないだ。

例　o-shigoto、Tanaka-san、25-sai

hana-ya、benkyō-shimasu

ただし、上記の内でも、造語性が弱いもの、また1語として数えたいものにはハイフンを用いない。

例　hitotsu、hitori、ocha、asagohan、oyasuminasai

5）文頭、および固有名詞とその複合語などの語頭に大文字を用いた。

6）外国人の名前は、その国で用いられている慣用的ローマ字表記に従った。

7）外来語の一部は原音に近い表記をした。

例　pātii、fōku

4．かっこの用法

分冊各国語版におけるかっこの用法は以下の通りである。

1）［ ］ ① その動詞と結び付きの強い語句の一例を示す。

例 kiemasu [denki ga ～]、okuremasu [jikan ni ～]

② 省略できる語句を示す。

例 Gokurōsama [deshita].

2）（ ） 同義あるいは類義の表現、語句を示す。

例 sebiro (sūtsu)

3）【 】 別の語句と置き換えができる部分を示す。

例 Yokattara,【issho ni iki】masen ka.

学習者の皆さんへ

1．言葉をよく覚え、文型を繰り返し練習しましょう。

この教科書の分冊には各課ごとに新しい言葉が提出されています。まず、その言葉をよく覚えましょう。その上で、文型の正しい意味を捕らえ、文の形がしっかり身につくまで繰り返し練習してください。特に「練習A，B」は実際に声を出して練習しましょう。

2．会話の練習を十分にしましょう。

文型練習の次は会話練習です。「会話」には日常生活で遭遇するさまざまな場面を取り上げました。こうした会話に慣れるために、まず「練習C」でよく練習しましょう。それから「会話」で場面や状況にふさわしいやり取りのコツを覚えましょう。

3．テープを何度も聞きましょう。

文型練習や会話練習の際は、正しい発音や抑揚などを身につけるために、テープを聞きながら、実際に声を出して練習しましょう。また、日本語の音やスピードに慣れ、内容を聞き取る力を養うためにも、テープを何度も聞きましょう。

4．必ず復習をしましょう。

授業で習ったことを忘れないためにも、必ずその日のうちに復習をしましょう。最後に「問題」で学んだことを確認し、聞き取りの力試しをしましょう。

5．実際に話してみましょう。

教室の中だけが学習の場ではありません。学んだ日本語を使って友達や一般の日本人に話しかけてみましょう。学んだものが役立てば、学習の励みにもなるでしょう。

以上のことを守って、この教科書の勉強を終えると、日常生活の基本的場面で必要とされる基本的語彙・表現が拡充され、初級日本語の基礎力が十分に養われます。焦らず根気よく勉強を続けてください。

Mokuji

Kono tekisuto no

Narong

Nagoya-jidōsha de jisshūchū

Watanabe

shain-ryō no kanrinin

Nagoya-jidōsha no shain

Takahashi

jisshū-tantōsha

Ishikawa

gijutsu-shidōin

Ikeda

jimuin

Lee

Ōsaka-kikai de jisshūchū

Nakamura

Ōsaka-kikai no gijutsu-shidōin

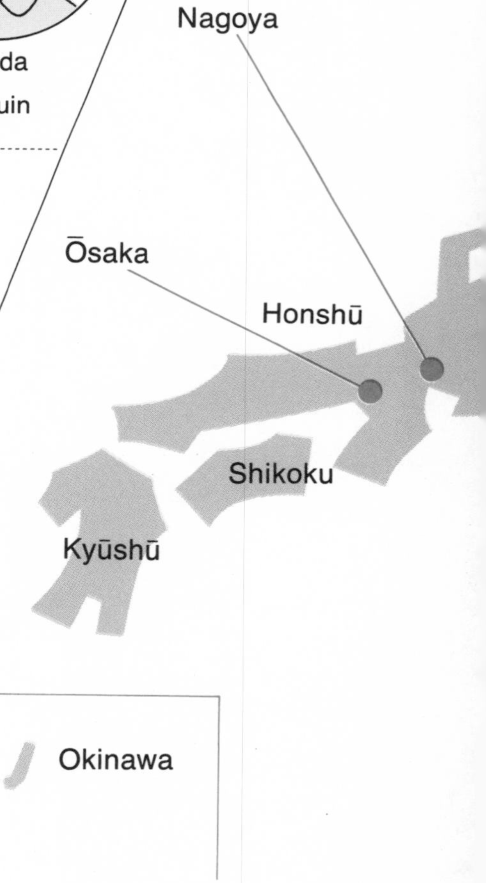

omona tōjō-jinbutsu

Karuizawa （提供ボンカラー）

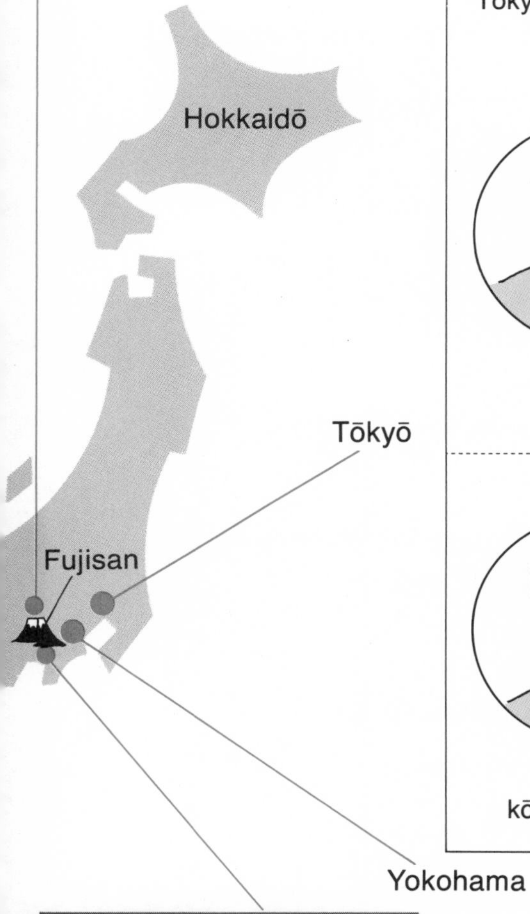

Hakone ©藤田麻生（提供ボンカラー）

Rao

Tōkyō-denki de jisshūchū

Tōkyō-denki no shain

Mori

buchō

Katō

jisshū-tantōsha

Satō

jimuin

AOTS de hataraite iru Nihon-jin

Tanaka

kōsu-tantōsha

Kimura

uketsuke no hito

Ali

Yokohama-kikai de jisshūchū

Ogawa

Yokohama-kikai no gijutsu-shidōin

Dai 26 ka

Bunkei

1. Kaze o hiita'n desu.
2. Michi ga wakaranai'n desu ga, oshiete kudasaimasen ka.

Reibun

1. Nihon-go ga jōzu desu ne.　Donokurai benkyō-shita'n desu ka.
   …Sentā de 1-kagetsu gurai benkyō-shimashita.

2. Kyō wa amari tabemasen ne.　Dō shita'n desu ka.
   …Onaka ga itai'n desu.

2

3. Konban pātii ni ikimasu ka.
   …Iie, ikimasen.　Kanai ga byōki na'n desu.

4. Sentakuki ga ugokanai'n desu ga, chotto mite kudasaimasen ka.
   …Wakarimashita.　Sugu ikimasu.

5. Tokei o kaitai'n desu ga, doko de kattara ii desu ka.
   …Eki no chikaku no tokei-ya ga ii to omoimasu.

Kaiwa

Ryō ni hairu

Takahashi: Kochira wa ryō no kanrinin-san desu.

Narong: Narong desu. Kyō kara osewa ni narimasu.
Dōzo yoroshiku onegai-shimasu.

Watanabe: Watanabe desu. Kochira koso dōzo yoroshiku.

Watanabe: Shokudō wa koko desu. Yūshoku wa 8-ji han made desu.

Narong: Jikan ni maniawanai toki, dō shitara ii desu ka.

Watanabe: Denwa de renraku-shite kudasai.

Narong: Hai.

Watanabe: O-furo wa koko de, sentakuki wa kono tonari desu.

Narong: Anō, o-furo no tsukai-kata ga yoku wakaranai'n desu ga・・・

Watanabe: Ja, ato de setsumei-shimasu. Saki ni heya e ikimashō.

Renshū A

1.

iku	'n desu
ikanai	
itta	
ikanakatta	

* kireina	'n desu
kirei ja nai	
kirei datta	
kirei ja nakatta	

samui	'n desu
samukunai	
samukatta	
samukunakatta	

* byōki na	'n desu
byōki ja nai	
byōki datta	
byōki ja nakatta	

2.

Itsu Nihon e	kita	'n desu ka.
Nihon de nani o	benkyō-suru	
Nihon ni donokurai	iru	

4

3. Dōshite tabenai'n desu ka. ……

Onaka ga	itai	'n desu.
Amari	suki ja nai	
Onaka ga	ippaina	

4. Watashi wa pātii ni ikimasen.

Tomodachi to yakusoku ga	aru	'n desu.
Jikan ga	nai	
Tsugō ga	warui	

5.

Kanji ga	wakaranai	'n desu ga,	oshiete	kudasaimasen ka.
Kikai ga	ugokanai		mite	
Denwa o	kaketai		kashite	

6.

Eki e	ikitai	'n desu ga,	dōyatte	itta	ra ii desu ka.
Kippu ga	denai		dō	shita	
Tokei ga	hoshii		doko de	katta	

Renshū B

1. Rei: ii tokei desu ne, doko de kaimashita ka

    ……Ii tokei desu ne. Doko de katta'n desu ka.

    1) Nihon-go ga jōzu desu ne, doko de naraimashita ka ……

    2) kireina shashin desu ne, doko de torimashita ka ……

    3) oishii okashi desu ne, dare ga tsukurimashita ka ……

    4) sugoi kuruma desu ne, itsu kaimashita ka ……

    5) nigiyaka desu ne, nani o yatte imasu ka ……

2. Rei: Dōshite tabenai'n desu ka. (oishikunai desu)

    ……Oishikunai'n desu.

    1) Dōshite kaisha o yasunda'n desu ka. (netsu ga arimashita) ……

    2) Dōshite terebi o minai'n desu ka. (tsumaranai desu) ……

    3) Dōshite jikan ni okureta'n desu ka. (basu ga kimasendeshita) ……

    4) Dōyatte gasu o tsukeru'n desu ka. (kōyatte tsukemasu) ……

    5) Dō shita'n desu ka. (doa ga akimasen) ……

3. Rei: Ashita pātii ni ikimasu ka. (tsugō ga warui desu)

    ……Iie, ikimasen. Tsugō ga warui'n desu.

    1) Jibun de ryōri o tsukurimasu ka. (ryō ni shokudō ga arimasu) ……

    2) Kesa shinbun o yomimashita ka. (jikan ga arimasendeshita) ……

    3) Katō-san wa imasu ka. (kyō wa yasumi desu) ……

    4) Sashimi o tabemasu ka. (sakana ga kirai desu) ……

    5) Konban dekakemasu ka. (repōto o kakanakereba narimasen) ……

4. Rei: sōjiki no tsukai-kata ga wakarimasen, oshiemasu

……Sōjiki no tsukai-kata ga wakaranai'n desu ga, oshiete kudasaimasen ka.

1) sūpā e ikitai desu, michi o oshiemasu ……

2) kikai no chōshi ga okashii desu, shirabemasu ……

3) terebi ga tsukimasen, mimasu ……

4) o-yu ga demasen, mimasu ……

5) kaisha ni renraku-shitai desu, denwa o kashimasu ……

5. Rei: eki e ikitai desu, dōyatte ikimasu ka

……Eki e ikitai'n desu ga, dōyatte ittara ii desu ka.

1) Yokohama-kōen e ikitai desu, dono basu ni norimasu ka ……

2) Tōkyō-tawā e ikitai desu, doko de chikatetsu o orimasu ka ……

3) kippu o kaitai desu, doko de kaimasu ka ……

6

4) komakai okane ga arimasen, dō shimasu ka ……

5) otsuri ga demasen, dō shimasu ka ……

Renshū C

1. A: Wā, ii kamera① desu ne. Doko de katta'n desu ka.
   B: Kore desu ka. Shinjuku② de kaimashita.
   A: Sō desu ka. Watashi mo sonna kamera① ga hoshii desu.

   1) ① kireina ningyō ② Kyōto
   2) ① sugoi rajikase ② Tōkyō

2. A: Kinō no pātii wa dō deshita ka.
   B: Totemo tanoshikatta desu yo.
   Dōshite konakatta'n desu ka.
   A: Kinō wa isogashikatta'n desu.

   1) chotto yakusoku ga arimashita
   2) karada no chōshi ga warukatta desu

3. A: Anō· · ·

B: Hai, nan desu ka.

A: Sentakuki no tsukai-kata ga wakaranai'n desu ga, oshiete kudasaimasen ka.

B: Sentakuki desu ka. Kōyatte tsukau'n desu yo.

A: Sō desu ka. Arigatō gozaimashita.

1) sōjiki no tsukai-kata

2) gasu no tsuke-kata

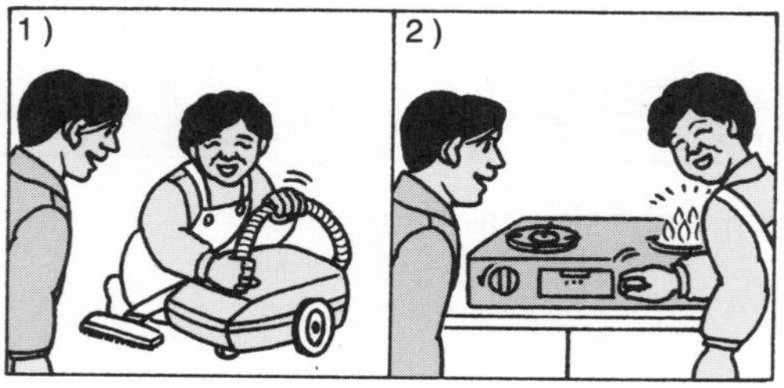

4. A: Sumimasen.

Ōsakajō e ikitai'n desu ga, dono basu ni nottara① ii desu ka.

B: 100-ban no basu② desu yo.

A: 100-ban no basu② desu ne. Dōmo.

1) ① doko de orimasu ka ② Kōen-mae

2) ① doko de norikaemasu ka ② Ōsaka-eki

Mondai

1\. 1) ______________________________

2) ______________________________

3) ______________________________

4) ______________________________

5) ______________________________

2\.

1) Narong-san wa Shinjuku de (   ) o { a. karimashita. / b. kaimashita. / c. kaemashita. }

2) Katō-san wa pātii ni { a. ikimashita. / b. kimashita. / c. kimasendeshita. }

Karada no chōshi ga (   ) desu kara.

3) Narong-san wa (   ) o yomu koto ga dekimasen.

{ a. Hiragana / b. Kanji / c. Nihon-go } ga wakarimasen kara.

4) Hiitā o { a. tsukeru / b. kesu / c. akeru } toki, (   ) o oshimasu.

5) (   ) no basu de { a. Yokohama-eki / b. Yokohama-kōen / c. Yokohama-kōjō } e iku koto ga dekimasu.

3.

Rei: ikimasu	iku'n desu	ikanai'n desu	itta'n desu	ikanakatta'n desu
hanashimasu				
yasumimasu				
arimasu				
tabemasu				
imasu				
shimasu				
(Nihon e) kimasu				
samui desu				
ii desu				
suki desu				
byōki desu				

4. Rei: Dōshite pātii ni ikanai'n desu ka. (konban wa tsugō ga warui desu)
……Konban wa tsugō ga warui'n desu.

1) Dō shita'n desu ka. (kaze o hikimashita)
……

2) Dōshite jikan ni okureta'n desu ka. (basu ga kimasendeshita)
……

3) Dōyatte kono sōjiki o tsukau'n desu ka. (kōyatte tsukaimasu)
……

4) Dōshite issho ni utawanai'n desu ka. (watashi wa uta ga heta desu)
……

5. Rei: Konban pātii ni ikimasu ka.
……Iie, ikimasen. Repōto o kakanakereba naranai'n desu.

1) Sashimi o tabemasu ka.
……Iie, tabemasen. ______________________

2) Kesa shinbun o yomimashita ka.
……Iie, yomimasendeshita. ______________________

3) Yoku kazoku ni denwa o kakemasu ka.
……Iie, amari kakemasen. ______________________

4) Nichi-yōbi asobi ni ikimasu ka.
……Iie, ikimasen. ______________________

6. Rei 1: kūrā no chōshi ga okashii desu
……Kūrā no chōshi ga okashii'n desu ga, mite kudasaimasen ka.
Rei 2: yasui wāpuro o kaitai desu
……Yasui wāpuro o kaitai'n desu ga, doko de kattara ii desu ka.
1) Tanaka-san no jūsho ga wakarimasen
…… ______________________ kudasaimasen ka.
2) shawā no o-yu ga demasen
…… ______________________ kudasaimasen ka.
3) Ginza e ikitai desu
…… ______________________ ii desu ka.
4) tokei o shūri-shitai desu
…… ______________________ ii desu ka.

7. Rei: Koko de tabako o (sutte mo, suttara, suu to) ii desu ka.
1) Hajimemashite. Rao desu. Indo kara (kimasu, kimashita, kita'n desu).
2) Ii tokei desu ne.
Doko de (kau'n desu ka, katta'n desu ka, kattara ii desu ka).
……Shinjuku de kaimashita.
3) Nichi-yōbi dokoka ikimashita ka.
……Iie, (ikimasendeshita, itta'n desu, ikanakatta'n desu).
Atama ga itakatta'n desu.
4) Dōshite butaniku o tabenai'n desu ka.
……(Kirai, Kiraina, Kirai da)'n desu.
5) Gasu no tsuke-kata ga (wakaranai'n desu ga, wakarimasen kara, wakaranai to), dōyatte tsuketara ii desu ka.

8. Rei: Doa (ga) shimarimasu.
1) Kaigi no jikan ( ) okurenai de kudasai.
2) Kaisha ( ) renraku-shitai'n desu ga, denwa o kashite kudasaimasen ka.
3) Suitchi ( ) irete mo, terebi ( ) tsukimasen.
4) Kono botan ( ) osu to, doa ( ) akimasu.

Dai 27 ka

Bunkei

1. Watashi wa Nihon-go ga sukoshi hanasemasu.
2. Watashi wa hiragana wa kakemasu ga, katakana wa kakemasen.

Reibun

1. Nihon-go de denwa ga kakeraremasu ka.
   …Hai. Demo, mada jōzu ni kakeraremasen.

2. Narong-san wa oyogemasu ka.
   …Hai. Demo, 20-mētoru gurai shika oyogemasen.

3. Nihon-ryōri ga taberaremasu ka.
   …Sukiyaki ya tenpura wa taberaremasu ga, sashimi wa taberaremasen.

4. Shinkansen kara Fujisan ga miemashita ka.
   …Iie, miemasendeshita. Tenki ga warukatta'n desu.

5. Watashi no koe ga yoku kikoemasu ka.
   …Iie. Sumimasen ga, mō sukoshi ōkii koe de itte kudasaimasen ka.

6. Eki no chikaku ni ōkii sūpā ga dekimashita ne.
   Itsu dekita'n desu ka.
   …Kotoshi no 4-gatsu desu.

Kaiwa

Michi o kiku

Narong: Anō, sumimasen. Ueda 1-chōme wa mada desu ka.

Otoko no hito: Ēto··· Mittsu-me desu yo.

Narong: Sumimasen. Soko ni tsuitara, oshiete kudasaimasen ka.

Otoko no hito: Ii desu yo.

Narong: Chotto sumimasen.
Supōtsu-sentā e ikitai'n desu ga···

Onna no hito: Supōtsu-sentā desu ka.
Ēto··· Mukō ni shingō ga miemasu ne.

Narong: Hai.

Onna no hito: Asoko o watatte, futatsu-me no kado o migi e magaru to, arimasu yo.

Narong: Futatsu-me no kado o migi desu ne.

Onna no hito: Sō desu. 5, 6-pun de ikemasu.

Narong: Sō desu ka. Dōmo arigatō gozaimashita.

Onna no hito: Iie.

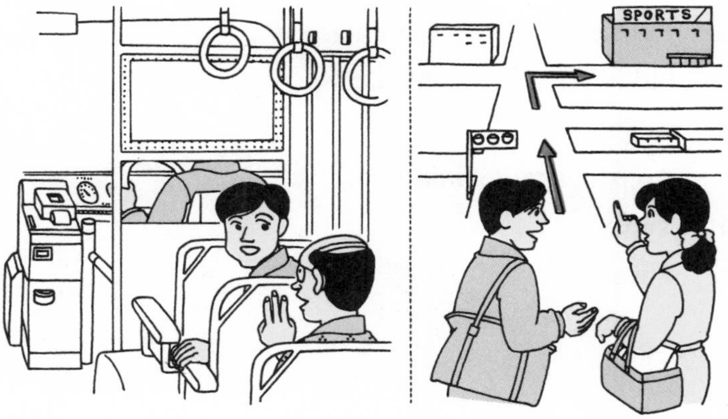

Renshū A

1.

				kanō		
I	i	ki	masu	i	ke	masu
	oyo	gi	masu	oyo	ge	masu
	no	mi	masu	no	me	masu
	yo	bi	masu	yo	be	masu
	to	ri	masu	to	re	masu
	tsuka	i	masu	tsuka	e	masu
	mo	chi	masu	mo	te	masu
	nao	shi	masu	nao	se	masu

			kanō		
II	tabe	masu	tabe	rare	masu
	kake	masu	kake	rare	masu
	ne	masu	ne	rare	masu
	kari	masu	kari	rare	masu

			kanō	
III	ki	masu	korare	masu
	shi	masu	* deki	masu

2. Watashi wa | kanji / sashimi / kuruma | ga | yomemasu. / taberaremasu. / unten-dekimasu.

Watashi wa	kanji	ga	yomemasu.
	sashimi		taberaremasu.
	kuruma		unten-dekimasu.

3.

Watashi wa mada	Nihon-go ga jōzu ni	hanasemasen.
	konpyūtā ga	sōsa-dekimasen.
	rōmaji shika	kakemasen.

4.

Hiragana	wa	kakemasu	ga,	katakana	wa	kakemasen.
Sukiyaki		taberaremasu		sashimi		taberaremasen.
Pinpon		dekimasu		tenisu		dekimasen.

5.

Heya kara	umi	ga	miemasu.
Koko kara	Fujisan		miemasu.
Jidōsha no	oto		kikoemasu.

6.

Atarashii	kōjō	ga dekimashita.
Chikaku ni	sūpā	
Kamera no	shūri	

Renshū B

1. Rei: o-sake o nomimasu ······ O-sake ga nomemasu.
   1) Nihon-go o jōzu ni hanashimasu ······
   2) hitori de doko demo ikimasu ······
   3) wāpuro o uchimasu ······
   4) konpyūtā o sōsa-shimasu ······

2. Rei: Katakana ga kakemasu ka. ······ Iie, mada kakemasen.
   1) Kuruma ga unten-dekimasu ka. ······
   2) Nihon no uta ga utaemasu ka. ······
   3) 500-mētoru oyogemasu ka. ······
   4) Nihon-go de denwa ga kakeraremasu ka. ······

3. Rei: rōmaji dake kakemasu ······ Rōmaji shika kakemasen.
   1) hiragana dake yomemasu ······
   2) taipu dake utemasu ······
   3) 20-mētoru dake oyogemasu ······
   4) Nihon-go ga sukoshi dake hanasemasu ······

4. Rei: okane ga arimasen, kamera o kaimasen
   ······ Okane ga arimasen kara, kamera ga kaemasen.
   1) kono nimotsu wa omoi desu, hitori de mochimasen ······
   2) Nihon-jin no namae wa muzukashii desu, nakanaka oboemasen ······
   3) yūbe wa atsukatta desu, nakanaka nemasendeshita ······
   4) 1-kagetsu shika benkyō-shimasendeshita, mada Nihon-go o jōzu ni hanashimasen ······

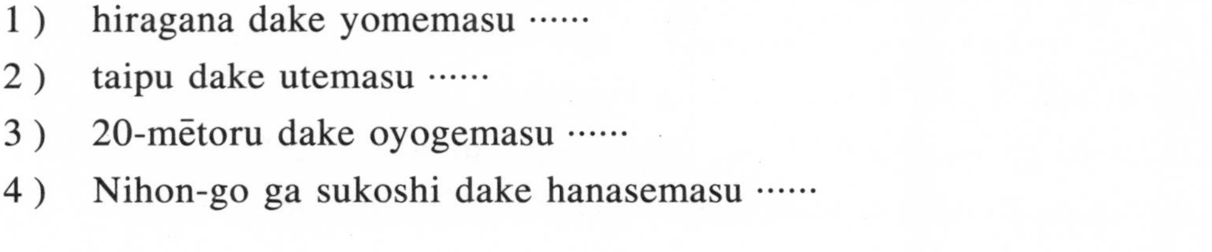

5. Rei: Hiragana ya katakana ga kakemasu ka.
……Hiragana wa kakemasu ga, katakana wa kakemasen.

1) Gyūniku ya butaniku ga taberaremasu ka. ……

2) Taipu ya wāpuro ga utemasu ka. ……

3) Tabako ya o-sake ga yameraremasu ka. ……

4) 200-man-en attara, kuruma ya uchi ga kaemasu ka. ……

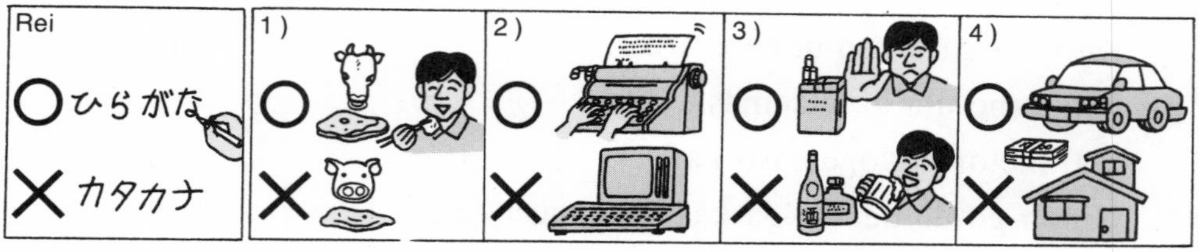

6. Rei: ji ga chiisai desu, yoku miemasen
……Ji ga chiisai desu kara, yoku miemasen.

16

1) oto ga chiisai desu, yoku kikoemasen ……

2) tenki ga warukatta desu, Fujisan ga miemasendeshita ……

3) terebi ga hakkiri miemasen, kāten o shimete kudasai ……

4) koe ga yoku kikoemasen, mō sukoshi ōkii koe de itte kudasai ……

7. Rei: Itsu ano hashi ga dekimashita ka. (2-nen mae)
……2-nen mae ni dekimashita.

1) Itsu shashin ga dekimasu ka. (kyō no yūgata) ……

2) Eki no soba ni nani ga dekimasu ka. (hoteru) ……

3) Itsu made ni kamera no shūri ga dekimasu ka. (ashita no yūgata) ……

4) Itsu made ni kuriiningu ga dekimasu ka. (asatte) ……

Renshū C

1. A: Nihon-go ga hanasemasu ka.
   B: Iie, mada amari hanasemasen.
   A: Daijōbu desu yo. Sugu jōzu ni narimasu yo.
   Ganbatte kudasai.

   1) katakana o kakimasu
   2) wāpuro o uchimasu

2. A: Nichi-yōbi uchi e asobi ni kimasen ka.
   B: Hai. Arigatō gozaimasu.
   A: Nihon-ryōri ga taberaremasu ka. (①)
   B: Tenpura (②) wa taberaremasu (①) ga, sashimi (③) wa dame desu.

   1) ① o-sake ga nomemasu ② biiru ③ uisukii
   2) ① niku ga taberaremasu ② gyūniku ③ butaniku

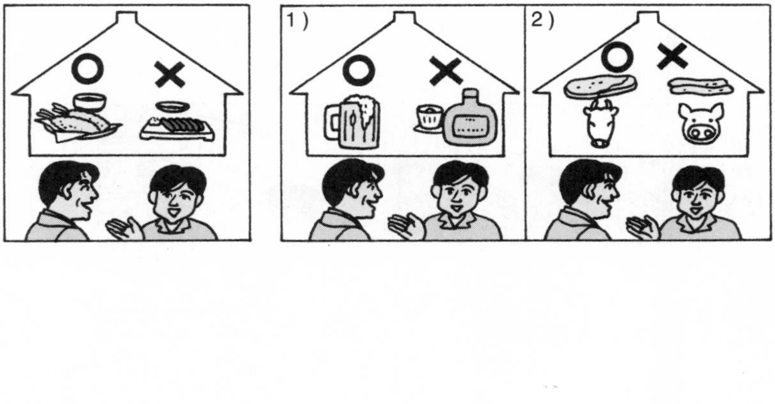

3. A: Chotto sumimasen. Yūbinkyoku e ikitai'n desu ga・・・

B: Yūbinkyoku desu ka. Mukō ni ginkō① ga miemasu ne.

A: Hai.

B: Ano ginkō no tonari② ni arimasu.

A: Sō desu ka. Dōmo.

1) ① shingō ② asoko o migi e magaru to, hidari-gawa

2) ① hashi ② ano hashi o wataru to, migi-gawa

4. A: Sumimasen. Kamera no shūri① o onegai-shimasu.

B: Hai.

A: Ashita② made ni dekimasu ka.

B: Ashita② wa chotto・・・

Asatte③ desu ne.

A: Wakarimashita. Ja, onegai-shimasu.

1) ① kuriiningu ② yūgata ③ ashita no gogo

2) ① tokei no shūri ② getsu-yōbi ③ ka-yōbi

Mondai

1\.
1) ______________________________
2) ______________________________
3) ______________________________
4) ______________________________
5) ______________________________

2\.

1) Lee-san wa (　　　　　) ga mada jōzu ni { a. tsukaemasu. / b. tsukaemasen. / c. renshū-dekimasu. }

2) Narong-san wa (　　　　　) wa taberaremasu ga,
sashimi ya sushi wa { a. taberaremasu. / b. taberaremasen. / c. suki desu. }

3) Yūbinkyoku wa shingō o { a. wataru / b. migi e magaru / c. hidari e magaru } to, (　　　　　) ni arimasu.

4) Kuruma no oto ga { a. miemasu / b. kikoemasu / c. kikoemasen } kara, yoru yoku (　　　　　).

5) { a. Senshū / b. Sengetsu / c. 3-gatsu ni } eki no chikaku ni (　　　　　) ga dekite kara,
benri ni narimashita.

3.

Rei: ikimasu	ikemasu	ikeru	yobimasu		
kakimasu			kaimasu		
oyogimasu			tabemasu		
hanashimasu			nemasu		
uchimasu			(Nihon e) kimasu		
nomimasu			shimasu		
kaerimasu			unten-shimasu		

4. Rei: koshō o naosu koto ga dekimasu ……Koshō ga naosemasu.

1) Eigo o hanasu koto ga dekimasu ……

2) konpyūtā o tsukau koto ga dekimasu ……

3) kotoba o nakanaka oboeru koto ga dekimasen
……

4) 10-ji no shinkansen ni noru koto ga dekimasendeshita
……

5. Rei 1: Hiragana ga kakemasu ka. (hai) ……Hai, kakemasu.

Rei 2: Kanji ga yomemasu ka. (iie, mada) ……Iie, mada yomemasen.

1) Gitā ga hikemasu ka. (hai) ……

2) Konpyūtā ga sōsa-dekimasu ka. (iie, mada) ……

3) 6-ji ni koraremasu ka. (hai) ……

4) Nihon-go de denwa ga kakeraremasu ka. (iie, mada) ……

6. Rei: wāpuro / konpyūtā, tsukaimasu
……Wāpuro wa tsukaemasu ga, konpyūtā wa tsukaemasen.

1) Eigo / Chūgoku-go, hanashimasu
……

2) sen-en satsu / ichi-man-en satsu, kaemasu
……

3) hiragana ya katakana / kanji, yomimasu
……

4) pinpon / tenisu, shimasu
……

7. 

Rei: Shingō o wataru to, kōen ga arimasu.

A: Chotto sumimasen.
Kono chikaku ni sūpā wa arimasen ka.

B: Sūpā desu ka. Ēto···, mukō ni shingō ga miemasu ne.
Asoko o watatte, ______ no ______ o ______ e magaru to, arimasu yo.

A: ______ no ______ o ______ desu ne.
Arigatō gozaimashita.

8. Rei: Watashi wa Nihon-go (o) hanasu koto ga dekimasu.

1) Narong-san wa hiragana (   ) kakemasu.
2) Sakkā (   ) dekimasu ga, tenisu (   ) dekimasen.
3) Kaisha no soba (   ) resutoran (   ) dekimashita.
4) Koko kara, 2, 3-pun (   ) eki (   ) tsukimasu.

9. Rei: ((Chotto), Hayaku, Amari) matte kudasai.

1) Takushii ga (hakkiri, nakanaka, massugu) kimasen.
2) Nihon-go ga mada (jōzu ni, saki ni, hontō ni) hanasemasen.
3) Chizu ga arimasu kara, hitori de (doko e, doko mo, doko demo) ikemasu.
4) Megane o kakeru to, mono ga (nakanaka, hakkiri, yukkuri) miemasu.

Dai 28 ka

Bunkei

1. Ongaku o kikinagara kōhii o nomimasu.
2. Himana toki, itsumo terebi o mite imasu.
3. Nimotsu mo ōi shi, ame mo futte iru shi, takushii de kaerimasu.

Reibun

1. Ocha o nominagara hanashimasen ka.
   …Sō desu ne. Ano kissaten ni hairimashō.

2. Kōjō no naka de wa arukinagara tabako o suwanai de kudasai.
   …Sumimasen. Korekara ki o tsukemasu.

3. Hiru-yasumi wa itsumo nani o shite imasu ka.
   …Terebi o mitari, minna to hanashitari shite imasu.

4. Ii tenki desu yo. Kyō wa dekakenai'n desu ka.
   …Ē. Repōto mo kakanakereba naranai shi, tegami mo kakitai shi, kyō wa ryō ni imasu.

5. Dōshite itsumo kono sūpā de kaimono-suru'n desu ka.
   …Nedan mo yasui shi, soreni shinamono mo ōi desu kara.

Kaiwa

Hanami

Narong:	Wā, kirei desu ne.
Ikeda:	Ē, hontō ni kirei desu ne.
Ishikawa:	Kotoshi wa nakanaka sakimasendeshita ga, yatto sakimashita.
Narong:	Sō desu ka. Zuibun hito ga ōi desu ne.
Ikeda:	Ē. Kyō wa nichi-yōbi da shi, tenki mo ii shi・・・
Ishikawa:	Soreni koko no sakura wa yūmei desu kara ne.
Narong:	Sō desu ka. Nihon-jin wa hana o minagara o-sake o nondari, utattari suru'n desu ne.
Ikeda:	Ē. Watashi-tachi mo ano sakura no shita de o-bentō o tabemashō.

Renshū A

1.

	Terebi o	mi	nagara	gohan o tabemasu.
	Kōhii o	nomi		hanashimasen ka.
		Aruki		tabako o suwanai de kudasai.

2.

Himana toki, itsumo	ongaku o	kiite	imasu.
	hon ya zasshi o	yonde	
	eiga o mitari, kaimono-shitari	shite	

3.

Kaze mo	tsuyoi	shi,	ame mo	futte iru	shi, doko mo ikimasen.
Atama mo	itai		netsu mo	aru	
Okane mo	nai		jikan mo	nai	

4. Dōshite itsumo kono sūpā de kaimono-suru'n desu ka.

……	Mise mo	kirei da	shi,
	Nedan mo	yasui	
	Basho mo	benri da	

soreni	hito mo	shinsetsu desu	kara.
	shinamono mo	ii desu	
	shinamono mo	ōi desu	

Renshū B

1. Rei: terebi o mimasu, gohan o tabemasu
   ……Terebi o minagara gohan o tabemasu.
   1) kōhii o nomimasu, shinbun o yomimasu ……
   2) rajio o kikimasu, kuruma o unten-shimasu ……
   3) tomodachi to hanashimasu, shokuji-shimasu ……
   4) gitā o hikimasu, uta o utaimasu ……
   5) arukimasu, iroiro kangaemasu ……

2. Rei: ocha o nomimasu, hanashimasen ka
   ……Ocha o nominagara hanashimasen ka.
   1) jisho de shirabemasu, senmon no hon o yomimashita ……
   2) memo o torimasu, kōgi o kiite kudasai ……
   3) manyuaru o mimasu, konpyūtā o sōsa-shite kudasai ……
   4) shigoto o shimasu, tabako o suwanai de kudasai ……
   5) kikai o sōsa-shimasu, hanasanai de kudasai ……

3. Rei: Himana toki, itsumo nani o shite imasu ka. (ongaku o kikimasu)
   ……Ongaku o kiite imasu.
   1) Yasumi no hi wa itsumo nani o shite imasu ka.
      (supōtsu o shimasu) ……
   2) Do-yōbi wa itsumo nani o shite imasu ka.
      (kaimono-shitari, eiga o mitari shimasu) ……
   3) Hiru-yasumi wa itsumo nani o shite imasu ka.
      (kōhii o nominagara minna to hanashimasu) ……
   4) Yoru wa itsumo nani o shite imasu ka.
      (hon o yondari, kazoku ni tegami o kaitari shimasu) ……
   5) Itsumo donna bangumi o mite imasu ka.
      (nyūsu ya dorama o mimasu) ……

4. Rei: iro ga ii desu, dezain ga ii desu, kono fuku o kaimasu

······ Iro mo ii shi, dezain mo ii shi, kono fuku o kaimasu.

1) katai desu, mazui desu, kono niku wa taberaremasen ······

2) kawaii desu, yasashii desu, kanojo to kekkon-shitai desu ······

3) majime desu, keiken ga arimasu, kare ni kono shigoto o tanomimasu ······

4) tsukaremashita, nodo ga kawakimashita, ano kissaten ni hairimashō ······

5) eki kara chikai desu, soba ni sūpā ga arimasu, koko wa benri desu ······

5. Rei: Dōshite itsumo kono mise de kaimono-suru'n desu ka.

(nedan ga yasui desu, shinamono ga ōi desu)

······ Nedan mo yasui shi, soreni shinamono mo ōi desu kara.

1) Dōshite itsumo kono resutoran de taberu'n desu ka.

(aji ga ii desu, menyū ga ōi desu) ······

2) Dōshite asagohan o tabenai'n desu ka.

(jikan ga arimasen, amari tabetakunai desu) ······

3) Dōshite doko mo ikanai'n desu ka.

(hon ga yomitai desu, tegami ga kakitai desu) ······

4) Dōshite kono hana o eranda'n desu ka.

(iro ga kirei desu, nioi ga ii desu) ······

5) Dōshite itsumo kono kissaten ni hairu'n desu ka.

(kōhii ga oishii desu, mise no hito ga shinsetsu desu) ······

Renshū C

1. A: Shibaraku desu ne.
   B: Ē.
   A: Dokoka de <u>ocha o nomi</u>① nagara hanashimasen ka.
   B: Ja, ano <u>kissaten</u>② ni hairimashō.

   1) ① shokuji-shimasu　② resutoran
   2) ① bangohan o tabemasu　② mise

2. A: <u>Kōjō</u>① no naka de wa <u>aruki</u>② nagara tabako o suwanai de kudasai.
   B: Wakarimashita. Doko de suttara ii desu ka.
   A: Asoko de onegai-shimasu.

   1) ① kōjō　② kikai o sōsa-shimasu
   2) ① jimusho　② shigoto o shimasu

3. A: Yoku kono resutoran e kuru'n desu ka.

B: Ē, koko wa ryōri mo oishii (①) shi, nedan mo yasui (②) shi, hiru wa itsumo koko de tabete imasu.

A: Sorede hito ga ōi'n desu ne.

1) ① menyū ga ōi desu ② aji ga ii desu

2) ① kaisha kara chikai desu ② ryōri ga sugu dekimasu

4. A: Korekara issho ni nomi ni ikimasen ka.

B: Sumimasen. Kyō wa chotto・・・

Kaze mo hiite iru shi, ashita Yokohama no kōjō e ikanakereba narimasen kara.

A: Sō desu ka, zannen desu ne.

1) mada shigoto ga owarimasen

2) karada no chōshi ga yokunai desu

Mondai

1\.
1) ______________________________
2) ______________________________
3) ______________________________
4) ______________________________
5) ______________________________

2\.
1) Kōjō no naka de wa kikai o (   )nagara tabako o
{ a. sutte kudasai. / b. sutte mo ii desu. / c. suwanai de kudasai. }

2) Lee-san wa ima (   )nagara Tanaka-san to
{ a. hanashite imasu. / b. shokuji-shite imasu. / c. sanpo-shite imasu. }

3) Hiru-yasumi wa tomodachi to (   )ri, kaisha no robii de
{ a. shinbun o yondari / b. kōhii o nondari / c. biiru o nondari } shite imasu.

4) Kono resutoran wa (   ) shi, { a. nedan mo yasui / b. nedan mo takai / c. hito mo ōi } desu kara, itsumo koko de tabete imasu.

5) Ame mo (   ) shi, nimotsu mo { a. omoi / b. ōi / c. ōkii } shi, eki made takushii de ikimasu.

3.

Rei: Terebi o minagara gohan o tabemasu.

1) ____________________

2) ____________________

3) ____________________

4) ____________________

4. Rei: (kaimono-shimasu)

Itsumo kono sūpā de (kaimono-shite imasu) ga, kinō wa yasumi deshita kara, hoka no mise de (kaimono-shimashita).

1) (okimasu)

Maiasa 6-ji han goro (   ) ga, kesa wa 7-ji han ni (   ).

2) (ikimasu)

Do-yōbi wa itsumo supōtsu-sentā e (   ) ga, ashita wa tsugō ga warui desu kara, (   ).

3) (tsukurimasu)

Watashi no kaisha wa jidōsha o (   ) ga, raigetsu kara atarashii taipu no kuruma o (   ).

4) (kekkon-shimasu)

Otōto wa 1-nen mae ni (   ) ga, watashi wa mada (   ).

5. Rei: Karada no (chōshi, koshō, onaka) ga warui desu kara, kaisha o yasumimasu.

1) Kono hana wa (aji, nioi, oto) ga ii desu.

2) Kono sūpā wa yasukute, ii (shinamono, nedan, keiken) ga ōi desu.

3) Kono mise no hanbāgu wa (dezain, seihin, aji) ga ii desu.

4) (Shumi, Iro, Mēkā) ga kirei desu kara, kono fuku o erabimashita.

6. Rei: samui desu, ame ga futte imasu, takushii de ikimasu

……Samui shi, ame mo futte iru shi, takushii de ikimasu.

1) majime desu, keiken ga arimasu, kare ni kono shigoto o tanomimasu

……

2) nedan ga yasui desu, dezain ga ii desu, kono kutsu o kaimasu

……

3) menyū ga ōi desu, ryōri ga sugu dekimasu, itsumo koko de tabete imasu

……

4) koko wa basu ga arimasen, takushii ga sukunai desu, fuben desu

……

7.

Narong-san wa Sentā de 6-shūkan Nihon-go o benkyō-shimashita. Ima Nagoya no kōjō de jisshū-shite imasu. Jisshū wa getsu-yōbi kara kin-yōbi made desu. Mainichi no jisshū wa 5-ji goro owarimasu. Jisshū ga owatte kara, sugu ryō e kaerimasu. Bangohan o tabete kara, itsumo repōto o kaitari, sono hi ni naratta kotoba o jisho de shirabetari shite imasu. Yasumi no hi wa yoku chikaku no kissaten e itte, kōhii o nominagara zasshi o yomimasu. Kono mise wa shizuka da shi, soreni mise no hito mo shinsetsu desu kara, Narong-san wa koko ga totemo suki desu.

Rei 1: Narong-san wa ima Sentā de benkyō-shite imasu. (×)

Rei 2: Narong-san wa ima Nagoya de jisshū-shite imasu. (○)

1) Itsumo ryō e kaette kara, repōto o kaite imasu. ( )

2) Bangohan o tabete kara, itsumo tegami o kaitari, Nihon-go o benkyō-shitari shite imasu. ( )

3) Narong-san ga yoku iku kissaten wa shizuka de, mise no hito mo shinsetsu desu. ( )

4) Kono mise de Narong-san wa ongaku o kikinagara zasshi o yomimasu. ( )

Dai 29 ka

Bunkei

1. Denki ga tsuite imasu.
2. Kono isu wa kowarete imasu.
3. Takushii ni kamera o wasurete shimaimashita.

Reibun

1. Kono heya wa samui desu ne.

   … Ē. A, mado ga sukoshi aite imasu yo.

   Hontō da. Shimemashō.

2. Kono taipu o tsukatte mo ii desu ka.

   … Sono taipu wa kowarete imasu kara, achira no o tsukatte kudasai.

3. Sumimasen. Karita kasa o nakushite shimaimashita.

   … Kamaimasen. Takai mono ja arimasen kara.

4. Dō shita'n desu ka.

   … Densha ni taisetsuna shorui o wasurete shimatta'n desu.

Kaiwa

Wasuremono

Rao: Sumimasen.

Ima no densha ni kaban o wasurete shimatta'n desu ga· · ·

Ekiin: Doko ni oita'n desu ka.

Rao: Ēto· · · 2-ryōme no amidana no ue desu.

Ekiin: Donna kaban desu ka.

Rao: Kuroi kaban desu. Kono kurai no· · ·

Ekiin: Nani ga haitte imasu ka.

Rao: Shorui to techō ga haitte imasu.

Ekiin: Ja, sugu renraku-shimasu kara, chotto matte ite kudasai.

Ekiin: Arimashita yo.

Rao: Ā, yokatta.

Ekiin: Ima Shinjuku-eki ni arimasu ga, dō shimasu ka.

Rao: Sugu tori ni ikimasu.

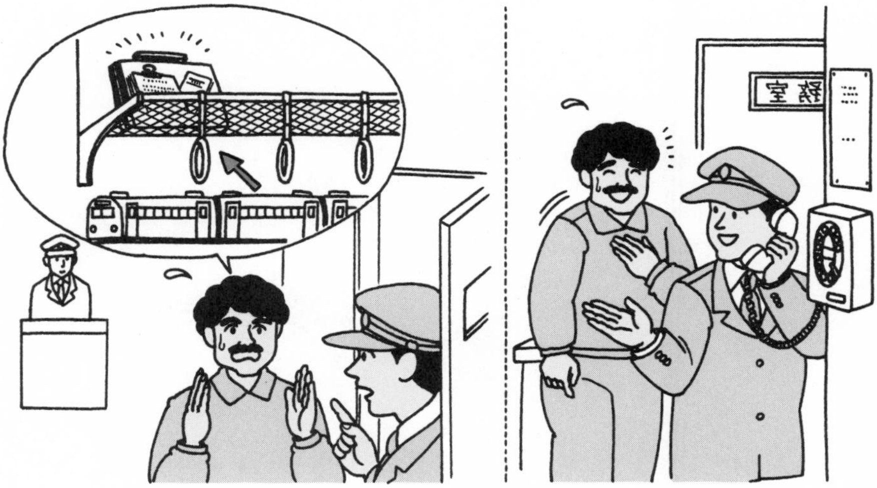

Renshū A

1.

Denki	ga	kiete	imasu.
Doa		shimatte	
Kagi		kakatte	

2.

Kono isu	wa	kowarete	imasu kara, tsukaemasen.
Kono fukuro		yaburete	
Sono kikai		koshō-shite	

3.

Kaban o	wasurete	shimaimashita.
Pasupōto o	nakushite	
Garasu ga	warete	

Renshū B

1. Rei: ······Denki ga tsuite imasu.
   1) ······
   2) ······
   3) ······
   4) ······
   5) ······
   6) ······
   7) ······

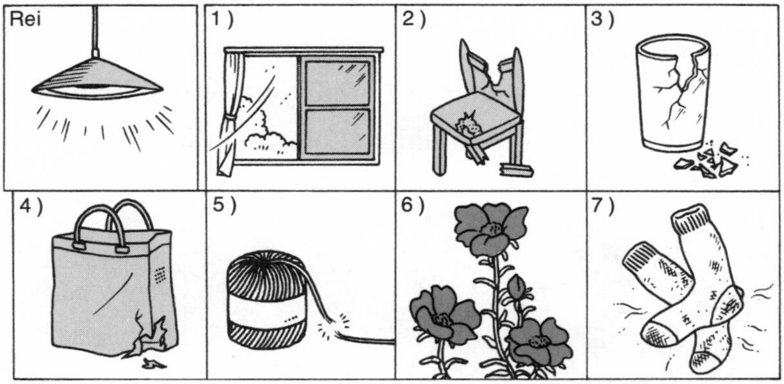

2. Rei: denki ga kiemasu, nani mo miemasen
   ······Denki ga kiete imasu kara, nani mo miemasen.
   1) garasu ga waremasu, abunai desu ······
   2) mado ga akimasu, samui desu ······
   3) kāten ga shimarimasu, kurai desu ······
   4) kagi ga kakarimasu, naka ni hairemasen ······
   5) michi ga komimasu, kuruma ga nakanaka ugokimasen ······

3. Rei: sara ga yogoremasu, araimasu
   ······Kono sara wa yogorete imasu kara, aratte kudasai.
   1) kikai ga koshō-shimasu, shūri-shimasu ······
   2) heya ga yogoremasu, sōji-shimasu ······
   3) fukuro ga yaburemasu, kaemasu ······
   4) isu ga kowaremasu, naoshimasu ······
   5) chawan ga waremasu, sutemasu ······

4. Rei: kippu o kaimashita, nakushimashita

……Kippu o kaimashita ga, nakushite shimaimashita.

1) jūsho o kikimashita, wasuremashita ……

2) chizu o motte ikimashita, michi o machigaemashita ……

3) takushii de ikimashita, jikan ni okuremashita ……

4) kesa heya o sōji-shimashita, mō yogoremashita ……

5) poketto ni saifu o iremashita, otoshimashita ……

5. Rei: Dōshite denwa o kakenakatta'n desu ka. (denwa-bangō o wasuremashita)

……Denwa-bangō o wasurete shimatta'n desu.

1) Dō shita'n desu ka. (teiki o nakushimashita) ……

2) Dōshite jikan ni okureta'n desu ka. (michi o machigaemashita) ……

3) Dō shita'n desu ka. (takushii ni kamera o wasuremashita) ……

4) Dōshite kuruma de konakatta'n desu ka. (koshō-shimashita) ……

5) Dōshite kamera o motte konakatta'n desu ka. (kowaremashita) ……

Renshū C

1. A: Watanabe-san, Watanabe-san, imasu ka.
   B: A, kagi ga kakatte imasu yo.
   A: Hontō da. Ja, imasen ne.
   B: Ē. Mata ato de kimashō.

   1) kāten ga shimarimasu
   2) denki ga kiemasu

2. A: Kono taipu① o tsukatte mo ii desu ka.
   B: A, sore wa kowarete② imasu yo.
   Achira no o tsukatte kudasai.
   A: Hai, dōmo.

   1) ① koppu ② yogoremasu
   2) ① sōjiki ② koshō-shimasu

3. A: Anō, karita kasa① o densha ni wasurete② shimaimashita.
   B: Ii desu yo. Takai mono ja arimasen kara.
   A: Dōmo sumimasen.

   1) ① tebukuro ② otoshimasu
   2) ① hon ② nakushimasu

38 4. A: Dō shita'n desu ka.
   B: Takushii ni kamera o wasurete① shimatta'n desu.
   A: Sore wa taihen desu ne.
   Sugu takushii no kaisha ni denwa de kiite② agemasu yo.
   B: Sumimasen. Yoroshiku onegai-shimasu.

   1) ① teiki o nakushimasu
      ② eki ni renraku-shimasu
   2) ① densha ni taisetsuna shorui o wasuremasu
      ② eki no hito ni kikimasu

Mondai

1\. 1) ______________________________

2) ______________________________

3) ______________________________

2\.

1) Mado no kagi ga (　　　　　) imasu kara, sugu { a. kaimasu. / b. kaemasu. / c. naoshimasu. }

2) Narong-san no heya wa kagi ga { a. kaite / b. kakete / c. kakatte } imasu.

Narong-san wa (　　　　　).

3) Kono sōjiki wa (　　　　　) imasu kara, { a. tsukaemasu. / b. tsukaemasen. / c. tsukatte imasu. }

4) Takushii ni (　　　　　) o (　　　　　) shimaimashita.

Sorede { a. Takahashi-san ni denwa de kiite moraimashita. / b. jibun de denwa o kakete, kikimashita. / c. sugu takushii no kaisha e ikimashita. }

5) Lee-san wa { a. michi de saifu o nakushite / b. kaisha de saifu o otoshite / c. dokoka de saifu o otoshite } shimaimashita.

Saifu no naka ni wa okane ga (　　　　　) gurai haitte imashita.

3.

Rei: mado o akemasu	mado ga akimasu
1) mado o shimemasu	
2) gasu o tsukemasu	
3) gasu o keshimasu	
4) kuruma o tomemasu	
5) himo o kirimasu	

4.

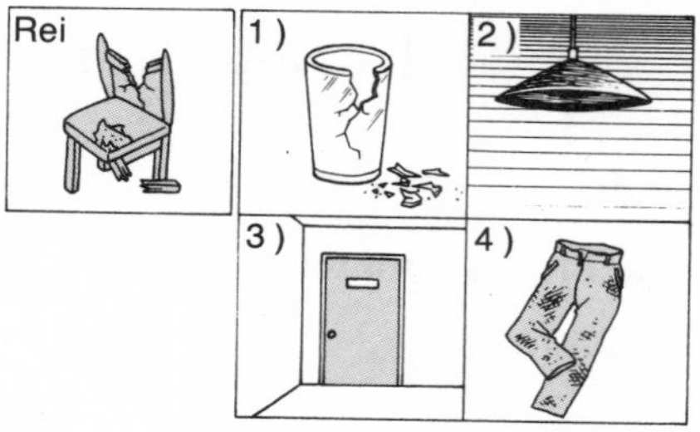

Rei: Isu ga kowarete imasu.

1) ____________________

2) ____________________

3) ____________________

4) ____________________

5. Rei: Hiitā ga tsuite imasu kara, (b)

1) Denki ga kiete imasu kara, (   )
2) Mado ga aite imasu kara, (   )
3) Bin ga warete imasu kara, (   )
4) Kaban ni shorui ga takusan haitte imasu kara, (   )

a. abunai desu.
b. atatakai desu.
c. samui desu.
d. omoi desu.
e. kurai desu.

6. Rei: Kono kikai wa koshō-shite imasu kara, (shūri-shite) kudasai.

1) Kono sara wa yogorete imasu kara, (   ) kudasai.
2) Kono bin wa warete imasu kara, (   ) kudasai.
3) Doa ga aite imasu kara, (   ) kudasai.
4) Robii no terebi ga tsuite imasu. Dare mo mite imasen kara, (   ) kudasai.

7. Rei: Kaisha ni (okuremasu··· okurete) shimaimashita.

1) Dokoka de saifu o (otoshimasu···   ) shimaimashita.
2) Sentakuki ga (kowaremasu···   ) shimaimashita.
3) Konpyūtā no sōsa o (machigaemasu···   ) shimaimashita.
4) Kinō katta teiki o (nakushimasu···   ) shimaimashita.

8. Rei: Koshō (o) naoshimasu.

1) Uchi no mae ni kuruma (   ) tomatte imasu.
Koko ni kuruma (   ) tomenai de kudasai.

2) Mado (   ) aite imasu.
Samui desu kara, mado (   ) shimete kudasai.

3) Sentakuki (   ) kowarete imasu.
Kono sentakuki (   ) kowarete imasu kara, tsukaemasen.

4) Densha (   ) kaban o wasurete shimaimashita.
Eki no mae (   ) saifu o hiroimashita.

9.

Kinō Narong-san wa saifu o otoshite shimaimashita. Saifu no naka ni wa okane to meishi to ryō no denwa-bangō o kaita kami ga haitte imashita.

Kinō wa 5-ji ni jisshū ga owatte kara, chikaku no sūpā de kaimono-shimashita. Sorekara ryō e kaette, fuku o kaeru toki, "A!" to omoimashita. Narong-san wa asa zubon no poketto ni saifu o iremashita. Keredomo, poketto ni wa nani mo haitte imasendeshita. Sugu sūpā made itte, mise no naka o yoku mimashita. Demo, saifu wa arimasendeshita.

Yoru shiranai onna no hito kara denwa ga arimashita. Sono onna no hito wa sūpā no chikaku de Narong-san no saifu o hirotta to iimashita.

Narong-san wa sono hito no jūsho o kiite, sugu saifu o morai ni ikimashita.

1) Narong-san wa doko de saifu o otoshimashita ka.

____

2) Dare ga saifu o hirotte kuremashita ka.

____

3) Saifu no naka ni wa nani ga haitte imashita ka.

____

4) Denwa o moratte kara, Narong-san wa dō shimashita ka.

____

Dai 30 ka

Bunkei

1. Kabe ni e ga kakete arimasu.
2. Ryokō ni iku mae ni, kippu o katte okimasu.

Reibun

1. Asoko ni posutā ga hatte arimasu ne.
   …Ē. Are wa ryokō no annai desu.

2. Sumimasen. Doraibā wa doko desu ka.
   …Sono hikidashi no naka ni shimatte arimasu yo.

3. Gogo no kaigi made ni nani o shite oitara ii desu ka.
   …Sō desu ne. Kono shiryō o yonde oite kudasai.

4. Sagyō ga owattara, dōgu o kichinto shimatte oite kudasai.
   …Hai, wakarimashita.

5. Kono nimotsu o katazukemashō ka.
   …Iie. Watashi ga yarimasu kara, sono mama ni shite oite kudasai.

Kaiwa

Kōgu o tsukau

Ogawa: Kyō wa kōgu no tsukai-kata o jisshū-shimasu.

Ali: Hai.

Ogawa: Manyuaru o mite, tsukau mono o sono dai no ue ni narabete kudasai.

Ali: Wakarimashita.
Anō, doriru wa doko desu ka.

Ogawa: Ano hako no naka ni shimatte arimasu yo.

Ogawa: Kyō wa kore de owarimasu.
Tsukatta kōgu o yoku fuite, moto no tokoro ni shimatte oite kudasai.

Ali: Hai, wakarimashita.

Ogawa: Ja, gokurōsama deshita.

Renshū A

1.

Robii	ni	terebi	ga	oite	arimasu.
Kabe		karendā		kakete	
Sōko		nimotsu		irete	

2.

Kaban	wa	tsukue no shita	ni	oite	arimasu.
Pasupōto		hikidashi		shimatte	
Fuku		hangā		kakete	

3.

Kaigi no mae ni, shiryō o	junbi-shite	okimasu.
	kopii-shite	
	yonde	

4. Kono nimotsu o katazukemashō ka.

……Iie, watashi ga yarimasu kara,		sono mama ni shite	oite
	soko ni	oite	
	soko ni	nosete	

kudasai.

Renshū B

1. Rei: nōto ni namae o kakimasu ······ Nōto ni namae ga kaite arimasu.

   1) asoko ni reizōko o okimasu ······

   2) tsukue no ue ni hon o narabemasu ······

   3) hikidashi ni buhin o shimaimasu ······

   4) kabe ni kōgu o kakemasu ······

   5) tana ni nimotsu o nosemasu ······

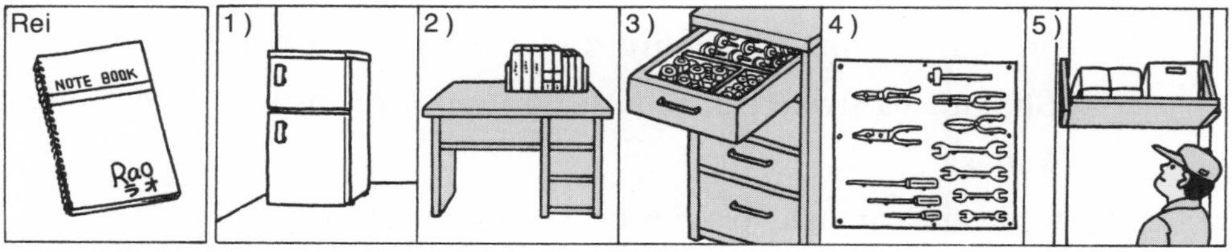

2. Rei: Tēburu no ue ni nani ga arimasu ka. (okimasu)

   ······ Kudamono ga oite arimasu.

   1) Tana no ue ni nani ga arimasu ka. (nosemasu) ······

   2) Tsukue no mae no kabe ni nani ga arimasu ka. (kakemasu) ······

   3) Tēburu no mawari ni nani ga arimasu ka. (okimasu) ······

   4) Denwa no soba ni nani ga arimasu ka. (harimasu) ······

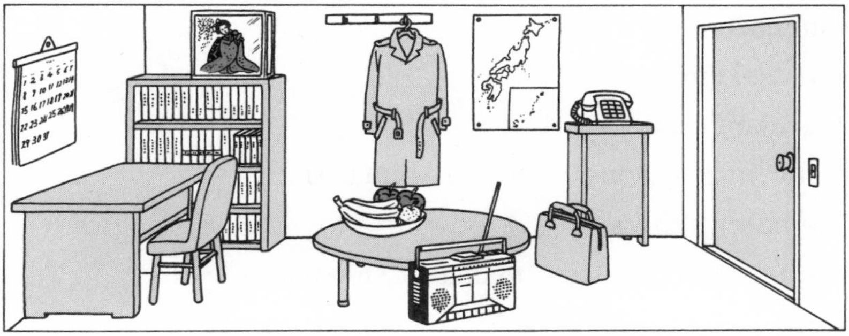

3. Rei: Tēburu wa doko desu ka. ······ Heya no mannaka ni oite arimasu.

   1) Hon wa doko desu ka. ······

   2) Denwa wa doko desu ka. ······

   3) Chizu wa doko desu ka. ······

   4) Kōto wa doko desu ka. ······

4. Rei: ryokō ni iku mae ni, kippu o kaimasu
……Ryokō ni iku mae ni, kippu o katte okimasu.
1) ryokō ni iku mae ni, nimotsu o junbi-shimasu ……
2) pātii no mae ni, nomimono o kaimasu ……
3) tomodachi ga kuru mae ni, heya o sōji-shimasu ……
4) kaigi no mae ni, shiryō o yoku yomimasu ……

5. Rei: shokuji ga owarimasu, tēburu no ue o kirei ni katazukemasu
……Shokuji ga owattara, tēburu no ue o kirei ni katazukete oite kudasai.
1) shigoto ga owarimasu, tsukue no ue o kichinto katazukemasu ……
2) hasami o tsukaimasu, moto no tokoro ni shimaimasu ……
3) kōgu o tsukaimasu, yoku fukimasu ……
4) sagyō ga owarimasu, heya o kirei ni sōji-shimasu ……

6. Rei: Mado o akemashō ka. (samui desu, shimemasu)
……Sumimasen. Samui desu kara, shimete oite kudasai.
1) Kono sara o katazukemashō ka.
(mada tabete imasu, soko ni okimasu) ……
2) Hiitā o keshimashō ka.
(samui desu, tsukemasu) ……
3) Kōgu o katazukemashō ka.
(mada tsukatte imasu, sono mama ni shimasu) ……
4) Doriru o shimaimashō ka.
(mata ato de tsukaimasu, sono mama ni shimasu) ……

Renshū C

1. A: Asoko ni posutā ga hatte① arimasu ne.
   Are wa nan desu ka.
   B: Ryokō no annai② desu.

   1) ① hon o narabemasu　② konpyūtā no manyuaru
   2) ① nimotsu o okimasu　② kuruma no buhin

2. A: Sumimasen. Hasami① wa doko desu ka.
   B: Hasami① desu ka.
   Ano hikidashi ni shimatte② arimasu yo.
   A: Sō desu ka. Dōmo.

   1) ① penchi　② kabe ni kakemasu
   2) ① hanmā　② soko ni okimasu

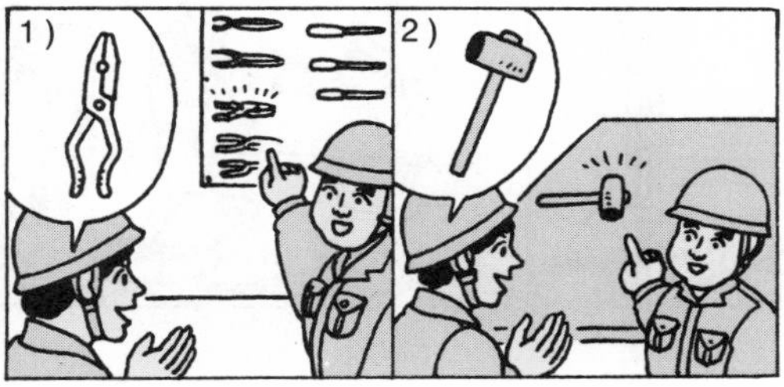

3. A: Raishū no kaigi made ni nani o shite oitara ii desu ka.
   B: Sō desu ne. Kono shiryō o yoku yonde oite kudasai.
   A: Wakarimashita.

   1) kono shiryō o kopii-shimasu
   2) sengetsu no kaigi no shiryō o mimasu

4. A: Kono kōgu o katazukemashō ka. ①
   B: A, mata ato de tsukaimasu kara, soko ni oite oite kudasai. ②
   A: Wakarimashita.

   1) ① atchi e motte ikimasu　　② sono mama ni shimasu
   2) ① hikidashi ni shimaimasu　　② soko ni okimasu

Mondai

1. 1) ______________________________________

   2) ______________________________________

   3) ______________________________________

   4) ______________________________________

   5) ______________________________________

2.

1) Asoko ni kami ga { a. oite arimasu. / b. hatte arimasu. / c. kakete arimasu. } (   ) to kaite arimasu.

2) (   ) wa dai no ue ni { a. narabete arimasu. / b. kakete arimasu. / c. oite arimasu. }

3) Kaigi no mae ni, (   ) o { a. yoku shirabete / b. tsukutte / c. kopii-shite, yoku yonde } okimasu.

4) Sagyō ga owattara, tsukatta kōgu o (   ) ni { a. shimatte / b. nosete / c. kakete } oite kudasai.

5) Hanmā ya doriru wa { a. mō tsukaimasen / b. mada tsukatte imasu / c. mō katazukemashita } kara, (   ) ni shite oite kudasai.

3. 

Rei: Tsukue no ue ni haizara ga oite arimasu.

1) ______

2) ______

3) ______

4) ______

4. 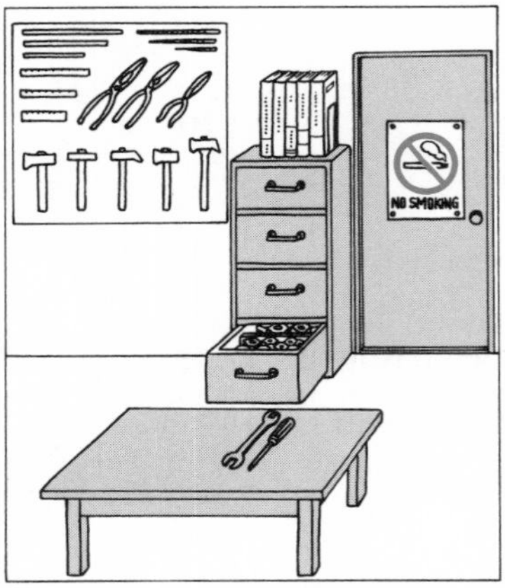

Rei: Dai no ue ni nani ga oite arimasu ka.
Doraibā to supana ga oite arimasu.

1) Hikidashi ni nani ga shimatte arimasu ka.
______

2) Hanmā wa doko ni kakete arimasu ka.
______

3) "Kin'en" no kami wa doko ni hatte arimasu ka.
______

4) Manyuaru wa doko desu ka.
______

5. Rei: Kūrā o keshimashō ka.
……Sumimasen. Atsui desu kara, tsukete oite kudasai.

1) Mado o akemashō ka.
……Sumimasen. Samui desu kara, ______

2) Hanmā o shimaimashō ka.
……Sumimasen. Mada tsukatte imasu kara,
dai no ue ni ______

3) Nimotsu o katazukemashō ka.
……Ato de watashi ga yarimasu kara,
sono mama ni ______

4) Terebi o keshimashō ka.
……Mada mite imasu kara, ______

6. Rei: Shiken no mae ni, hon ya nōto o yoku mite okimasu.
   1) Pātii no mae ni, ______________________________
   2) Kaigi no mae ni, ______________________________
   3) Shokuji ga owattara, ______________________________
   4) Sagyō ga owattara, ______________________________

7. Rei: Asoko ni shashin ga hatte (imasu, (arimasu), okimasu).
   1) Kagi ga kakatte (imasu, arimasu, okimasu) kara, heya ni hairemasen.
   2) Haizara wa doko desu ka.
   ……Tēburu no ue ni oite (imasu, arimasu, okimasu).
   3) Zuibun kireina heya desu ne.
   ……Ē, anata ga kuru mae ni, sōji-shite (ita, atta, oita)'n desu.
   4) Kono hasami wa doko ni shimattara ii desu ka.
   ……Tsukue no hikidashi ni shimatte (ite, atte, oite) kudasai.

8. Rei: Takushii ga ((nakanaka), sorosoro, yatto) kimasen.
   1) Shigoto ga owattara, tsukue no ue o (zutto, kitto, kichinto) katazukete okimasu.
   2) Kōgi wa owarimashita ka.
   ……Iie, (mō, mada, yatto) yatte imasu.
   3) Tēburu ga yogorete imasu kara, (hakkiri, jōzu ni, kirei ni) fuite oite kudasai.
   4) Fukuro ni mono o ireru toki wa, (saki ni, hajimete, korekara) omoi mono o irete, ato de karui mono o iremasu.

9. Rei: Denki (ga) tsuite imasu.
   1) Kabe ( ) e ( ) kakete arimasu.
   2) Kaban wa tsukue no shita ( ) oite arimasu.
   3) Ryokō ni iku mae ni, nimotsu ( ) junbi-shite okimasu.
   4) Heya o sōji-shimashō ka.
   ……Iie, watashi ( ) yarimasu kara, sono mama ni shite oite kudasai.

Fukushū F

1. Rei: Kaigi no jikan (ni) okurete shimaimashita.
   1) Sōjiki ( ) tsukai-kata ga wakaranai'n desu ( ), oshiete kudasaimasen ka.
   2) Watashi wa mada wāpuro ( ) hayaku utemasen.
   3) Sukiyaki ( ) taberaremasu ga, sashimi ( ) taberaremasen.
   4) Koe ( ) yoku kikoemasen. Mō sukoshi ōkii koe ( ) itte kudasai.
   5) Shinkansen kara Fujisan ( ) miemashita.
   6) Nedan ( ) yasui shi, shinamono ( ) ōi shi, itsumo kono sūpā de kaimono-shite imasu.
   7) Denki ( ) tsuite imasu kara, keshite kudasai.
   8) Kono kikai ( ) koshō-shite imasu kara, tsukaemasen.
   9) Asoko ( ) posutā ( ) hatte arimasu.
   10) Kaban ( ) tsukue no shita ( ) oite arimasu.

2. Rei: Ame ga (furimasu … futta)ra, pikunikku ni ikimasen.
   1) Dōshite kinō kaisha o (yasumimasu …)'n desu ka.
   …Atama ga (itai desu …)'n desu.
   2) Watashi wa pātii ni ikimasen.
   Kanai ga (byōki desu …)'n desu.
   3) Tōkyō-tawā e ikitai'n desu ga, dōyatte (ikimasu …)ra ii desu ka.
   4) Itsumo rajio o (kikimasu …)nagara kuruma o unten-shite imasu.
   5) Iro mo (kirei desu …) shi, dezain mo (ii desu …) shi, kono fuku ni shimasu.
   6) Dō shita'n desu ka.
   …Saifu o (otoshimasu …) shimaimashita.
   7) Hasami o tsukattara, moto no tokoro ni (shimaimasu …) oite kudasai.

3. (   ) no naka ni "imasu", "arimasu", "okimasu", "shimaimashita" no dore ga hairimasu ka.

1) Yasumi no hi wa itsumo nani o shite imasu ka.
…Supōtsu-sentā e itte, oyoide (   ).

2) Watashi no kōto wa doko desu ka.
…Asoko no hangā ni kakete (   ).

3) Terebi o keshite mo ii desu ka.
…Sumimasen. Mada mite imasu kara, tsukete (   ) kudasai.

4) Takushii ni kaban o wasurete (   ).
…Ja, sugu takushii no kaisha ni renraku-shite agemashō.

5) Kaisha no mae ni tomete (   ) kuruma wa dare no desu ka.
…Kāto-san no desu.

6) Samui desu ne.
…A, asoko no mado ga aite (   ) yo.

7) Dō shita'n desu ka.
…Pasupōto o nakushite (   )'n desu.

8) Kaigi no mae ni, nani o shite oitara ii desu ka.
…Kono shiryō o kopii-shite, yoku yonde (   ) kudasai.

4. Rei: Kono mizu wa yogorete imasu kara, (nomemasen).

1) Kono sentakuki wa kowarete imasu kara, (   ).

2) Kagi ga kakatte imasu kara, heya ni (   ).

3) Hako no naka ni hon ga takusan haitte imasu. Omoi desu kara, (   ).

4) Kippu o katte okimashita kara, sugu shinkansen ni (   ).

5) Denwa-bangō ga kaite aru techō o otoshite shimaimashita kara, tomodachi ni denwa ga (   ).

F

Dai 31 ka

Bunkei

1. Issho ni shashin o torō.
2. Ashita Ōsakajō e ikō to omotte imasu.
3. Rainen kekkon-suru tsumori desu.

Reibun

1. Onaka ga suita ne. Nanika tabenai?
   …Un, tabeyō.

2. Kondo no nichi-yōbi wa nani o shimasu ka.
   …Tomodachi to tenisu o shiyō to omotte imasu.

3. Jisshū no repōto wa mō kakimashita ka.
   …Iie, mada kaite imasen.
   Korekara kakō to omotte imasu.

4. Kimura-san wa kekkon-shitara, shigoto o yamemasu ka.
   …Iie, tsuzukeru tsumori desu.

5. Ashita kanai ga Nihon e kimasu.
   …Sō desu ka. Nan-ji goro kūkō ni tsuku'n desu ka.
   Yūgata 5-ji goro tsuku yotei desu.

Kaiwa

Natsu-yasumi no keikaku

Takahashi:	Mōsugu natsu-yasumi desu ne. Dokoka ikimasu ka.
Ishikawa:	Ē. Inaka e kaette, yukkuri yasumu tsumori desu. Takahashi-san wa?
Takahashi:	Tomodachi to Karuizawa e ikō to omotte imasu.
Ishikawa:	Karuizawa desu ka. Ii nā.
Narong:	Donna tokoro na'n desu ka.
Ishikawa:	Suzushikute, totemo ii tokoro desu yo.
Takahashi:	Narong-san no yotei wa?
Narong:	Mada nani mo kimete imasen.
Takahashi:	Ja, yokattara, issho ni Karuizawa e ikimasen ka.
Narong:	E, ii'n desu ka.
Takahashi:	Ē, kamaimasen yo. Kuruma de ikimasu kara.
Narong:	Arigatō gozaimasu. Tanoshimi ni shite imasu.

Renshū A

1.

	masu-kei			ikō-kei	
I	i	ki	masu	i	kō
	iso	gi	masu	iso	gō
	no	mi	masu	no	mō
	yo	bi	masu	yo	bō
	owa	ri	masu	owa	rō
	ma	chi	masu	ma	tō
	a	i	masu	a	ō
	hana	shi	masu	hana	sō

	masu-kei		ikō-kei	
II	tabe	masu	tabe	yō
	hajime	masu	hajime	yō
	dekake	masu	dekake	yō
	mi	masu	mi	yō

	masu-kei		ikō-kei	
III	ki	masu	ko	yō
	shi	masu	shi	yō

2. Issho ni | ocha o / eiga o | nomō. / miyō. / shokuji-shiyō.

3. Nichi-yōbi wa | Tōkyō-tawā e / eiga o / depāto de | ikō / miyō / kaimono-shiyō | to omotte imasu.

4. Repōto wa mada | matomete / kaite / dashite | imasen.

Korekara | matomeyō / kakō / dasō | to omotte imasu.

5. Watashi wa | tabako o / 30-sai made ni / buchō ni | yameru / kekkon-suru / sōdan-suru | tsumori desu.

31

Renshū B

1. Rei: Issho ni gohan o tabemashō.
   ……Issho ni gohan o tabeyō.
   1) Issho ni tenisu o shimashō. ……
   2) Konban issho ni o-sake o nomimashō. ……
   3) Sukoshi kyūkei-shimashō. ……
   4) Konban issho ni eiga o mi ni ikimashō. ……

2. Rei: nichi-yōbi wa tomodachi to Ōsakajō e ikimasu
   ……Nichi-yōbi wa tomodachi to Ōsakajō e ikō to omotte imasu.
   1) ashita tomodachi to dekakemasu ……
   2) nichi-yōbi wa uchi de yukkuri yasumimasu ……
   3) natsu-yasumi ni Hokkaidō o ryokō-shimasu ……
   3) natsu-yasumi ni kazoku to inaka e kaerimasu ……

3. Rei: Hirugohan wa mō tabemashita ka. (korekara)
   ……Iie, mada tabete imasen. Korekara tabeyō to omotte imasu.
   1) Repōto wa mō matomemashita ka. (konban) ……
   2) Natsu-yasumi no yotei wa mō kimemashita ka. (ashita made ni) ……
   3) Ano eiga wa mō mimashita ka. (kondo no nichi-yōbi) ……
   4) Wāpuro no shūri wa mō tanomimashita ka. (korekara) ……

4. Rei: tabako o yamemasu

……Tabako o yameru tsumori desu.

1) rainen kekkon-shimasu ……

2) 40-sai made ni uchi o tatemasu ……

3) isshōkenmei gijutsu o naraimasu ……

4) kuni e kaettara, naratta gijutsu o minna ni oshiemasu ……

5. Rei: Itsu kekkon-shimasu ka. (rainen kekkon-shimasu)

……Rainen kekkon-suru tsumori desu.

1) Dare ni kono shigoto o tanomimasu ka. (Katō-san ni tanomimasu) ……

2) Daigaku o detara, dō shimasu ka. (enjinia ni narimasu) ……

3) Kaisha o yamete, dō shimasu ka. (chichi no shigoto o tetsudaimasu) ……

4) Itsu jisshū no yotei o kimemasu ka. (raishū buchō ni sōdan-shimasu) ……

6. Rei: Han-san wa itsu kuni e kaerimasu ka. (8-gatsu no owari ni)

……8-gatsu no owari ni kaeru yotei desu.

1) Buchō wa itsu Ōsaka e shutchō-shimasu ka. (raishū no getsu-yōbi) ……

2) Katō-san wa itsu Tai e ikimasu ka. (ashita no gogo) ……

3) Hikōki wa nan-ji ni kūkō ni tsukimasu ka. (yūgata 6-ji) ……

4) Itsu kara konpyūtā no sōsa o jisshū-shimasu ka. (raishū) ……

Renshū C

1. A: Ashita hima dattara, dokoka ikanai?

   B: Ii ne. Doko e iku?

   A: Shinjuku e itte, eiga o miyō.

   B: Un, sō shiyō.

   1) shokuji-shimasu

   2) o-sake o nomimasu

2. A: Natsu-yasumi ni dokoka ikimasu ka.

   B: Mada nani mo kimete imasen.

   A: Sō desu ka. Watashi wa Fujisan e ikō to omotte imasu. Yokattara, issho ni ikimasen ka.

   B: Hontō desu ka. Arigatō gozaimasu.

   1) inaka e kaerimasu

   2) Hokkaidō o ryokō-shimasu

3. A: Raishū kuni e kaerimasu. Iroiro osewa ni narimashita.
   B: Iie.
   A: Kuni e kaettara, isshōkenmei hataraku tsumori desu.
   B: Sō desu ka. Ganbatte kudasai.

   1) naratta gijutsu o minna ni oshiemasu
   2) motto konpyūtā o benkyō-shimasu

4. A: Katō-san wa itsu Tai e ikimasu ka. (①)
   B: Kongetsu no owari ni (②) iku (①) yotei desu.
   A: Donokurai iru'n desu ka.
   B: 1-shūkan gurai no yotei desu.

   1) ① Tai e shuppatsu-shimasu ② raishū
   2) ① Ōsaka e shutchō-shimasu ② raigetsu no hajime ni

Mondai

1. 1) ______________________________
   2) ______________________________
   3) ______________________________
   4) ______________________________
   5) ______________________________

2.

1) Futari wa korekara ( ) de { a. shokuji-shimasu. / b. jūsu o nomimasu. / c. terebi o mimasu. }

2) Kimura-san wa kondo no ( )
{ a. tomodachi no uchi e asobi ni ikimasu. / b. tomodachi to kaimono ni ikimasu. / c. tomodachi to eiga o mi ni ikimasu. }

3) Narong-san wa natsu-yasumi no ( ) o
{ a. mō kimemashita. / b. mō kangaemashita. / c. mada kimete imasen. }

4) Kuni e kaettara, ( ) o { a. minna ni oshieru / b. isshōkenmei benkyō-suru / c. oshiete morau }.
tsumori desu.

5) Buchō wa ashita yūgata ( ) no hikōki de Tai e
{ a. kaeru / b. shutchō-suru / c. kuru } yotei desu.

3.

Rei: ikimasu	ikō	yobimasu		yamemasu	
kakimasu		kaimasu		mimasu	
isogimasu		machimasu		shimasu	
yasumimasu		dashimasu		sōdan-shimasu	
kaerimasu		tabemasu		tsurete kimasu	

4. Rei: Hirugohan wa mō tabemashita ka. (korekara)
……Iie, mada tabete imasen. Korekara tabeyō to omotte imasu.
1) Kamera wa mō kaimashita ka. (kondo no nichi-yōbi)
……
2) Repōto wa mō matomemashita ka. (korekara)
……
3) Nimotsu wa mō okurimashita ka. (ashita)
……
4) Tegami wa mō kakimashita ka. (konban)
……

5. Rei: Kuni e kaettara, sugu (kekkon-shimasu…kekkon-suru) tsumori desu.
1) Konban tomodachi to (dekakemasu…) to omotte imasu.
2) Nichi-yōbi wa uchi de yukkuri (yasumimasu…) to omotte imasu.
3) Daigaku o detara, ginkō de (hatarakimasu…) tsumori desu.
4) Rainen 3-gatsu no owari made Nihon ni (imasu…) yotei desu.

6. Rei: Watashi wa kinō Kyōto e kenbutsu ni (ikimasu, ikimashita, iku tsumori desu).
1) Buchō wa ashita kara Hiroshima e shutchō-(shite imasu, shiyō to omotte imasu, suru yotei desu).
2) Watashi wa konban eiga o mi ni (iku, ikanai, ikō) to omotte imasu. Tabun Rao-san mo (iku, ikanai, ikō) to omoimasu.
3) Issho ni biiru o nomanai?
……Un, ii ne. (Nomanai, Nomō, Nonde).
4) Lee-san wa doko desu ka.
……Mō 12-ji desu kara, tabun shokudō ni iru (yotei desu, tsumori desu, to omoimasu).

7. Rei: 12-ji kara 1-ji (made) kyūkei-shimasu.

1) Mondai ga attara, buchō (   ) sōdan-shimasu.

2) Ashita kara Ōsaka (   ) shutchō-shimasu.

3) Kono shinkansen wa 6-ji ni Tōkyō (   ) shuppatsu-shite, 8-ji han ni Ōsaka (   ) tsukimasu.

4) 8-gatsu no hajime (   ) kanai (   ) Nihon e kimasu.

8.

> Atsuku narimashita ga, Tanaka-san, o-genki desu ka. Kochira e jisshū ni kite kara, 1-kagetsu ni narimasu. Kaisha no hito wa shinsetsu de, ryō no Watanabe-san mo ii hito desu kara, ima wa nani mo mondai ga arimasen. Ryō ni wa wakai hito ga takusan sunde imasu. Tomodachi wa 2, 3-nin dekimashita ga, korekara motto iroirona hito to tomodachi ni naritai to omotte imasu. Konoaida kaisha no hito to Kyōto e ikimashita. Totemo kireina tokoro deshita. Raishū kuni kara imōto ga Nihon e kuru yotei desu. Imōto ga kitara, Kyōto e tsurete ikō to omotte imasu.
>
> Jisshū wa isogashii desu ga, omoshiroi desu. Nihon wa hontō ni gijutsu ga susunde iru to omoimasu. Korekara Nihon no gijutsu o isshōkenmei narau tsumori desu.
>
> Ja, mata tegami o kakimasu. Tanaka-san mo mainichi isogashii to omoimasu ga, dōzo o-genki de.
>
> 6-gatsu tōka
> Tanaka Ichirō-sama
>
> Narong

* ～-sama : ～-san

Rei 1: Narong-san wa Tanaka-san ni tegami o kakimashita. (○)

Rei 2: Tanaka-san wa Narong-san ni tegami o kakimashita. (×)

1) Narong-san wa 1-kagetsu mae ni kaisha e kimashita. (   )

2) Narong-san wa kaisha e kite kara, tomodachi ga takusan dekimashita. (   )

3) Narong-san wa imōto-san o Kyōto e tsurete iku tsumori desu. (   )

4) Narong-san wa kuni e kaette kara, Nihon no gijutsu o isshōkenmei narau tsumori desu. (   )

Dai 32 ka

Bunkei

1. Sugu byōin e itta hō ga ii desu.
2. Ashita wa tabun ii tenki deshō.
3. Gogo kara yuki ga furu kamo shiremasen.

Reibun

1. Dō shita'n desu ka.

   …Ototoi kara zutto netsu ga aru'n desu.

   Ja, byōin e itta hō ga ii desu yo.

2. O-furo ni haitte mo ii desu ka.

   …Iie, hairanai hō ga ii desu. Netsu ga arimasu kara.

3. Ashita no tenki wa dō deshō ka.

   …Zutto ii tenki desu kara, ashita mo hareru deshō.

4. Dō shita'n desu ka.

   …Nodo ga itai'n desu.

   Tabun kaze deshō. Sugu kusuri o nonda hō ga ii desu yo.

5. Zuibun michi ga konde imasu ne.

   …Sō desu ne. Yakusoku no jikan ni maniawanai kamo shiremasen.

6. Mōtā no oto ga okashii desu ne.

   …Ē. Koshō kamo shiremasen. Sugu shirabete moraimashō.

Kaiwa

Byōin de

Isha: Dō shimashita ka.

Narong: Ototoi kara nodo ga itakute, seki ga deru'n desu.
Soreni onaka mo itai desu.

Isha: Ja, shatsu o nuide, soko ni yoko ni natte kudasai.

Isha: Kaze desu ne.

Narong: Sō desu ka.

Isha: Arerugii wa arimasen ka.

Narong: Arimasen.

Isha: Ja, kusuri o mikka-bun dashimasu.

Narong: Anō, kaisha e itte mo ii desu ka.

Isha: Ē, daijōbu deshō.

Narong: O-furo wa?

Isha: Kyō wa hairanai hō ga ii desu ne.

Narong: Wakarimashita. Arigatō gozaimashita.

Isha: Odaiji ni.

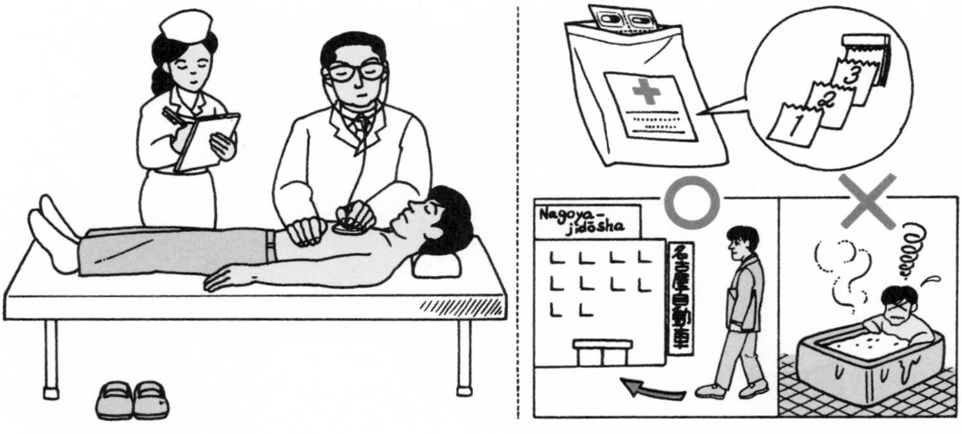

Renshū A

1.

Kusuri o	nonda	hō ga ii desu.
Netsu o	hakatta	
O-sake o	nomanai	
O-furo ni	hairanai	

2.

Ashita wa tabun	ame ga	furu	deshō.
		atsui	
	ii	tenki	

3.

Kare wa	okureru	kamo shiremasen.
	konai	
	byōki	

Renshū B

1. Rei 1: karada ni warui desu, tabako o yamemasu

   ……Karada ni warui desu kara, tabako o yameta hō ga ii desu.

   Rei 2: kaze desu, o-furo ni hairimasen

   ……Kaze desu kara, o-furo ni hairanai hō ga ii desu.

   1) michi ga konde imasu, densha de ikimasu ……
   2) ano mise wa takai desu, kaimasen ……
   3) koko wa kuruma ga ōi desu, ki o tsukemasu ……
   4) karada ni warui desu, o-sake o nomimasen ……
   5) kikai no chōshi ga okashii desu, shirabete moraimasu ……

2. Rei: Kinō kara nodo ga itai'n desu. (kusuri o nomimasu)

   ……Ja, sugu kusuri o nonda hō ga ii desu yo.

   1) Ototoi kara zutto netsu ga aru'n desu. (byōin e ikimasu) ……
   2) Karada no chōshi ga warui'n desu. (isha ni mite moraimasu) ……
   3) Te ni kega o shite shimatta'n desu. (kusuri o tsukemasu) ……
   4) Densha ni kaban o wasurete shimatta'n desu. (eki no hito ni iimasu) ……
   5) Pasupōto o nakushite shimatta'n desu. (kaisha no hito ni sōdan-shimasu) ……

3. Rei: yūgata kara ame ga furimasu ……Yūgata kara ame ga furu deshō.

   1) ashita wa ii tenki desu ……
   2) nichi-yōbi wa haremasu ……
   3) ashita no asa wa samui desu ……
   4) gogo wa ame ga yamimasu ……
   5) korekara dandan atsuku narimasu ……

4. Rei: kare wa byōki desu, tabun pātii ni kimasen

……Kare wa byōki desu kara, tabun pātii ni konai deshō.

1) kusuri o nomimashita, sugu naorimasu ……

2) netsu ga sagarimashita, mō daijōbu desu ……

3) zutto ii tenki desu, ashita mo kitto haremasu ……

4) kyō wa nichi-yōbi desu, michi ga suite imasu ……

5) kyō wa michi ga suite imasu, hayaku tsukimasu ……

5. Rei: Dō shita'n desu ka. (enjin no oto ga okashii desu, koshō desu)

……Enjin no oto ga okashii desu kara, koshō kamo shiremasen.

1) Do-yōbi made ni kuruma no shūri ga dekimasu ka.

(kono buhin wa ima arimasen, dekimasen) ……

2) Konban pātii ni ikimasu ka.

(mada shigoto ga owarimasen, ikemasen) ……

3) Dō shita'n desu ka.

(sukoshi netsu ga arimasu, kaze desu) ……

4) Ashita no tenki wa dō deshō ka.

(kyō wa totemo samui desu, yuki ga furimasu) ……

5) 6-ji no shinkansen ni maniaimasu ka.

(michi ga konde imasu, maniaimasen) ……

Renshū C

1. A: Dō shita’n desu ka.
   B: Kinō kara seki ga deru’n desu. (①: Kinō kara seki ga deru)
   A: Ja, byōin e itta hō ga ii desu yo. (②: byōin e itta)
   B: Ē.

   1) ① yakedo o shimashita　② kusuri o tsukemasu
   2) ① atama ga itai desu　② kusuri o nomimasu

2. A: O-furo ni haitte mo ii desu ka.
   B: Iie, hairanai hō ga ii desu ne.
   Netsu ga arimasu kara.
   A: Wakarimashita.

   1) shawā o abimasu
   2) ryokō ni ikimasu

3. A: Ashita issho ni Fujisan e ikimasen ka.
   B: Ii desu ne. Demo, tenki wa dō deshō ka.
   A: <u>Tabun ii tenki</u> deshō. Zutto ii tenki desu kara.

   1) kitto haremasu
   2) tabun daijōbu desu

4. A: Zuibun michi ga konde imasu ne.
   B: Ē. <u>1-ji made ni Tōkyō-denki ni tsukanai</u> kamo shiremasen.
   A: Ja, denwa de renraku-shita hō ga ii desu ne.
   B: Sō shimashō.

   1) 1-ji no shinkansen ni maniaimasen
   2) yakusoku no jikan ni okuremasu

Mondai

1\. 1) ______________________________

2) ______________________________

3) ______________________________

4) ______________________________

5) ______________________________

2\.

1) (　　　　　) de kamera o { a. miseta / b. katta / c. kawanai } hō ga ii desu.

2) Kyō shawā o { a. abita / b. abiru / c. abinai } hō ga ii desu.

(　　　　　) ga arimasu kara.

3) Narong-san no byōki wa tabun (　　　　　) deshō.

{ a. Sugu byōin e itta / b. Isha ni mite moratta / c. Kusuri o nonde, yasunda } hō ga ii desu.

4) Zutto (　　　　　) desu kara, ashita mo tabun

{ a. hareru / b. ame ga yamu / c. ame ga furu } deshō.

5) Yakusoku no jikan ni (　　　　　) kamo shiremasen kara,

{ a. densha de itta / b. isoida / c. denwa o kaketa } hō ga ii desu.

3. Rei: Atama ga itai'n desu ga· · ·

······Ja, (byōin e itta) hō ga ii desu yo.

1) Te ni sukoshi yakedo o shite shimaimashita.

······Ja, ( ) hō ga ii desu yo.

2) Kusuri o nonde mo, nakanaka netsu ga sagarimasen.

······Ja, ( ) hō ga ii desu yo.

3) Botan o oshite mo, otsuri ga denai'n desu ga· · ·

······Ja, ( ) hō ga ii desu yo.

4) Takushii ni shorui o wasurete shimatta'n desu ga· · ·

······Ja, ( ) hō ga ii desu yo.

4. Rei: Kyō wa atsui desu. Ashita mo tabun (atsui) deshō.

1) Buchō wa, konban no pātii ni ikimasu ka.

······Tabun ( ) deshō.

Ashita no asa hayaku Ōsaka e shutchō-suru yotei desu kara.

2) Depāto wa kyō suite imasu ka.

······Iie. Nichi-yōbi desu kara, kitto ( ) deshō.

3) Konban wa zuibun samui desu ne.

······Ē. Yuki ga ( ) kamo shiremasen ne.

4) Sentakuki no oto ga okashii desu.

······( ) kamo shiremasen ne. Chotto mite moraimashō.

5. Rei: Ashita wa kitto (hareru, harete, hareta) deshō.

1) Narong-san wa kyō mo kaisha o yasunde imasu.

(Byōki, Byōki da, Byōki no) kamo shiremasen.

2) Kazoku wa minna (genki, genki da, genkina) to omoimasu.

3) Konshū wa tabun ii (tenki, tenki da, tenki no) deshō.

Raishū wa tenki ga waruku (nari, natte, naru) kamo shiremasen.

4) Michi ga konde imasu kara,

isoide mo, (maniau, maniawanai, maniatta) kamo shiremasen.

6. Rei: Atama ga (itai) desu.

1) Senshū kaze o hiite shimaimashita ga, mō ( ).

2) Naifu de kega o ( ) shimaimashita.

3) Watashi wa arerugii ga ( ) kara, kono kusuri wa nomemasen.

4) Chotto netsu o ( ) kudasai.

7.

> Senshū wa taihen samukatta desu. Sorede Narong-san wa kaze o hiite shimaimashita. Chikaku no kusuri-ya de kusuri o katte, nomimashita ga, nakanaka naorimasendeshita. Seki mo deru shi, nodo mo itai shi, kyō wa kaisha o yasumimashita.
>
> Gogo kara byōin e itte, isha ni mite moraimashita. Isha wa netsu ga aru kara, kyō wa o-furo ni hairanai hō ga ii to iimashita. Narong-san wa kusuri o mikka-bun moratte, ryō e kaerimashita. Soshite moratta kusuri o nonde, hayaku nemashita.

Rei 1: Narong-san wa kaze o hikimashita. (○)

Rei 2: Narong-san wa genki desu. (×)

1) Kusuri o nonde mo, kaze wa nakanaka naorimasendeshita. ( )

2) Kaze o hiite, sugu byōin e ikimashita. ( )

3) Byōin de kusuri o mikka-bun moraimashita. ( )

4) Narong-san wa ryō e kaette, o-furo ni haitte, sorekara sugu nemashita. ( )

Dai 33 ka

33

Bunkei

1. Kisoku o mamore.
2. Suitchi ni sawaru na.

Reibun

1. Asoko ni nan to kaite aru'n desu ka.

   … "Tomare" to kaite arimasu.

2. Ano kanji wa nan to yomu'n desu ka.

   … "Shiyō-kinshi" desu.

   Dōiu imi desu ka.

   … Tsukau na to iu imi desu.

3. Kono nimotsu wa jama da kara, katazukete kure.

   … Wakarimashita. Sugu yarimasu.

4. Sakki honsha no Yoshida-san kara denwa ga arimashita.

   … Sō desu ka. Nanika itte imashita ka.

   Kaigi no shiryō o okutte kure to itte imashita.

Kaiwa

Anzen-shidō o ukeru

Nakamura: Kyō kara kono rokkā o tsukatte kudasai.

Lee: Hai.

Nakamura: Kōjō ni hairu toki wa, kanarazu kono herumetto o kabutte, anzengutsu o haite kudasai.

Lee: Wakarimashita.

Nakamura: Ja, sugu kigaete kudasai.
Junbi ga dekitara, kōjō no naka o annai-shimasu.

Lee: Sumimasen. Are wa nan to yomu'n desu ka.

Nakamura: "Tachiiri-kinshi" desu. Koko ni hairu na to iu imi desu yo.

Lee: Kōjō no naka ni wa kisoku ga takusan arimasu ne.

Nakamura: Ē. Anzen ga daiichi desu kara.
Lee-san mo yoku mamotte kudasai.

Renshū A

1.

	masu-kei			meirei-kei		kinshi-kei	
I	i	ki	masu	i	ke	i	ku	na
	iso	gi	masu	iso	ge	iso	gu	na
	yasu	mi	masu	yasu	me	yasu	mu	na
	yo	bi	masu	yo	be	yo	bu	na
	to	ri	masu	to	re	to	ru	na
	tsuka	i	masu	tsuka	e	tsuka	u	na
	mo	chi	masu	mo	te	mo	tsu	na
	mawa	shi	masu	mawa	se	mawa	su	na

	masu-kei		meirei-kei		kinshi-kei		
II	tome	masu	tome	ro	tome	ru	na
	ire	masu	ire	ro	ire	ru	na
	mi	masu	mi	ro	mi	ru	na
	i	masu	i	ro	i	ru	na

	masu-kei		meirei-kei	kinshi-kei	
III	ki	masu	koi	kuru	na
	shi	masu	shiro	suru	na

2.

Chotto	mate.
Hayaku	shiro.
Kikai ni	sawaru na.
Koko ni nimotsu o	oku na.

3. Kono kanji wa tomare / chūi-shiro / tsukau na to iu imi desu.

4. Kono nimotsu wa jama da kara,

	katazukete	kure.
atchi e	motte itte	
sōko ni	shimatte	

5. Sakki honsha no Yoshida-san kara denwa ga arimashita.

Ashita honsha e	kite kure	to itte imashita.
1-ji kara kaigi ga	aru	
Kaigi no shiryō o	okutta	

Renshū B

1. Rei 1: suitchi o iremasu …… Suitchi o irero.

   Rei 2: kuruma o tomemasen …… Kuruma o tomeru na.

   1) suitchi o kirimasu ……
   2) kisoku o mamorimasu ……
   3) rebā o agemasu ……
   4) suitchi o tashikamemasu ……
   5) buhin o motte kimasu ……
   6) koko ni gomi o sutemasen ……
   7) kōjō no naka o hashirimasen ……
   8) kikai ni sawarimasen ……

33

2. Rei 1: Ano kanji wa dōiu imi desu ka. (chūi-shimasu)
   …… Chūi-shiro to iu imi desu.

   Rei 2: Ano kanji wa dōiu imi desu ka. (tabako o suimasen)
   …… Tabako o suu na to iu imi desu.

   1) Ano kanji wa dōiu imi desu ka. (kichinto katazukemasu) ……
   2) Ano kanji wa dōiu imi desu ka. (suitchi o tashikamemasu) ……
   3) Ano kanji wa dōiu imi desu ka. (tsukaimasen) ……
   4) Ano kanji wa dōiu imi desu ka.
   (koko ni hairimasen) ……
   5) Ano kanji wa dōiu imi desu ka.
   (shashin o torimasen) ……

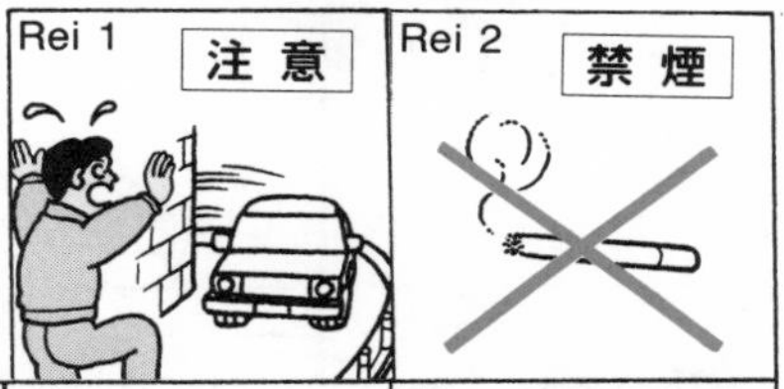

3. Rei: nimotsu o hakobimasu, tetsudaimasu
   …… Nimotsu o hakobu kara, tetsudatte kure.

   1) ima ikimasu, chotto machimasu ……
   2) kono nimotsu wa omoi desu, issho ni mochimasu ……
   3) kono nimotsu wa jama desu, katazukemasu ……
   4) kono buhin wa tsukaimasen, shimaimasu ……
   5) kono hako wa irimasen, tana ni nosemasu ……

4. Rei: Tanaka-san wa denwa de nan to itte imashita ka.
(Sentā ni denwa-shite kudasai)
...... Sentā ni denwa-shite kure to itte imashita.

1) Mori-san wa denwa de nan to itte imashita ka.
(kaigi no jikan o shirasete kudasai) ......

2) Yamada-san wa denwa de nan to itte imashita ka.
(10-ji ni honsha e kite kudasai) ......

3) Yoshida-san wa denwa de nan to itte imashita ka.
(fakkusu de shiryō o okutte kudasai) ......

4) Takahashi-san wa denwa de nan to itte imashita ka.
(honsha e shorui o motte kite kudasai) ......

5) Katō-san wa denwa de nan to itte imashita ka.
(okutta shiryō o mite kudasai) ......

5. Rei: Takahashi-san wa itsu Ōsaka e shutchō-shimasu ka. (ka-yōbi)
...... Ka-yōbi shutchō-suru to itte imashita.

1) Takahashi-san wa nan de Ōsaka e ikimasu ka. (hikōki) ......

2) Yoshida-san wa nan-ji ni kochira e kimasu ka. (gogo 1-ji) ......

3) Narong-san wa konban nan-ji ni ryō e kaerimasu ka. (11-ji goro) ......

4) Narong-san wa dare to Karuizawa e ikimasu ka. (Takahashi-san) ......

5) Takahashi-san wa donokurai Karuizawa ni imasu ka. (1-shūkan gurai) ......

Renshū C

1. A: Abunai. Suitchi o kire.

   B: Hai.

   A: Akai ranpu ga tsuitara, sugu suitchi o kitte kudasai.

   B: Wakarimashita.

   1) kikai o tomemasu

   2) rebā o sagemasu

2. A: Sumimasen. Ano kanji wa nan to yomu'n desu ka.

   B: "Shiyō-kinshi" desu. ①

   A: Dōiu imi desu ka.

   B: Tsukau na to iu imi desu. ②

   1) ① tachiiri-kinshi ② koko ni hairimasen

   2) ① seiri-seiton ② kirei ni katazukemasu

3. A: Torakku ga tsukimashita.
   B: Ja, nimotsu o oroshite kure.
   A: Wakarimashita. Sugu yarimasu.

   1) hakobimasu
   2) sōko e motte ikimasu

4. A: Sakki Yoshida-san kara denwa ga arimashita yo.
   B: Sō desu ka. Nanika itte imashita ka.
   A: Shiryō o okutte kure to itte imashita.
   B: Wakarimashita.

   1) denwa-shimasu
   2) okutta shiryō o mimasu

Mondai

1. 1) ______________________

2) ______________________

3) ______________________

2.

1) (   ) ga tsuitara, kanarazu suitchi o { a. irero. / b. kire. / c. tashikamero. }

2) Ano kami ni wa (   ) to kaite arimasu.

{ a. Suu na / b. Hairu na / c. Tsukau na } to iu imi desu.

3) Ano kanji wa { a. "kiken" / b. "kisoku" / c. "chūi" } to yomimasu.

(   ) to iu imi desu.

4) Kono nimotsu wa { a. jama da / b. tsukawanai / c. omoi } kara, sōko e (   ) kure.

5) Shachō wa { a. kyō / b. ashita / c. asatte } Ōsaka e (   ) to itte imashita.

3.

Rei: ikimasu	ike	iku na	tsukaimasu		
isogimasu			tabemasu		
yasumimasu			shimemasu		
asobimasu			mimasu		
torimasu			shimasu		
machimasu			unten-shimasu		
keshimasu			(Nihon e) kimasu		

4.

Rei 1: suitchi o iremasu ······ Suitchi o irero.

Rei 2: suitchi o iremasen ······ Suitchi o ireru na.

1) suitchi o kirimasu ······

2) rebā o agemasu ······

3) buhin o motte kimasu ······

4) suitchi o mō ichido tashikamemasu ······

5) kōjō no naka o hashirimasen ······

6) koko ni gomi o sutemasen ······

5. Rei: Torakku ga tsuita kara, <u>nimotsu o oroshite kure.</u>

1) Kono nimotsu wa omoi kara, chotto ____________________

2) Kono kōgu wa tsukawanai kara, ____________________

3) Kono kami wa iranai kara, ____________________

4) Kono kikai wa koshō-shite iru kara, ____________________

6. Rei: Tanaka-san wa nan to itte imashita ka. (ato de denwa-shite kudasai)
…… Ato de denwa-shite kure to itte imashita.

1) Buchō wa nan to itte imashita ka. (kaigi no shiryō o tsukutte kudasai)
……

2) Yamada-san wa nan to itte imashita ka. (shiryō o okutte kudasai)
……

3) Shachō wa nan to itte imashita ka. (gogo kaigi ga arimasu)
……

4) Shachō wa itsu Tai e shutchō-suru to itte imashita ka. (ashita ikimasu) ……

7. Rei: Kono nimotsu wa jama da. Sugu katazukete (kure, kudasai, kudasaimasen ka).

1) Sumimasen ga, mō sukoshi yukkuri (hanase, hanashite kure, hanashite kudasai).

2) Eki e ikitai'n desu ga, michi o oshiete (agemasen ka, moraimasen ka, kudasaimasen ka).

3) A, abunai. Sono suitchi ni (sawarō, saware, sawaru na).

4) Isha wa karada ni warui kara tabako o (yamenai, yamero, yameru na) to itte imashita.

8.

Rei 1: Asa 7-ji kara 9-ji made tabako ga suemasen. (○)

Rei 2: Asa 7-ji kara 9-ji made tabako o sutte mo ii desu. (×)

1) Kuruma wa koko de tomaranakereba narimasen. ( )

2) Koko de michi o watatte mo ii desu. ( )

3) Migi e magaru na, massugu ike to iu imi desu. ( )

4) Koko ni kuruma o tomeru na to iu imi desu. ( )

Dai 34 ka

Bunkei

1. Ima watashi ga yatta tōri ni, enjin o kumitatete kudasai.
2. Shigoto ga owatta ato de, kaisha no hito to shokuji ni ikimasu.
3. Eigo o tsukawanai de, Nihon-go dake de jisshū-shimasu.

Reibun

1. Sōsa no junjo ga chigaimasu yo.
   Sakki watashi ga setsumei-shita tōri ni, yatte kudasai.
   ··· Hai, wakarimashita.

2. Kikai ga ugokanai'n desu ga···
   ··· Ja, watashi ga mite imasu kara, mō ichido manyuaru no tōri ni, sōsa-shite kudasai.

3. Kinō kachō ga kaetta ato de, honsha kara denwa ga arimashita.
   ··· Wakarimashita. Sugu renraku-shimasu.

4. Jisshū ni tsuite nanika mondai wa arimasen ka.
   ··· Iie. Mainichi sagyō no ato de, miitingu o shite imasu kara.

5. Kikai no sōsa wa mō oboemashita ka.
   ··· Hai, daitai oboemashita. Wakaranai toki wa, kono manyuaru o mite yatte imasu.
   Ja, kyō kara dekiru dake minai de yatte kudasai.

6. Nichi-yōbi dokoka ikimasu ka.
   ··· Iie. Doko mo ikanai de, uchi de yukkuri yasumimasu.

Kaiwa

Mōtā o kumitateru

Ogawa: Kyō wa mōtā o kumitateru jisshū desu.

Ali: Hai.

Ogawa: Watashi ga yatta ato de, Ali-san ni kumitatete moraimasu kara, yoku mite ite kudasai.

Ali: Hai.

Ogawa: Mazu koko ni kono buhin o toritsukete, tsugi ni pakkingu o hamete, sorekara boruto de shikkari shimemasu.

Ja, koko made watashi ga yatta tōri ni, kumitatete kudasai.

Ali: Hai.

A, ikenai. Machigaeta.

Ogawa: Awatenai de, yukkuri yatte kudasai.

Ali: Sumimasen··· Kore de ii desu ka.

Ogawa: Ē. Umaku ikimashita ne.

Renshū A

1.

Ima watashi ga	yatta	tōri ni, kikai o sōsa-shite kudasai.
Sakki watashi ga	itta	
Kono	bangō no	
Kono	manyuaru no	

2.

Hirugohan o	tabeta	ato de,	barēbōru o shimasu.
Sagyō ga	owatta		miitingu o shimasu.
	Shigoto no		eiga o mi ni ikimasu.
	Shokuji no		yoku ryō no tomodachi to hanashimasu.

3.

Asagohan o	tabete	kaisha e ikimasu.
Manyuaru o	mite	kikai o sōsa-shimasu.
Asagohan o	tabenai de	kaisha e ikimasu.
Manyuaru o	minai de	kikai o sōsa-shimasu.

4.

Doko mo	ika	nai de,	yukkuri yasumimasu.
Ryō e	kaera		tomodachi no uchi ni tomarimasu.
Basu ni	nora		aruite ikimasu.

Renshū B

1. Rei: watashi ga yarimashita, enjin o bunkai-shimasu

……Ima watashi ga yatta tōri ni, enjin o bunkai-shite kudasai.

1) watashi ga iimashita, kikai o sōsa-shimasu ……

2) watashi ga setsumei-shimashita, puroguramu o tsukurimasu ……

3) watashi ga oshiemashita, mōtā o kumitatemasu ……

4) bideo de mimashita, buhin o toritsukemasu ……

2. Rei: bangō, botan o oshimasu

……Kono bangō no tōri ni, botan o oshite kudasai.

1) zu, hako o kumitatemasu ……

2) sen, kami o kirimasu ……

3) manyuaru, konpyūtā o sōsa-shimasu ……

4) sanpuru, buhin o tsukurimasu ……

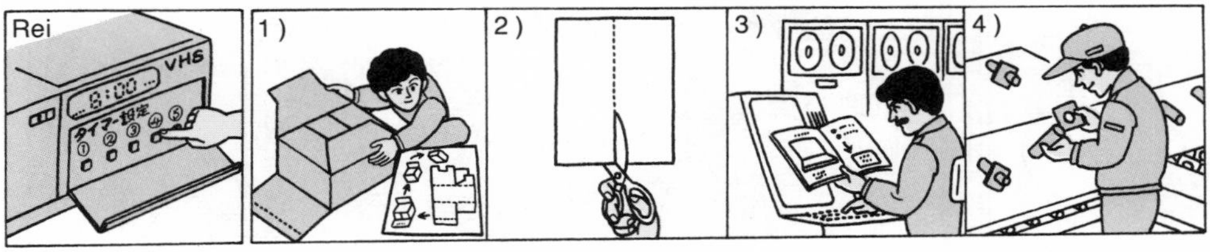

3. Rei 1: miitingu ga owarimasu, ryō e kaerimasu

……Miitingu ga owatta ato de, ryō e kaerimasu.

Rei 2: shigoto desu, kaisha no hito to shokuji ni ikimasu

……Shigoto no ato de, kaisha no hito to shokuji ni ikimasu.

1) o-furo ni hairimasu, bangohan o tabemasu ……

2) bangohan o tabemashita, terebi o mimashita ……

3) kōgi desu, 1-jikan kyūkei-shimasu ……

4) sagyō desu, dōgu o katazukete oite kudasai ……

4. Rei: Sugu shokuji-shimasu ka. (shawā o abimasu)
……Iie, shawā o abita ato de, shokuji-shimasu.

1) Sugu byōin e ikimasu ka. (hirugohan o tabemasu) ……
2) Sugu ryō e kaerimasu ka. (kono hon o kopii-shimasu) ……
3) Sugu sagyō o hajimemasu ka. (asa no miitingu desu) ……
4) Sugu honsha e ikimasu ka. (kaigi desu) ……

5. Rei: asagohan o tabete kaisha e ikimasu
……Asagohan o tabenai de kaisha e ikimasu.

1) basu ni notte eki e ikimasu ……
2) kasa o motte dekakemasu ……
3) manyuaru o mite konpyūtā o sōsa-shimasu ……
4) hasami o tsukatte kirimasu ……

6. Rei: ashita wa yasumimasen, hatarakimasu
……Ashita wa yasumanai de, hatarakimasu.

1) ashita wa dekakemasen, yukkuri yasumimasu ……
2) konban wa ryō e kaerimasen, tomodachi no uchi ni tomarimasu ……
3) nichi-yōbi wa doko mo ikimasen, ryō de terebi o mimasu ……
4) yūbe wa nemasendeshita, repōto o kakimashita ……

Renshū C

1. A: Enjin o kumitatemashita. Kore de ii desu ka.
   B: Ā, koko ga sukoshi chigaimasu yo.
   Sakki watashi ga kumitateta tōri ni, yatte kudasai.
   A: Hai, wakarimashita.

   1) mōtā o bunkai-shimasu
   2) buhin o toritsukemasu

2. A: Sumimasen. Kikai ga ugokanai'n desu ga・・・
   B: Ja, watashi ga mite imasu kara, mō ichido manyuaru no tōri ni, yatte kudasai.
   A: Hai, wakarimashita.

   1) bangō
   2) zu

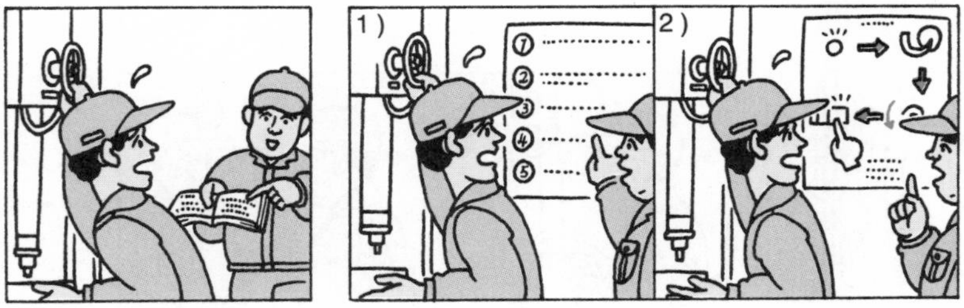

3. A: Jisshū ga owatta① ato de, itsumo nani o shite imasu ka.

   B: Ryō e kaette, benkyō-shitari,② repōto o matometari③ shite imasu.

   A: Sō desu ka. Taihen desu ne.

   1) ① ryō e kaerimasu
      ② repōto o kakimasu ③ kotoba o shirabemasu

   2) ① bangohan o tabemasu
      ② Nihon-go o benkyō-shimasu ③ senmon no hon o yomimasu

4. A: Kikai no sōsa wa mō oboemashita ka.

   B: Hai, oboemashita.

   A: Ja, kyō wa kono zu o mi nai de sōsa-shite kudasai.

   B: Hai, wakarimashita.

   1) setsumeisho o yomimasu

   2) manyuaru o mimasu

Mondai

1\. 1) ______________________

2) ______________________

3) ______________________

4) ______________________

5) ______________________

2\.

1) Sakki { a. kōgi de kiita / b. bideo de mita / c. watashi ga yatta } tōri ni, mōtā o (   ) kudasai.

2) Kono { a. zu / b. hyō / c. sanpuru } no tōri ni, kikai o (   ) kudasai.

3) Bangohan o (   ) ato de, terebi o mitari,
{ a. naratta kotoba o shirabetari / b. senmon no hon o yondari / c. Nihon-go o benkyō-shitari } shite imasu.

4) (   ) no ato de, itsumo
{ a. kōgi o kikimasu. / b. miitingu ga arimasu. / c. kaisha no hito to nomi ni ikimasu. }

5) Kyō wa (   ) o { a. minagara / b. mite / c. minai de } enjin o bunkai-shite kudasai.

3.

Rei 1: ima watashi ga yarimashita, buhin o kumitatemasu

……Ima watashi ga yatta tōri ni, buhin o kumitatete kudasai.

Rei 2: kono bangō, botan o oshimasu

……Kono bangō no tōri ni, botan o oshite kudasai.

1) ima watashi ga toritsukemashita, buhin o toritsukemasu

……

2) ima watashi ga shimemashita, boruto o shikkari shimemasu

……

3) kono manyuaru, konpyūtā o sōsa-shimasu

……

4) kono sanpuru, buhin o tsukurimasu

……

4. Rei: Hirugohan o tabete (mae ni, kara, ato de), barēbōru o shimasu.

1) Kinō shigoto ga owatta (mae ni, kara, ato de), shokuji ni ikimashita.

2) Rajio o (kiki, kiite, kiku)nagara benkyō-shimasu.

3) Pātii no (mae ni, owari ni, ato de), nomimono o junbi-shite oite kudasai.

4) Ōsaka e (iku, itta, ikanakatta) toki, Ōsakajō de kono shashin o torimashita.

5. Rei: Ashita kaisha o yasumimasu ka. (hatarakimasu)
……Iie, yasumanai de, hatarakimasu.

1) Yūbe yoku nemashita ka. (isshōkenmei benkyō-shimashita)
……

2) Konban dekakemasu ka. (uchi de terebi o mimasu)
……

3) Kondo no nichi-yōbi dokoka ikimasu ka. (yukkuri yasumimasu)
……

4) Depāto de nanika kaimashita ka. (uchi e kaerimashita)
……

6. Rei: Gohan o (tabete, tabenai de, tabenai to) kimashita.
Sorede onaka ga sukimashita.

1) Kyō wa ame ga furu to itte imashita kara, kasa o (motte, motanai de, motanakute) dekakemasu.

2) Basu ni (notte, noranai de, noranakute), aruite ikimashita.

3) Kega wa mō naorimashita kara, byōin e (itte, ikanakute, ikanai to) mo ii desu.

4) Kanji ga (wakaru to, wakaranai to, wakaranai de), Nihon no shinbun ga yomemasen.

7. 34 ka no kaiwa o yonde, shitsumon ni kotaete kudasai.

1) Kyō wa nan no jisshū desu ka.

____

2) Ali-san wa nani mo minai de sugu mōtā o kumitatemashita ka.

____

3) Ali-san wa machigaenai de mōtā ga kumitateraremashita ka.

____

4) Mōtā o kumitateru junjo (1, 2, 3) o kaite kudasai.

(   ) Boruto de shikkari shimeru.

(   ) Buhin o toritsukeru.

(   ) Pakkingu o hameru.

Dai 35 ka

Bunkei

1. Kono setsumeisho o yomeba, tsukai-kata ga wakarimasu.
2. Nedan ga yasukereba, kaimasu.
3. Kamera nara, Shinjuku ga yasui desu.

Reibun

1. Furasshu ga tsukanai'n desu ga···
   ···Koko o oseba, tsukimasu yo.

2. Kyō no kōgi ni tsuite nanika shitsumon ga arimasu ka.
   ···Iie, arimasen.
   Nakereba, kore de owarimasu.

3. Koko kara Fujisan ga miemasu ka.
   ···Ē, tenki ga yokereba, miemasu.

4. Bideo-kamera ga tsukaemasu ka.
   ···Hai, sōsa ga kantan nara, tsukaemasu.

5. Wāpuro o kaitai'n desu ga, doko no mēkā ga ii desu ka.
   ···Sō desu ne. Wāpuro nara, Tōkyō-denki ga ii to omoimasu. Shurui mo ōi shi, nedan mo yasui desu kara.

Kaiwa

Bideo o kau

Ten'in: Irasshaimase.

Rao: Bideo ga hoshii'n desu ga· · ·

Ten'in: Kochira ni iroiro gozaimasu.

Rao: Kore to sore to, nedan ga chigaimasu ne.

Dō chigau'n desu ka.

Ten'in: Kochira wa rimokon de bangumi ga yoyaku-dekimasu.

Rao: Rimokon de yoyaku-dekireba, benri desu ne.

Ten'in: Ē. Ima kono taipu ga ichiban yoku urete imasu.

Rao: Kore, motto yasuku narimasen ka.

Ten'in: Iya, kore ijō wa muri desu ne.

Rao: Sō desu ka. Ja, kore o kudasai.

Sumimasen ga, haitatsu o onegai-dekimasu ka.

Ten'in: Hai, kashikomarimashita.

Renshū A

1.

	masu-kei			jōken-kei		
I	i	ki	masu	i	ke	ba
	iso	gi	masu	iso	ge	ba
	tano	mi	masu	tano	me	ba
	yo	bi	masu	yo	be	ba
	a	ri	masu	a	re	ba
	ka	i	masu	ka	e	ba
	ma	chi	masu	ma	te	ba
	hana	shi	masu	hana	se	ba

	masu-kei		jōken-kei		
II	shirabe	masu	shirabe	re	ba
	kae	masu	kae	re	ba
	mi	masu	mi	re	ba
	i	masu	i	re	ba

	masu-kei		jōken-kei	
III	ki	masu	kure	ba
	shi	masu	sure	ba

2.

Setsumeisho o	yomeba,	sōsa no shi-kata ga wakarimasu.
Mise no hito ni	kikeba,	
Manyuaru o	mireba,	

3.

Denchi ga	nakereba,	ugokimasen.
Katarogu o	minakereba,	nedan ga wakarimasen.
Tsukai-kata ga	wakaranakereba,	setsumeisho o yonde kudasai.

4.

Nedan ga	yasukereba,	kaimasu.
Tsukai-kata ga	yasashikereba,	
Oto ga	yokereba,	

5.

Sōsa ga	kantan	nara, kaimasu.
Oto ga	shizuka	
Tōkyō-denki no	wāpuro	

Renshū B

1. Rei: kono botan o oshimasu, terebi ga tsukimasu

    ……Kono botan o oseba, terebi ga tsukimasu.

    1) taimā ga arimasu, benri desu ……
    2) denchi o kaemasu, kono tokei wa mada tsukaemasu ……
    3) kono setsumeisho o yomimasu, tsukai-kata ga wakarimasu ……
    4) kono tsumami o mawashimasu, oto ga chōsetsu-dekimasu ……

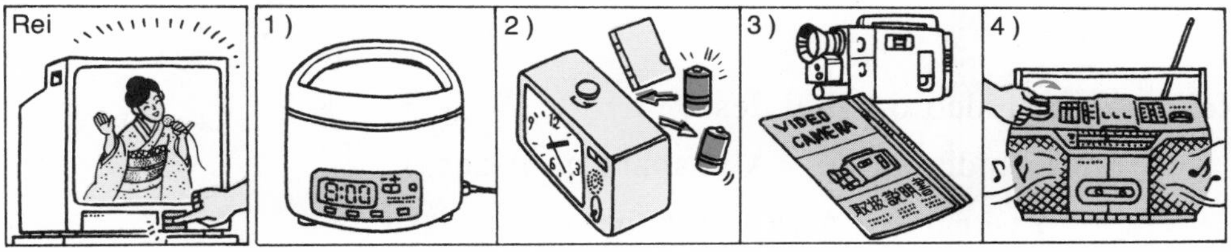

2. Rei: rimokon ga arimasen, fuben desu

    ……Rimokon ga nakereba, fuben desu.

    1) shūri-shimasen, kono rajikase wa tsukaemasen ……
    2) furasshu ga arimasen, koko de wa shashin ga toremasen ……
    3) tsukai-kata ga wakarimasen, setsumeisho o yonde kudasai ……
    4) ashita haitatsu-dekimasen, asatte haitatsu-shite kudasai ……

3. Rei 1: Futa ga akimasen. (koko o oshimasu, akimasu)

    ……Koko o oseba, akimasu yo.

    Rei 2: Sentakuki ga ugokimasen. (kono botan o oshimasen, ugokimasen)

    ……Kono botan o osanakereba, ugokimasen yo.

    1) Otsuri ga demasen.
    (kono botan o oshimasu, demasu) ……
    2) Gasu ga tsukimasen.
    (kono tsumami o mawashimasen, tsukimasen) ……
    3) Kamera ga kowarete shimaimashita.
    (katta mise e motte ikimasu, naoshite kuremasu) ……
    4) 10-ji made ni honsha e ikanakereba narimasen.
    (8-ji ni ryō o demasen, maniaimasen) ……

4. Rei: Terebi no oto ga chiisai desu. (kono botan de chōsetsu-dekimasu)
……Oto ga chiisakereba, kono botan de chōsetsu-dekimasu.

1) Sentakuki no chōshi ga okashii desu. (sugu shūri-shite moraimasu)
……

2) Kono katarogu ga hoshii desu. (agemasu) ……

3) Heya ga kurai desu. (denki o tsukete kudasai) ……

4) Do-yōbi wa tsugō ga warui desu. (nichi-yōbi ikimashō) ……

5. Rei: Yasui bideo o kaitai desu.
(yasui bideo desu, Akihabara ga ii desu)
……Yasui bideo nara, Akihabara ga ii desu.

1) Kono sentakuki wa oto ga shizuka desu.
(oto ga shizuka desu, kaitai desu) ……

2) Wāpuro ga koshō desu.
(koshō desu, shūri-shite moraimasu) ……

3) Kono bideo-kamera wa sōsa ga kantan desu.
(sōsa ga kantan desu, kaitai desu) ……

4) Konpyūtā no hon o kaitai desu.
(konpyūtā no hon desu, eki no mae no hon-ya de utte imasu) ……

6. Rei: Maiban terebi o mimasu ka. (jikan ga arimasu)
……Ē, jikan ga areba, mimasu.

1) Bideo o kaimasu ka. (yasui desu) ……

2) Kono tokei wa mada tsukaemasu ka. (denchi o kaemasu) ……

3) Raishū no pātii ni ikimasu ka. (hima desu) ……

4) Setsumeisho ga yomemasu ka. (Eigo desu) ……

Renshū C

1. A: Sumimasen. Bideo ga tsukanai'n desu ga・・・
   B: Kono botan o oseba, tsukimasu yo.
   A: Wakarimashita.

   (In the dialogue "Bideo ga tsuka" and "tsuki" are underlined and marked ①; "Kono botan o oseba" is underlined and marked ②.)

   1) ① oto ga ōkiku narimasu
      ② koko o oshimasu
   2) ① iro ga chōsetsu-dekimasu
      ② kono tsumami o mawashimasu

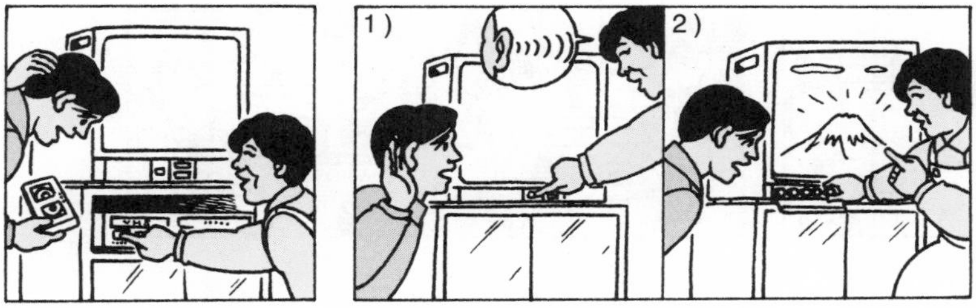

2. A: Sentakuki ga ugokanai'n desu ga, chotto mite kudasaimasen ka.
   B: Ā, kono botan o osanakereba, ugokimasen yo.
   A: A, sō desu ka. Dōmo sumimasen.

   1) kono tsumami o mawashimasu
   2) futa o shimemasu

35

3. A: Kono bideo wa ikaga desu ka.
   B: Sō desu ne. Rimokon ga tsuite ireba, kaimasu ga・・・
   A: Ē, tsuite imasu yo.
   B: Ja, kore o kudasai.

(In the dialogue above, "bideo" is underlined and marked ①; "Rimokon ga tsuite ireba" and "tsuite imasu" are underlined and marked ②.)

1) ① sentakuki ② oto ga shizuka desu
2) ① kamera ② sōsa ga kantan desu

4. A: Wāpuro o kaitai'n desu ga, doko no mēkā ga ii desu ka.
   B: Sō desu ne. Wāpuro nara, Tōkyō-denki ga ii to omoimasu. Shurui mo ōi shi, nedan mo yasui desu kara.

(In the dialogue above, both occurrences of "Wāpuro" are underlined and marked ①; "Tōkyō-denki" is underlined and marked ②.)

1) ① kamera ② Mirion
2) ① pasokon ② NTC

Mondai

1. 1) ______________________________
   2) ______________________________
   3) ______________________________
   4) ______________________________
   5) ______________________________

2.

1) Kono botan o (　　　　　　),
- a. oto ga chiisaku narimasu.
- b. oto ga ōkiku narimasu.
- c. iro ga chōsetsu-dekimasu.

2) (　　　　　　) o
- a. shimenakereba,
- b. akenakereba,
- c. mawasanakereba,

sentakuki ga ugokimasen.

3) Kono bideo wa atarashii taipu de, yoku (　　　　　　).

Nedan ga
- a. takakatta desu kara,
- b. yasukatta desu kara,
- c. 30,000-en ika deshita kara,

kaimashita.

4) (　　　　　　) nara, NTC no ga ii desu.

Sōsa mo kantan da shi,
- a. nedan mo yasui desu.
- b. shurui mo ōi desu.
- c. rimokon mo tsuite imasu.

5)
- a. Konban
- b. Ashita
- c. Asatte

made ni shinakereba naranai shigoto ga arimasu ga,

jikan ga (　　　　　　), pātii ni ikimasu.

35

3.

Rei: ikimasu	ikeba	ikanakereba	tsukaimasu		
isogimasu			hanashimasu		
machimasu			tabemasu		
yobimasu			mimasu		
nomimasu			dekimasu		
arimasu			shimasu		
wakarimasu			(Nihon e) kimasu		

Rei: yasui desu	yasukereba
chiisai desu	
hoshii desu	
ii desu	

Rei: shizuka desu	shizuka nara
hima desu	
kantan desu	
ame desu	

4. Rei: Terebi ga tsukanai'n desu ga· · ·
……Kono botan o (oseba), tsukimasu yo.

1) Rajio no oto ga chōsetsu-dekinai'n desu ga· · ·
……Kono tsumami o ( ), chōsetsu-dekimasu yo.

2) Tokei ga ugokanai'n desu ga· · ·
……Denchi o ( ), ugokimasu yo.

3) Bideo-kamera no tsukai-kata ga wakaranai'n desu ga· · ·
……Kono setsumeisho o ( ), wakarimasu yo.

4) Kono terebi ni wa rimokon ga tsuite imasu.
……Rimokon ga ( ), benri desu ne.

5. Rei: Okane ga (nakereba), nani mo kaemasen.

1) Kono sōjiki wa ( ), tsukaemasen.
2) Kikai no tsukai-kata ga ( ), kono manyuaru o mite kudasai.
3) Sentakuki no futa o ( ), ugokimasen yo.
4) Sugu basu ga ( ), takushii de ikimasu.

6. Rei 1: Nedan ga (yasukereba), shinamono ga yoku uremasu.

Rei 2: (Ii tenki nara), Tōkyō kara Fujisan ga miemasu.

1) Enjin no chōshi ga okashii'n desu ga· · ·

……Chōshi ga (   ), Ogawa-san ni mite moraimashō.

2) Shinkansen kara Fujisan ga miemasu ka.

……Ē, tenki ga (   ), miemasu yo.

3) Kono bideo wa sōsa ga kantan desu.

……Sōsa ga (   ), kore o kaitai desu.

4) Ashita made ni haitatsu-dekimasu ka.

……Ashita made ni wa muri desu ga, (   ) haitatsu-dekimasu.

7. Rei: Kuruma nara, Nagoya-jidōsha no kuruma ga ii desu.

Enjin mo ii shi, iroirona taipu no kuruma ga arimasu kara.

1) Denki-seihin nara, ______________________________.

______________________________ kara.

2) Watashi no kuni no omiyage nara, ______________________________.

______________________________ kara.

8. Rei: Isshōkenmei benkyō-sureba, Nihon-go ga jōzu ni narimasu.

……Isshōkenmei benkyō-shita ra, Nihon-go ga jōzu ni narimasu.

1) Akai botan o oseba, kikai ga tomarimasu.

……Akai botan o ____________ to, kikai ga tomarimasu.

2) Isoganakereba, kaigi no jikan ni okuremasu.

…… ____________ to, kaigi no jikan ni okuremasu.

3) Nedan ga yasukereba, kaimasu.

……Nedan ga ____________ra, kaimasu.

4) Do-yōbi nara, tsugō ga ii desu.

……Do-yōbi ____________ra, tsugō ga ii desu.

Fukushū G

1.

Rei: kaku	kakeru	kakō	kake	kakeba
oyogu				
yomu				
yobu				
toru				
kau				
motsu				
hanasu				
taberu				
suru				
kuru				

G

2. Rei: Pasupōto wa hikidashi ni (shimaimasu ··· shimatte) arimasu.
   1) Kekkon-shite mo, shigoto o (tsuzukemasu ···) tsumori desu.
   2) Hikōki wa yūgata 6-ji ni kūkō ni (tsukimasu ···) yotei desu.
   3) Repōto wa mada (matomemasu ···) imasen.
   Konban (matomemasu ···) to omotte imasu.
   4) Netsu ga arimasu kara, byōin e (ikimasu ···) hō ga ii desu.
   5) Kaze desu kara, o-furo ni (hairimasu ···)nai hō ga ii desu.
   6) Enjin no oto ga okashii desu. (Koshō desu ···) kamo shiremasen.
   7) "Seiri-seiton" wa kichinto (katazukemasu ···) to iu imi desu.
   8) "Tachiiri-kinshi" wa koko ni (hairimasu ···) na to iu imi desu.
   9) Kachō wa sugu fakkusu o (okutte kudasai ···) to itte imashita.
   10) Ima watashi ga (yarimashita ···) tōri ni, enjin o kumitatete kudasai.
   11) Bangohan o (tabemasu ···) ato de, terebi o mimashita.
   12) Nichi-yōbi wa doko mo (ikimasu ···)nai de, uchi de yukkuri yasumimasu.

13) Kono botan o (oshimasu ···)ba, terebi ga tsukimasu.

14) Oto ga (chiisai desu ···)ba, kono tsumami de chōsetsu-dekimasu.

15) Sōsa ga (kantan desu ···) nara, kono bideo o kaitai desu.

3. Rei: Kinō no shiken wa muzukashikatta desu ga, kyō no shiken wa { a. takusan / b. amari / (c.) zuibun } yasashikatta desu.

1) Kondo no nichi-yōbi wa uchi de { a. dandan / b. yukkuri / c. hakkiri } yasumō to omotte imasu.

2) Konshū wa { a. motto / b. zutto / c. yatto } ii tenki desu kara, ashita mo { a. kitto / b. kichinto / c. zehi } hareru deshō.

3) Kōjō ni hairu toki wa, { a. kanarazu / b. tabun / c. nakanaka } herumetto o kabutte kudasai.

4) Korekara buhin no toritsuke-kata o setsumei-shimasu.

Mazu koko ni buhin o toritsukete, { a. hajime ni / b. tsugi ni / c. owari ni } pakkingu o hamete, { a. sorede / b. sorekara / c. soreni } boruto de { a. hakkiri / b. shikkari / c. mōsugu } shimemasu.

5) { a. Isshōkenmei / b. Massugu / c. Umaku } benkyō-sureba, Nihon-go ga jōzu ni narimasu.

Dai 36 ka

Bunkei

1. Nihon-go ga jōzu ni naru yō ni, isshōkenmei benkyō-shimasu.
2. Nihon-go ga hanaseru yō ni narimashita.
3. Jikan ni okurenai yō ni shite kudasai.

Reibun

1. Minna ga yoku wakaru yō ni, ōkina koe de happyō-shite kudasai.
   …Hai, wakarimashita.

2. Wasurenai yō ni, memo o totte kudasai.
   …Hai, wakarimashita.

3. Nihon no tabemono ni wa mō naremashita ka.
   …Hai, hajime wa amari taberaremasendeshita ga,
   ima wa nan demo taberareru yō ni narimashita.

4. Kanji ga kakeru yō ni narimashita ka.
   …Iie, mada kakemasen. Hayaku kakeru yō ni naritai desu.

5. Osokatta desu ne.
   …Sumimasen. Basu ga nakanaka konakatta'n desu.
   Okureru toki wa, kanarazu renraku-suru yō ni shite kudasai.

6. Kono botan o osu to, kikai ga zenbu tomarimasu. Zettai ni sawaranai yō ni shite kudasai.
   …Wakarimashita. Ki o tsukemasu.

Kaiwa

Repōto no kaki-kata

Katō:	Konpyūtā no sōsa ni zuibun naremashita ne.
Rao:	Ē, okagesama de kantanna puroguramu ga tsukureru yō ni narimashita.
Katō:	Yokatta desu ne.
	Tokorode, repōto no koto desu ga· · ·
Rao:	Hai.
Katō:	Jisshū no naiyō wa kuwashiku kaite aru'n desu ga, kansō ga kaite arimasen ne.
Rao:	Sumimasen.　Donna koto o kaitara ii desu ka.
Katō:	Tatoeba koko ga yokatta toka, muzukashikatta toka· · ·
Rao:	Wakarimashita.
Katō:	A, sō sō, hizuke mo wasurenai yō ni shite kudasai.
Rao:	Sumimasen.　Korekara ki o tsukemasu.

Renshū A

1.

Shinbun ga	yomeru	yō ni,	kanji o benkyō-shimasu.
Yoku	wakaru		zu de setsumei-shimasu.
Kaze o	hikanai		sētā o kimasu.
Kazoku ga	shinpai-shinai		tegami o kakimasu.

2.

Kanji ga kanari	kakeru	yō ni narimashita.
Nihon-go de denwa ga	kakerareru	
Konpyūtā no sōsa ga	dekiru	

3.

Kanarazu jikan o	mamoru	yō ni shite kudasai.
Maishū kin-yōbi ni repōto o	dasu	
Kono suitchi ni zettai ni	sawaranai	
Kikai no sōsa o	machigaenai	

Renshū B

1. Rei: yoku wakarimasu, yukkuri hanashite kudasai

    ……Yoku wakaru yō ni, yukkuri hanashite kudasai.

    1) hakkiri miemasu, ōkina ji de kaite kudasai ……

    2) yoku kikoemasu, ōkina koe de hanashite kudasai ……

    3) Nihon-go ga jōzu ni narimasu, isshōkenmei benkyō-shite imasu ……

    4) wāpuro ga hayaku utemasu, mainichi renshū-shite imasu ……

2. Rei: wasuremasen, techō ni kaite okimasu

    ……Wasurenai yō ni, techō ni kaite okimasu.

    1) okuremasen, hayaku ikimashō ……

    2) yogoremasen, pasokon ni kabā o kakete okimasu ……

    3) nimotsu ga ochimasen, kichinto nosete kudasai ……

    4) michi o machigaemasen, chizu o motte ikimasu ……

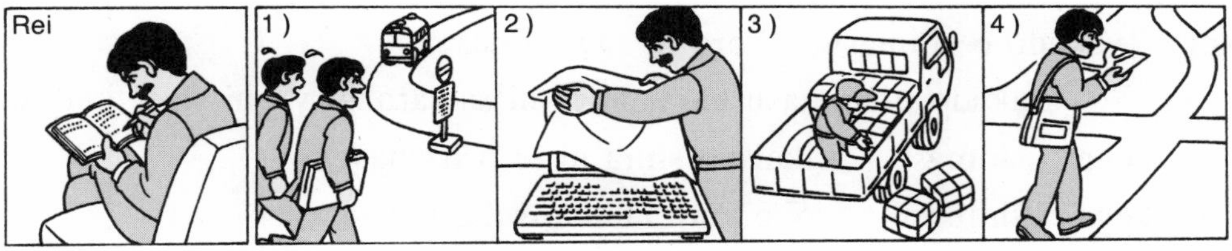

3. Rei: Nihon-ryōri ga taberaremasu (nan demo)

    ……Nihon-ryōri ga nan demo taberareru yō ni narimashita.

    1) katakana ga kakemasu (hotondo) ……

    2) Nihon-jin no hanashi ga wakarimasu (sukoshi) ……

    3) Nihon-go ga hanasemasu (kanari) ……

    4) kantanna puroguramu ga tsukuremasu (yatto) ……

4. Rei: Konpyūtā no sōsa ga dekiru yō ni narimashita ka.
……Iie, mada dekimasen. Hayaku dekiru yō ni naritai desu.

1) Senmon no kōgi ga wakaru yō ni narimashita ka. ……
2) Wāpuro ga uteru yō ni narimashita ka. ……
3) Puroguramu ga tsukureru yō ni narimashita ka. ……
4) Enjin ga kumitaterareru yō ni narimashita ka. ……

5. Rei: shigoto no yari-kata o hayaku oboemasu
……Shigoto no yari-kata o hayaku oboeru yō ni shite kudasai.

1) jikan o mamorimasu ……
2) kaisha o yasumu toki wa, kanarazu denwa de renraku-shimasu ……
3) repōto ni wa kanarazu kansō o kakimasu ……
4) repōto wa maishū kin-yōbi ni dashimasu ……

6. Rei: yakedo o shimasu, kore ni sawarimasen
……Yakedo o shimasu kara, kore ni sawaranai yō ni shite kudasai.

1) kega o shimasu, kikai no shita ni te o iremasen ……
2) kega o shimasu, koko kara atama o dashimasen ……
3) kiken desu, mono o otoshimasen ……
4) kiken desu, nimotsu o takusan nosemasen ……

Renshū C

1. A: Happyō no toki wa, yoku kikoeru① yō ni, ōkina koe de hanashite② kudasai.

   B: Hai, wakarimashita.

   1) ① miemasu ② ōkina ji de kakimasu

   2) ① wakarimasu ② kantan ni setsumei-shimasu

2. A: Nihon no seikatsu ni wa mō naremashita ka.

   B: Ē, yatto naremashita.

   A: Nihon no tabemono① wa mō daijōbu desu ka.

   B: Hai, hajime wa zenzen taberare②masendeshita ga, ima wa sukoshi taberareru② yō ni narimashita.

   1) ① Nihon-go ② hanasemasu

   2) ① kanji ② yomemasu

3. A: Konpyūtā no sōsa ga dekiru yō ni narimashita ka.
   B: Iie, mada dekimasen.
   Hayaku dekiru yō ni naritai desu.
   A: Sō desu ka. Ganbatte kudasai.

   1) puroguramu ga tsukuremasu
   2) wāpuro ga utemasu

4. A: A, abunai.
   Kikai no shita ni te o ireru ① to, kega o shimasu ② yo.
   B: Hai.
   A: Zettai ni te o irenai ① yō ni shite kudasai.
   B: Wakarimashita. Ki o tsukemasu.

   1) ① kore ni sawarimasu ② yakedo o shimasu
   2) ① paipu o otoshimasu ② shita no hito ga kega o shimasu

Mondai

1\. 1) ____________________

2) ____________________

3) ____________________

4) ____________________

5) ____________________

2\.

1) Yoku (   ) yō ni, { a. kuwashiku / b. kantan ni / c. ōkina koe de } shitsumon-shite kudasai.

2) Narong-san wa kanji ga { a. zenzen kakemasen. / b. sukoshi kakemasu. / c. kanari kakemasu. }

Motto kanji ga (   ) yō ni, mainichi benkyō-shite imasu.

3) Narong-san wa Nihon no seikatsu ni daitai (   ).

Ima wa { a. mada Nihon-ryōri ga zenzen taberaremasen. / b. mada sashimi ga taberaremasen. / c. sushi ya sashimi ga taberareru yō ni narimashita. }

4) Repōto wa { a. maishū kin-yōbi made ni / b. mainichi 5-ji made ni / c. jisshū no ato de, itsumo } (   ) yō ni shite kudasai.

5) Sono { a. paipu / b. taipu / c. koppu } ni sawaru to, yakedo o shimasu kara, zettai ni (   ) yō ni shite kudasai.

3. Rei 1: Yoku (wakaru) yō ni, mō sukoshi yukkuri hanashite kudasai.

Rei 2: Kaze o (hikanai) yō ni, takusan fuku o kimasu.

1) Terebi ga hakkiri ( ) yō ni, kāten o shimete kudasai.

2) Nihon-go ga motto jōzu ni ( ) yō ni, isshōkenmei benkyō-shimasu.

3) ( ) yō ni, memo o totte kudasai.

4) Denwa-bangō o ( ) yō ni, kakeru mae ni, yoku tashikamemasu.

4. Rei: Kanji ga yomemasu ka. (sukoshi)

……Hai, sukoshi yomeru yō ni narimashita.

1) Nihon-go ga hanasemasu ka. (kanari)

……

2) Katakana ga kakemasu ka. (hotondo)

……

3) Nihon-ryōri ga taberaremasu ka. (nan demo)

……

4) Nihon-jin no kangae-kata ga wakarimasu ka. (zuibun)

……

5. Rei 1: Kaisha o yasumu toki wa, kanarazu denwa de (renraku-suru) yō ni shite kudasai.

Rei 2: Repōto ni wa namae o (wasurenai) yō ni shite kudasai.

1) Hayaku kaeru toki wa, kanarazu kaisha no hito no kyoka o ( ) yō ni shite kudasai.

2) Repōto ni wa kanarazu jisshū no naiyō to kansō o ( ) yō ni shite kudasai.

3) Miitingu no jikan ni ( ) yō ni shite kudasai.

4) Kega o shimasu kara, kikai no shita ni te o ( ) yō ni shite kudasai.

6. Rei: Kaisha ni (maniawanai, okurenai, isoganai) yō ni, hayaku okimasu.

1) Shashin ga kirei ni (toru, toreru, torenai) yō ni, furasshu o tsukaimasu.

2) Nihon-go de denwa ga (kaku, kakeru, kakerareru) yō ni narimashita.

3) Heya o deru toki wa, (kitto, kanarazu, hotondo) denki o kesu yō ni shite kudasai.

4) Abunai desu kara, (zettai ni, kanarazu, zehi) koko ni hairanai yō ni shite kudasai.

7.

Shinkansen wa 1964-nen ni dekimashita. Tōkyō to Ōsaka no aida wa sore made 8-jikan ijō kakarimashita ga, ima wa 2-jikan han gurai de ikeru yō ni narimashita.

Shinkansen ni wa “Nozomi” ya “Hikari” ya “Kodama” ga arimasu. “Nozomi” to “Hikari” wa ōkina eki ni shika tomarimasen kara, hayaku tsukimasu. Shinkansen no naka ni wa tabemono ya nomimono o utte iru tokoro ga arimasu. Sorekara denwa mo kakeraremasu.

Shinkansen wa anzen o kangaete, tsukutte arimasu. Tatoeba mado no garasu ga warenai yō ni, 11.6 mm (miri) no garasu o tsukatte imasu. Tsuyoi kaze ya yuki no toki wa, konpyūtā de tomattari, ugoitari shimasu.

2000-nen goro ni wa shinkansen yori motto hayai riniya-ekusupuresu ga dekiru yotei desu. Kono riniya-ekusupuresu ga dekireba, Nihon no iroirona tokoro e motto hayaku ikeru yō ni narimasu.

riniya-ekusupuresu

* “Nozomi”, “Hikari”, “Kodama”: shinkansen no namae

1) Tōkyō kara Ōsaka made nan-jikan de ikeru yō ni narimashita ka.

____

2) Shinkansen no naka de tabemono ya nomimono ga kaemasu ka.

____

3) Dōshite 11.6 mm no garasu o tsukatte iru'n desu ka.

____

4) Riniya-ekusupuresu ga dekireba, dō narimasu ka.

____

Dai 37 ka

Bunkei

1. Watashi wa kachō ni shikararemashita.
2. Watashi wa otōto ni kamera o kowasaremashita.
3. Kono biru wa kyonen tateraremashita.

Reibun

37

1. Doko ni ita'n desu ka.
   …Kachō ni yobarete, jimusho ni imashita.
   Repōto ni tsuite iroiro kikaremashita.

2. Kinō dorobō ni okane o toraremashita.
   …Ikura torareta'n desu ka.
   50,000-en gurai desu.

3. O-sake to biiru wa dō chigau'n desu ka.
   …Genryō ga chigaimasu.
   O-sake wa kome kara, biiru wa mugi kara tsukuraremasu.

4. Koko wa kumitate-rain desu.
   Koko de wa kuruma no bodii ga yōsetsu-saremasu.
   …Zenbu robotto ga yatte iru'n desu ne.

5. Kono kōjō no seihin wa donokurai yushutsu-sarete imasu ka.
   …50-pāsento gurai yushutsu-sarete imasu.

Kaiwa

Seisan-rain no kengaku

Narong: Kono kōjō wa itsu taterareta'n desu ka.

Ishikawa: 1965-nen desu. Ima 7,000-nin no hito ga hataraite imasu.

Narong: Sō desu ka. Hontō ni ōkii kōjō desu ne.

Ishikawa: Ē. Ja, seisan-rain o annai-shimashō.

Narong: Hai.

Ishikawa: Koko de wa enjin ga toritsukeraremasu.
Sorekara asoko de wa mado-garasu ya taiya ga toritsukeraremasu.

Narong: Zuibun hayaku dekimasu ne.
1-nichi ni nan-dai gurai seisan-sarete imasu ka.

Ishikawa: Yaku 1,500-dai desu. 3-pun ni 1-dai kansei-shimasu.

Narong: Sō desu ka. Sugoi desu ne.

Renshū A

1.

						ukemi
I	ki	ki	masu	ki	ka	remasu
	yo	mi	masu	yo	ma	remasu
	hako	bi	masu	hako	ba	remasu
	to	ri	masu	to	ra	remasu
	tsuka	i	masu	tsuka	wa	remasu
	kowa	shi	masu	kowa	sa	remasu

			ukemi	
II	tabe	masu	tabe	raremasu
	home	masu	home	raremasu
	mi	masu	mi	raremasu

			ukemi	
III	ki	masu	ko	raremasu
	shi	masu	sa	remasu

2. Watashi wa buchō ni yobaremashita. / homeraremashita. / shitsumon-saremashita.

3. Watashi wa dorobō / kodomo / imōto ni okane / tokei / shorui o toraremashita. / kowasaremashita. / suteraremashita.

4. Ano biru wa 30-nen mae ni / sengetsu / raigetsu tateraremashita. / uraremashita. / kowasaremasu.

5. Koko de bodii / enjin / kuruma ga yōsetsu-saremasu. / toritsukeraremasu. / kensa-saremasu.

6. Kono hon / Nihon no konpyūtā / ATM no kuruma wa iroirona kuni de yomarete / tsukawarete / seisan-sarete imasu.

37

Renshū B

1. Rei: kachō wa watashi o shikarimashita
    ……Watashi wa kachō ni shikararemashita.
    1) buchō wa watashi o homemashita ……
    2) Katō-san wa watashi o yobimashita ……
    3) Katō-san wa watashi ni iroiro shitsumon-shimashita ……
    4) kachō wa watashi ni repōto ni tsuite kikimashita ……

2. Rei: kodomo wa tokei o kowashimashita
    ……Kodomo ni tokei o kowasaremashita.
    1) tomodachi wa tegami o yomimashita ……
    2) tomodachi wa kasa o machigaemashita ……
    3) dorobō wa kaban o torimashita ……
    4) haha wa taisetsuna shorui o sutemashita ……

3. Rei: Itsu kaban o toraremashita ka. (kesa)
    ……Kesa toraremashita.
    1) Densha no naka de nani o toraremashita ka. (saifu) ……
    2) Dare ni kono shigoto o tanomaremashita ka. (Takahashi-san) ……
    3) Kachō ni nani o kikaremashita ka. (jisshū no kansō) ……
    4) Isha ni nan to iwaremashita ka. (tabako o yamero) ……

4. Rei: 2-nen mae ni ano biru o tatemashita

……Ano biru wa 2-nen mae ni tateraremashita.

1) kome kara o-sake o tsukurimasu ……

2) tankā de sekiyu o hakobimasu ……

3) hako ni seihin o iremasu ……

4) kikai de seihin o wakemasu ……

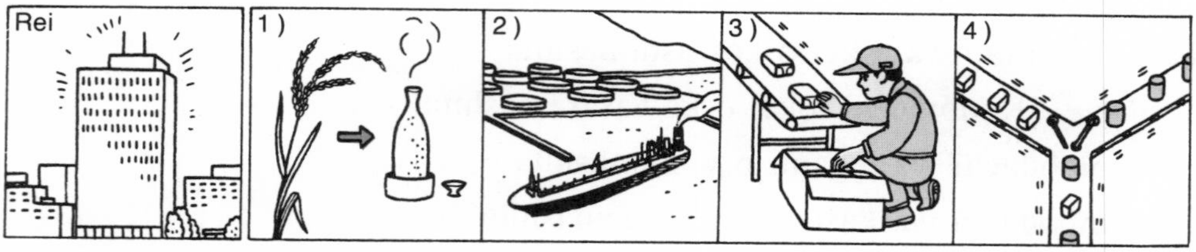

5. Rei: kōhan o kirimasu

……Koko de kōhan ga kiraremasu.

1) bodii o yōsetsu-shimasu ……

2) bodii o kumitatemasu ……

3) enjin o toritsukemasu ……

4) kansei-shita kuruma o kensa-shimasu ……

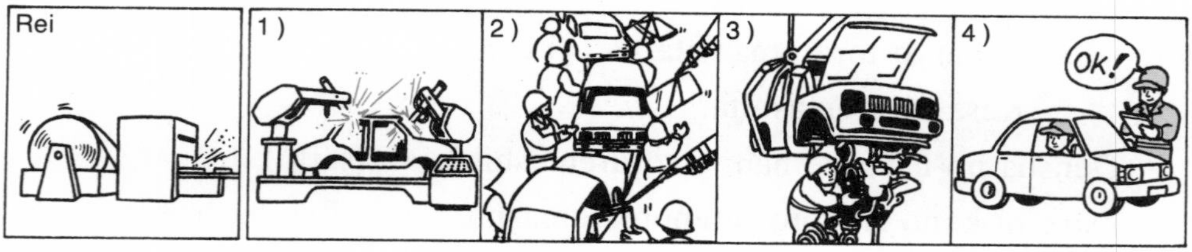

6. Rei: iroirona tokoro de konpyūtā o tsukatte imasu

……Konpyūtā wa iroirona tokoro de tsukawarete imasu.

1) iroirona kuni de Eigo o hanashite imasu ……

2) Nihon de kono hon o yoku yonde imasu ……

3) Amerika ya Yōroppa e Nihon no kuruma o yushutsu-shite imasu ……

4) Tōnan-Ajia kara genryō o yunyū-shite imasu ……

Renshū C

1. A: Doko ni ita'n desu ka.

   B: Kachō ni yobarete, jimusho ni imashita.

   Repōto ni tsuite iroiro kikaremashita.

   1) homemasu

   2) shitsumon-shimasu

2. A: Dō shita'n desu ka.

   B: Dareka ni kaban o machigaerareta'n desu.

   A: Hontō desu ka. Taihen desu ne.

   1) kasa o motte ikimasu

   2) taisetsuna shorui o sutemasu

3. A: Koko wa kumitate-rain desu.
   Koko de wa bodii ga yōsetsu-saremasu.
   B: Zenbu robotto ga yatte iru'n desu ne.

   1) bodii o kumitatemasu
   2) iroirona buhin o toritsukemasu

4. A: Kono kōjō de wa 1-nichi ni nan-dai gurai jidōsha ga seisan-sarete① imasu ka.
   B: Yaku 1,500②-dai desu.
   A: Seihin wa doko e yushutsu-sarete imasu ka.
   B: Amerika ya Yōroppa ya Tōnan-Ajia nado desu.

   1) ① kamera o tsukurimasu ② yaku 1,200
   2) ① terebi o seisan-shimasu ② yaku 800

Mondai

1. 1) ______________________________
   2) ______________________________
   3) ______________________________
   4) ______________________________
   5) ______________________________

2. 1) Rao-san wa (   ) ni yobarete, jimusho e ikimashita.

   Soshite { a. repōto no naiyō ni tsuite shitsumon-saremashita. / b. jisshū no kansō o kikaremashita. / c. repōto no naiyō ga warui to iwaremashita. }

   2) Dareka ni (   ) o { a. toraremashita. / b. machigaeraremashita. / c. motte ikaremashita. }

   3) Kono kōjō wa (   ) ni tateraremashita.

   Ima wa yaku { a. 7,000-nin / b. 5,300-nin / c. 3,500-nin } hataraite imasu.

   4) Koko de wa bodii ga (   ).

   Zenbu { a. hito / b. robotto / c. konpyūtā } ga yatte imasu.

   5) Kono kōjō de wa 1-nichi ni yaku (   )-dai terebi ga

   { a. yushutsu-sarete / b. tsukawarete / c. tsukurarete } imasu.

3.

Rei: kikimasu	kikaremasu	homemasu	
kowashimasu		iremasu	
yobimasu		wakemasu	
yomimasu		tatemasu	
shikarimasu		shimasu	
tsukaimasu		(Nihon e) kimasu	

4. Rei: tomodachi wa kamera o nakushimashita
……Tomodachi ni kamera o nakusaremashita.

1) kachō wa shigoto o tanomimashita ……
2) dorobō wa kaban o torimashita ……
3) otōto wa kamera o kowashimashita ……
4) imōto wa taisetsuna shorui o sutemashita ……

5.

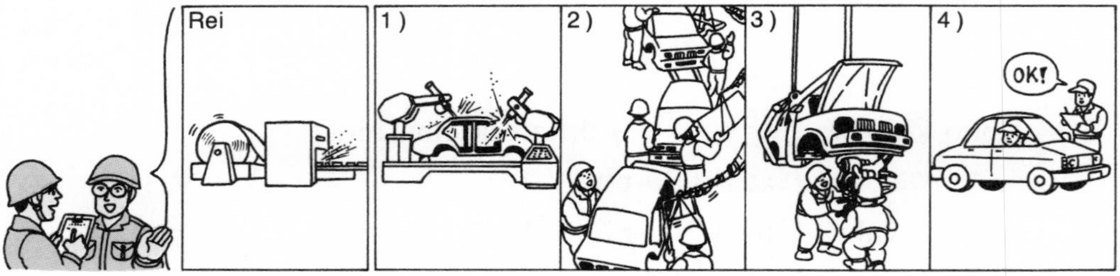

E o mite, kuruma no seisan-rain o setsumei-shite kudasai.

Rei: Koko de kōhan ga kiraremasu.

1) Koko de ______________________
2) Koko de ______________________
3) Koko de ______________________
4) Koko de ______________________

6. Rei: Watashi wa buchō (ni) homeraremashita.

1) Kodomo no toki, yoku sensei ( ) shikararemashita.
2) Densha no naka de dorobō ( ) saifu ( ) torarete shimaimashita.
3) O-sake wa kome ( ) tsukuraremasu.
4) Nihon no kuruma ( ) iroirona kuni ( ) yushutsu-sarete imasu.

7. Nihon wa gaikoku kara genryō ya zairyō o yunyū-shite, sono genryō ya zairyō kara seihin o tsukutte, gaikoku e yushutsu-shite imasu.

Zu ① o mireba, Nihon ga genryō ya zairyō o yunyū-shite iru kuni ga yoku wakarimasu. Genryō ya zairyō wa tōi gaikoku kara fune de Nihon e hakobaremasu.

Tsugi ni, Nihon ga gaikoku e yushutsu-shite iru seihin wa zu ② o mireba, yoku wakarimasu. Nihon de tsukurareta seihin wa fune de gaikoku e hakobarete, uraremasu. Nihon no seihin wa ima iroirona tokoro de tsukawarete imasu.

zu ①

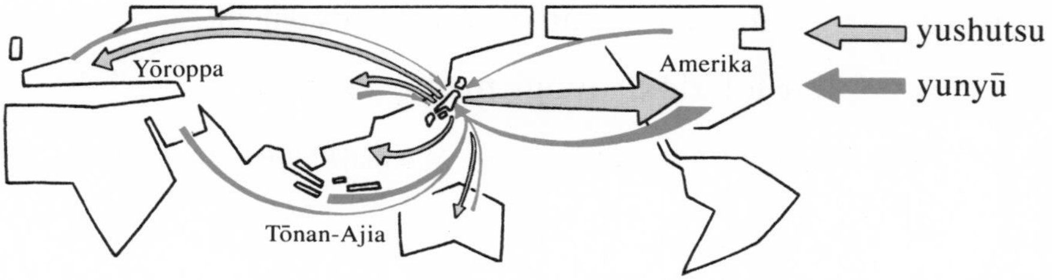

zu ②

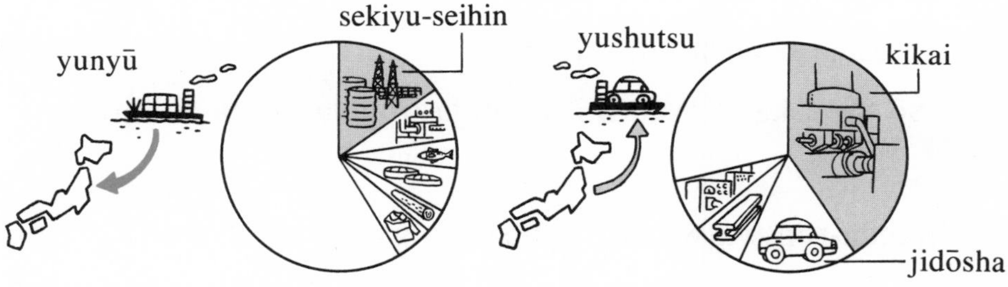

Rei 1: Genryō ya seihin wa fune de hakobaremasu. (○)

Rei 2: Genryō ya seihin wa hikōki de hakobaremasu. (×)

1) Genryō ya zairyō wa Amerika ya Tōnan-Ajia nado kara yunyū-sarete imasu. (　　)

2) Nihon ga ichiban takusan yunyū-shite iru mono wa kome ya mugi desu. (　　)

3) Nihon ga ichiban takusan yushutsu-shite iru mono wa jidōsha desu. (　　)

4) Nihon de tsukurareta seihin wa Amerika e takusan yushutsu-sarete imasu. (　　)

Dai 38 ka

38

Bunkei

1. Minna de shokuji-suru no wa tanoshii desu.
2. Watashi wa hon o yomu no ga suki desu.
3. Repōto ni namae o kaku no o wasuremashita.

Reibun

1. Katō-san wa nanika supōtsu o shite imasu ka.

   …Ē. Yoru tokidoki oyogi ni itte imasu.

   Shigoto no ato de oyogu no wa kimochi ga ii desu yo.

2. Shumi wa nan desu ka.

   …Eiga o miru koto desu.

   Sō desu ka. Watashi mo eiga o miru no ga suki desu.

3. Ikeda-san wa wāpuro o utsu no ga hayai desu ne.

   …Iie, sore hodo demo arimasen.

4. A, ikenai.

   …Dō shita'n desu ka.

   Hiitā o kesu no o wasuremashita.

5. Kimura-san ga kekkon-shita no o shitte imasu ka.

   …Iie, shirimasendeshita. Itsu desu ka.

   Senshū no nichi-yōbi desu.

Kaiwa

Kaisha no kaeri ni

Lee: Nakamura-san wa yoku kono mise e kuru'n desu ka.

Nakamura: Ē. Kaisha no kaeri ni yoku kimasu.
Ima goro densha ni noru to, rasshu ga sugoi desu kara ne.

Lee: Uchi made donokurai kakarimasu ka.

Nakamura: Densha de 2-jikan gurai desu.

Lee: Ja, mainichi kayou no wa taihen desu ne.

Nakamura: Ē. Demo, hon o yondari, tēpu o kiitari shite imasu.

Lee: Nihon-jin wa jikan o muda ni shimasen ne.

Nakamura: Demo, nete iru hito mo ōi desu yo.

Lee: Sō desu ne.

Nakamura: Lee-san, mō ippai dō desu ka.

Lee: Iie, watashi wa mō kekkō desu.

Renshū A

1.

Nihon-go o	hanasu	no wa	muzukashii desu.
Tabako o	suu		karada ni warui desu.
Asa hayaku	sanpo-suru		kimochi ga ii desu.

2.

Watashi wa	e o	kaku	no ga suki desu.
	hon o	yomu	
	hitori de ryokō o	suru	

3.

Ikeda-san wa	hanasu	no ga hayai desu.
	aruku	
	keisan-suru	

4.

Hiitā o	kesu	no o wasuremashita.
Repōto o	dasu	
Kamera o	motte kuru	

5.

Ashita kaigi ga	aru	no o shitte imasu ka.
Mario-san ga kuni e	kaetta	
Kimura-san ga	kekkon-shita	

Renshū B

1. Rei: kazoku to shokuji-shimasu, tanoshii desu
……Kazoku to shokuji-suru no wa tanoshii desu.

1) Nihon-go de shitsumon ni kotaemasu, muzukashii desu ……
2) tabako o suimasu, karada ni warui desu ……
3) minna no mae de hanashimasu, hazukashii desu ……
4) mainichi zangyō-shimasu, taihen desu ……
5) asa hayaku sanpo-shimasu, kimochi ga ii desu ……

2. Rei: watashi wa kitte o atsumemasu, suki desu
……Watashi wa kitte o atsumeru no ga suki desu.

1) watashi wa yakyū o mimasu, daisuki desu ……
2) watashi wa rasshu no densha ni norimasu, kirai desu ……
3) Narong-san wa shashin o torimasu, jōzu desu ……
4) Takahashi-san wa shigoto o shimasu, hayai desu ……
5) watashi wa wāpuro o uchimasu, osoi desu ……

3. Rei 1: senmon no kotoba o oboemasu, muzukashii desu
……Senmon no kotoba o oboeru no wa muzukashii desu ka.

Rei 2: Nakamura-san wa karaoke de utaimasu, suki desu
……Nakamura-san wa karaoke de utau no ga suki desu ka.

1) mainichi densha de kayoimasu, taihen desu ……
2) tabako o yamemasu, muzukashii desu ……
3) kachō wa mainichi uchi e kaerimasu, osoi desu ……
4) Takahashi-san wa wāpuro o uchimasu, hayai desu ……
5) Lee-san wa ryōri o tsukurimasu, jōzu desu ……

4. Rei: repōto ni namae o kakimasu

……Repōto ni namae o kaku no o wasuremashita.

1) denki o keshimasu ……

2) kagi o kakemasu ……

3) kasa o motte kimasu ……

4) mado o shimemasu ……

5) Katō-san ni shorui o watashimasu ……

5. Rei: raishū honsha de kaigi ga arimasu

……Raishū honsha de kaigi ga aru no o shitte imasu ka.

1) ashita buchō ga kōjō e kimasu ……

2) shachō ga Amerika e shutchō-shimasu ……

3) Takahashi-san ga kachō ni narimashita ……

4) Kimura-san ga kekkon-shimashita ……

5) Ishikawa-san ni otoko no ko ga umaremashita ……

Renshū C

1. A: Katō-san wa nanika supōtsu o shite imasu ka.

   B: Ē. Shigoto no ato de, yoku pūru e itte① imasu.

   Oyogu② no wa karada ni ii shi, kimochi mo ii desu kara.

   1) ① supōtsu-sentā e ikimasu ② undō-shimasu

   2) ① jogingu o shimasu ② hashirimasu

2. A: Shumi wa nan desu ka.

   B: Ongaku o kiku① koto desu.

   A: Sō desu ka. Watashi mo ongaku o kiku① no ga suki desu.

   B: Ja, kondo no do-yōbi issho ni konsāto② ni ikimasen ka.

   A: Ē, ii desu ne.

   1) ① eiga o mimasu ② eiga

   2) ① uta o utaimasu ② karaoke

3. A: A, ikenai.

B: Dō shita'n desu ka.

A: Hiitā o kesu no o wasuremashita.

Sumimasen ga, chotto matte ite kudasai.

1) kagi o kakemasu

2) saifu o motte kimasu

4. A: Kimura-san ga kekkon-shita no o shitte imasu ka.
①
B: Iie, shirimasendeshita. Itsu desu ka.

A: Senshū no nichi-yōbi desu.
②
B: Ja, oiwai o shimashō.

1) ① Ishikawa-san ni otoko no ko ga umaremashita

② ototoi

2) ① Takahashi-san ga kachō ni narimashita

② sengetsu

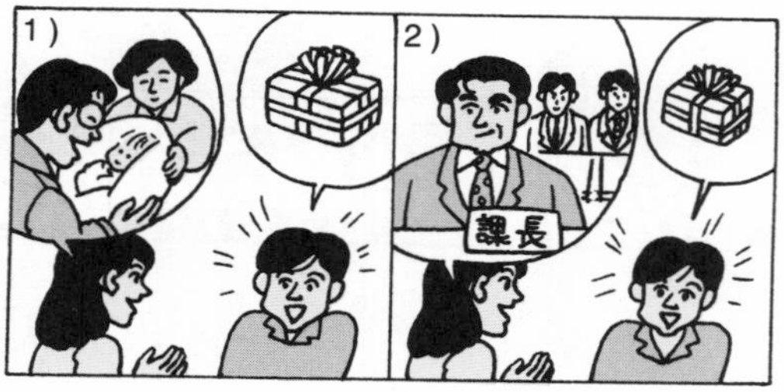

Mondai

1\. 1) ______________________________

2) ______________________________

3) ______________________________

4) ______________________________

5) ______________________________

2\.

1) Nakamura-san wa yoku { a. yakyū o shite imasu. / b. jogingu o shite imasu. / c. pūru de oyoide imasu. }

( ) no wa karada ni ii shi, kimochi mo ii desu kara.

2) Futari no shumi wa ( ) koto desu.

Futari wa kitte o { a. harimasu. / b. kaimasu. / c. kaemasu. }

3) Ikeda-san wa { a. wāpuro o utsu / b. taipu o utsu / c. keisan-suru } no ga totemo ( ) desu.

4) { a. Gasu / b. Kagi / c. Hiitā } o ( ) no o wasurete shimaimashita.

5) Narong-san wa Ishikawa-san ni { a. ototoi otoko no ko / b. ototoi onna no ko / c. kinō onna no ko } ga

( ) no o shirimasendeshita.

3. Rei 1: kanji o yomimasu, muzukashii desu

……Kanji o yomu no wa muzukashii desu.

Rei 2: watashi wa kitte o atsumemasu, suki desu

……Watashi wa kitte o atsumeru no ga suki desu.

1) kotoba o oboemasu, muzukashii desu

……

2) asa hayaku sanpo-shimasu, kimochi ga ii desu

……

3) watashi no kodomo wa terebi o mimasu, daisuki desu

……

4) Lee-san wa e o kakimasu, totemo jōzu desu

……

4. Rei: A, ikenai. Hiitā o (kesu) no o wasuremashita.

1) Repōto ni namae o ( ) no o wasurete shimaimashita.

2) Senshū Kimura-san ga ( ) no o shitte imasu ka.

3) Ashita honsha de kaigi ga ( ) no o shitte imasu ka.

4) Katō-san ga sengetsu kachō ni ( ) no o shirimasendeshita.

5. Rei: Nihon-go de shitsumon ni kotaeru no wa muzukashii desu.

1) ______________________ kimochi ga ii desu.

2) ______________________ suki desu.

3) ______________________ wasuremashita.

4) ______________________ shitte imasu ka.

6. Rei: Nihon-jin wa hanasu ((no), koto) ga hayai desu.

1) Watashi wa hiragana o kaku (no, koto) ga dekimasu.

2) Watashi no shumi wa eiga o miru (no, koto) desu.

3) Tegami ni jūsho o kaku (no, koto) o wasurete shimaimashita.

4) Watashi wa shinkansen ni notta (no, koto) ga arimasen.

7.

Katō-san no kazoku wa 4-nin desu. Katō-san wa 2-nen mae ni uchi o katte, Chiba ni sunde imasu.

Mainichi densha de Tōkyō no kaisha ni kayotte imasu. Kaisha made 2-jikan gurai kakarimasu kara, asa hayaku okinakereba narimasen. Densha wa iki mo kaeri mo itsumo konde imasu. Rasshu no densha ni noru no wa hontō ni taihen desu.

Kaisha wa 5-ji made desu. Shigoto no ato de, 1-shūkan ni 1-kai kaisha no chikaku no supōtsu-sentā e itte imasu. Oyogu no wa karada ni ii shi, kimochi mo ii desu kara. Shigoto ga isogashii toki wa, zangyō-shinakereba narimasen. Zangyō no toki wa, kantanna shokuji o shite, 10-ji goro made hatarakimasu. Yoru osoku made shigoto o suru no wa karada ni warui to okusan ni yoku iwaremasu.

Zangyō ga nai toki wa, kaisha no hito to nomi ni ikimasu. Katō-san wa karaoke de utau no ga suki desu. Shigoto o shitari, nomi ni ittari shite, Katō-san wa itsumo uchi e kaeru no ga osoi desu.

1) Katō-san wa itsumo nan de kaisha ni kayotte imasu ka.

____

2) Densha wa suite imasu ka.

____

3) Katō-san wa shigoto ga owatte kara, itsumo sugu uchi e kaerimasu ka.

____

4) Zangyō-suru toki wa, bangohan o tabenai de shigoto o shimasu ka.

____

Dai 39 ka

Bunkei

1. Tegami o yonde, anshin-shimashita.
2. Yōji ga aru node, hayaku kaerimasu.

Reibun

1. Kinō Kyūshū de ōkina jishin ga atta no o shitte imasu ka.
   …Ē. Watashi mo kesa nyūsu o kiite, bikkuri-shimashita.

2. Ashita issho ni eiga o mi ni ikimasen ka.
   …Ashita wa chotto tsugō ga warukute, ikemasen.

3. Pasokon no tsukai-kata wa mō oboemashita ka.
   …Iie, sōsa ga fukuzatsu de, mada oboeraremasen.

4. Osoku natte, sumimasen.
   …Dō shita'n desu ka.
   Jiko de densha ga okureta'n desu.

5. Kibun ga warui node, kaette mo ii desu ka.
   …Ii desu yo. Odaiji ni.

6. Kono michi wa itsumo konde imasu ga, kyō wa suite imasu ne.
   …Ē. Nichi-yōbi na node, kuruma ga sukunai'n desu.

Kaiwa

Sōtai no kyoka o morau

Rao: Katō-san, ima o-isogashii desu ka.

Katō: Iie. Dōzo.

Rao: Chotto onegai ga aru'n desu ga・・・

Katō: Nan desu ka.

Rao: Jitsu wa raishū no kin-yōbi ni taishikan de pātii ga aru'n desu.

Katō: Sō desu ka.

Rao: 4-ji made ni ikanakereba naranai node, gogo kara kaette mo ii desu ka.

Katō: Taishikan no pātii desu ka. Soreja shikata ga arimasen ne.

Rao: Mōshiwake arimasen. Yoroshiku onegai-shimasu.

Renshū A

1.

Tegami o	yonde,	anshin-shimashita.
Nyūsu o	kiite,	bikkuri-shimashita.
Tegami ga	konakute,	sabishii desu.
Pātii ni	ikenakute,	zannen desu.

2.

	Takakute,	kaemasen.
	Karakute,	taberaremasen.
Sōsa ga	fukuzatsu de,	yoku wakarimasen.

3.

Koshō	de	kikai ga tomarimashita.
Byōki		kaisha o yasumimashita.
Kōtsū-jiko		hito ga shinimashita.

4.

Tomodachi to yakusoku ga	aru	node,	saki ni kaerimasu.
Basu ga sugu	konakatta		okuremashita.
Atama ga	itai		kaisha o yasumimasu.
Konban wa	himana		asobi ni ikimasu.
Ashita wa	yasumi na		tomodachi to dekakemasu.

Renshū B

1. Rei: tegami o yomimashita, anshin-shimashita

  ……Tegami o yonde, anshin-shimashita.

 1) nyūsu o kikimashita, bikkuri-shimashita ……

 2) shashin o mimashita, kazoku o omoidashimashita ……

 3) Katō-san no hanashi o kikimashita, minna waraimashita ……

 4) kachō ni homeraremashita, ureshikatta desu ……

2. Rei: koibito ni aemasen, sabishii desu

  ……Koibito ni aenakute, sabishii desu.

 1) pātii ni ikemasen, zannen desu ……

 2) tomodachi ga imasen, sabishii desu ……

 3) Nihon-go ga wakarimasen, komatte imasu ……

 4) kazoku kara tegami ga kimasendeshita, shinpai-shimashita ……

3. Rei: kono hon wa muzukashii desu, yoku wakarimasen

  ……Kono hon wa muzukashikute, yoku wakarimasen.

 1) kono nimotsu wa omoi desu, motemasen ……

 2) kuruma no oto ga urusai desu, yoku neraremasen ……

 3) shigoto ga isogashii desu, doko mo ikemasen ……

 4) hanasu no ga hayai desu, yoku wakarimasen ……

4. Rei: shinkansen ga tomarimashita (yuki)

······Yuki de shinkansen ga tomarimashita.

1) uchi ga kowaremashita (jishin) ······

2) hoteru ga yakemashita (kaji) ······

3) ki ga taoremashita (taifū) ······

4) hito ga kega o shimashita (kōtsū-jiko) ······

5. Rei: chotto yōji ga arimasu, saki ni kaerimasu

······Chotto yōji ga aru node, saki ni kaerimasu.

1) byōin e ikitai desu, hayaku kaette mo ii desu ka ······

2) onaka ga itai desu, sukoshi yasunde mo ii desu ka ······

3) basu ga nakanaka kimasendeshita, kaisha ni okuremashita ······

4) repōto o kakanakereba narimasen, kyō wa sugu kaerimasu ······

6. Rei: Doko mo dekakenai'n desu ka. (karada no chōshi ga warui desu)

······Ē, karada no chōshi ga warui node, dekakemasen.

1) Kinō kaisha o yasunda'n desu ka.
(atama ga itakatta desu) ······

2) Kono hon o yomanakatta'n desu ka.
(jikan ga arimasendeshita) ······

3) Kinō no ban shinkansen ga tomatta'n desu ka.
(takusan yuki ga furimashita) ······

4) Kono michi wa kuruma ga tōrenai'n desu ka.
(ima kōjichū desu) ······

Renshū C

1. A: Kinō Kyūshū de ōkina jishin ① ga atta no o shitte imasu ka.

   B: Ē. Watashi mo kesa nyūsu o kiite ②, bikkuri-shimashita.

   Jishin ① wa hontō ni kowai desu ne.

   1) ① chikaku de kaji

   ② shinbun o yomimashita

   2) ① kaisha no chikaku de kōtsū-jiko

   ② terebi o mimashita

2. A: Ashita Shinjuku e kaimono ni ikimasen ka.

   B: Ashita desu ka. Ashita wa chotto tsugō ga warukute, ikemasen.

   A: Ja, do-yōbi wa dō desu ka.

   B: Do-yōbi nara, ii desu.

   1) shigoto ga isogashii desu

   2) jikan ga arimasen

3. A: Osoku natte, sumimasen.

   B: Dō shita'n desu ka.

   A: Jiko① de densha ga tomatte shimatta②'n desu.

   B: Sore wa taihen deshita ne.

   1) ① kōtsū-jiko ② michi ga konde imashita

   2) ① yuki ② basu ga nakanaka kimasendeshita

4. A: Chotto onegai ga aru'n desu ga· · ·

   B: Nan desu ka.

   A: Jitsu wa raishū no kin-yōbi ni taishikan de pātii ga aru① node, hayaku kaette② mo ii desu ka.

   B: Wakarimashita. Ii desu yo.

   1) ① tomodachi no kekkonshiki ga arimasu

   ② yasumimasu

   2) ① byōin e ikanakereba narimasen

   ② sukoshi okuremasu

Mondai

1. 1) Narong-san wa kesa (   ) no nyūsu o

{ a. rajio de kiite, / b. terebi de mite, / c. shinbun de yonde, } bikkuri-shimashita.

2) Lee-san wa konban { a. yōji ga atte, / b. pātii ga atte, / c. shigoto ga isogashikute, } issho ni shokuji ni

(   ).

3) Narong-san wa (   ) no

{ a. kanji ga yomenakute, / b. naiyō ga muzukashikute, / c. kotoba no imi ga wakaranakute, } komatte imasu.

4) (   ) de { a. shinkansen ga koshō-shita / b. shinkansen ga tomatta / c. hikōki ga shuppatsu-dekinakatta } node,

kaigi no jikan ni okurete shimaimashita.

5) Raishū no kin-yōbi ni (   ) ga arimasu.

5-ji made ni hoteru e { a. inakereba naranai / b. kaeranakereba naranai / c. ikanakereba naranai } node, hayaku

kaeritai desu.

2. Rei: Tegami o (moratte), ureshikatta desu.

1) Rajio de jishin no nyūsu o (   ), bikkuri-shimashita.

2) Kazoku no tegami o (   ), anshin-shimashita.

3) Kōtsū-jiko o (   ), kowaku narimashita.

4) Nihon ni tomodachi ga (   ), sabishii desu.

3. Rei: Kono ryōri wa karakute, taberaremasen.
   1) Kono nimotsu wa omokute, ______________________
   2) Kono setsumeisho wa kanji ga ōkute, ______________________
   3) Kōji no oto ga urusakute, ______________________
   4) Tōkyō no chikatetsu wa fukuzatsu de, ______________________

4. 

   Rei: Byōki de kaisha o yasumimashita.
   1) ______________________
   2) ______________________
   3) ______________________
   4) ______________________

5. Rei: Onaka ga (itakatta desu … itakatta) node, kaisha o yasumimashita.
   1) Netsu ga (arimasu …) node, hayaku kaette mo ii desu ka.
   2) Kyō wa (nichi-yōbi desu …) node, byōin wa yasumi desu.
   3) Michi ga (konde imashita …) node, jikan ni okurete shimaimashita.
   4) Kinō wa karada no chōshi ga (warukatta desu …) node, doko mo ikimasendeshita.
   5) Basu ga sugu (kimasendeshita …) node, takushii de kimashita.

6. Rei: Hikōki-jiko no nyūsu o (kiite, kiite kara, kiita node), bikkuri-shimashita.
   1) (Kaze de, Kaze da, Kaze na node), kaisha o yasumimashita.
   2) Kono sūpā wa nedan mo (yasui node, yasui shi, yasui kara), shinamono mo ōi shi, itsumo koko de kaimono-shite imasu.
   3) Ii jisho ga (nai de, nakute, nakute mo), komatte imasu.
   4) Taishikan no pātii ni (ikitai kara, ikitai node, ikitakute), hayaku kaette mo ii desu ka.

7. Tsugi no bun o yonde, ato no shitsumon ni kotaete kudasai.

Nihon wa kuruma ga ōi desu. Sorede kōtsū-jiko mo taihen ōi desu. Mainichi takusan no hito ga shindari, kega o shitari shite imasu. Shita no hyō o mireba, kono koto ga yoku wakarimasu.

Wakai hito no baiku no jiko mo ōku natte imasu. 1990-nen wa 1-nen de yaku 1,500-nin no hito ga baiku no jiko de shinimashita. Shita no zu o mite kudasai. Kuruma o unten-shite iru hito ni wa, ushiro no baiku ga yoku mienai node, jiko ni narimasu. Desukara, kuruma o unten-suru toki wa, mae ya ushiro o yoku mite, anzen-unten o shinakereba narimasen.

	kōtsū-jiko	shinda hito	kega o shita hito
1989-nen	552,788	9,261	681,346
1990-nen	579,190	9,317	712,330
1991-nen	590,134	9,347	720,495

1) 1991-nen ni kōtsū-jiko de kega o shita hito wa nan-nin desu ka. (Hyō o mite, kotaete kudasai.)

2) 1990-nen ni baiku no jiko de shinda hito wa donokurai imasu ka.

3) Dōshite jiko ni narimasu ka.

4) Kuruma o unten-suru hito wa donna koto ni ki o tsukenakereba narimasen ka.

Dai 40 ka

Bunkei

1. Kaigi wa nan-ji ni owaru ka, wakarimasen.
2. Pātii ni korareru ka dō ka, shirasete kudasai.
3. Nihon no o-sake o nonde mimasu.

Reibun

1. Narong-san wa doko e ikimashita ka.
   …Sā, doko e itta ka, wakarimasen.
   Watanabe-san ni kiite kudasai.

2. Kono hako no nakami wa nan desu ka.
   …Sā, nani ka, wakarimasen. Akete shirabemashō.

3. Omosa ga donokurai aru ka, hakatte kudasai.
   …Hai, wakarimashita. Sugu hakarimasu.

4. Ashita no pātii ni ikimasu ka.
   …Sō desu ne. Shigoto ga isogashii node, ikeru ka dō ka, wakarimasen.

5. Koko de donna kensa o suru'n desu ka.
   …Bin ni kizu ga nai ka dō ka, shirabemasu.

6. Sumimasen. Kono zubon o haite mite mo ii desu ka.
   …Hai. Achira de dōzo.

Kaiwa

Jisshū no yotei ni tsuite

Takahashi: Kore wa jisshū no yotei-hyō desu.
Korekara donna jisshū o suru ka, yoku mite kudasai.

Narong: Hai.

Takahashi: Sukejūru ni tsuite nanika kibō ga attara, itte kudasai.

Narong: Anō, 9-gatsu kara 2-kagetsu hanbaiten de jisshū-suru'n desu ka.

Takahashi: Sō desu.

Narong: Watashi no senmon to amari kankei ga nai to omoimasu ga· · ·

Takahashi: Iya. O-kyaku-san no niizu o shiru no mo taisetsu desu yo.

Narong: Sō desu ka. Wakarimashita.

Takahashi: Shikashi, 2-kagetsu wa nagai kamo shiremasen ne.
Mō sukoshi mijikaku naru ka dō ka, buchō ni sōdan-shite mimasu.

Narong: Sumimasen. Yoroshiku onegai-shimasu.

Renshū A

1.

Narong-san wa	doko ni	iru	ka,	wakarimasen.
Hako ga	ikutsu	aru		kazoete kudasai.
Pātii wa	itsu ga	ii		kangaete kudasai.
Kōbe wa	donna	machi		shirimasen.

2.

Lee-san wa	kuru	ka dō ka,	wakarimasen.
Machigai ga	nai		shirabete kudasai.
Suitchi o	kitta		tashikamete kudasai.
Sono hanashi wa	hontō		wakarimasen.

3.

Buchō ni iken o	kiite	mimasu.
Koshō no gen'in o	shirabete	
Dekiru ka dō ka,	yatte	

Renshū B

1. Rei: Kōgi wa nan-ji ni owarimasu ka.
   ……Sā, nan-ji ni owaru ka, wakarimasen.
   1) Narong-san wa nani o shite imasu ka. ……
   2) Katō-san wa itsu kaerimashita ka. ……
   3) Lee-san wa doko e ikimashita ka. ……
   4) Ano hito wa dare desu ka. ……

2. Rei: ringo ga nan-ko arimasu ka, kazoemasu
   ……Ringo ga nan-ko aru ka, kazoete kudasai.
   1) nagasa ga donokurai arimasu ka, hakarimasu ……
   2) hanmā ga doko ni arimasu ka, sagashimasu ……
   3) dō shitara ii desu ka, kangaemasu ……
   4) dōshite koshō-shimashita ka, shirabemasu ……

3. Rei: Shinkansen ni maniaimasu ka. (michi ga konde imasu)
   ……Sā, maniau ka dō ka, wakarimasen.
   Michi ga konde imasu kara.
   1) Ali-san wa genki desu ka. (tegami ga kimasen) ……
   2) Biiru wa tarimasu ka. (o-kyaku-san ga ōi desu) ……
   3) Hoteru wa yoyaku-dekimasu ka. (natsu-yasumi desu) ……
   4) Kare wa pātii ni kimasu ka. (isogashii to itte imashita) ……

4. Rei: genki desu, tegami de shirasemasu

……Genki ka dō ka, tegami de shirasete kudasai.

1) ringo ga tarimasu, kazoemasu ……

2) pātii ni koraremasu, renraku-shimasu ……

3) kotae ga tadashii desu, mō ichido tashikamemasu ……

4) kizu ga arimasen, kensa-shimasu ……

5. Rei 1: minna ni iken o kikimasu

……Minna ni iken o kiite mimasu.

Rei 2: zehi Fujisan e ikitai desu

……Zehi Fujisan e itte mitai desu.

1) buchō ni sōdan-shimasu ……

2) mō ichido gen'in o shirabemasu ……

3) zehi Nihon-ryōri o tabetai desu ……

4) zehi sukii o shitai desu ……

6. Rei: oishii desu, chotto tabemasu

……Oishii ka dō ka, chotto tabete mite kudasai.

1) saizu ga aimasu, chotto kimasu ……

2) machigai ga arimasen, mō ichido chekku-shimasu ……

3) depāto wa yasumi desu, denwa de kikimasu ……

4) shūri-dekimasu, yarimasu ……

Renshū C

1. A: Hako ga ikutsu arimasu ka.
   B: Sā, ikutsu aru ka, wakarimasen. ①
   A: Ja, kazoete kudasai. ②
   B: Wakarimashita.

   1) ① buhin ga ikutsu nokotte imasu ka ② kazoemasu
   2) ① omosa ga nan-kiro arimasu ka ② hakarimasu

2. A: Akai ranpu ga tsukimashita. Dō shitara ii desu ka.
   B: Koshō desu ne.
   Sugu kikai o tomete, doko ga okashii ka, shirabete kudasai.
   A: Wakarimashita.

   1) nani ga gen'in desu ka
   2) dōshite koshō-shimashita ka

3. A: Koko de wa donna kensa o suru'n desu ka.
   B: Kizu ga nai① ka dō ka, chekku-shimasu.
   A: Moshi kizu ga atta②ra, dō shimasu ka.
   B: Kono hako ni iremasu.

   1) ① gomi ga haitte imasen ② haitte imasu
   2) ① saizu ga atte imasu ② atte imasen

4. A: Sumimasen. Kono fuku o kite mite mo ii desu ka.
   B: Hai, dōzo・・・ Ikaga desu ka.
   A: Pittari desu. Kore o kudasai.

   1) kutsu o hakimasu
   2) bōshi o kaburimasu

Mondai

1\.
1) ______________________________
2) ______________________________
3) ______________________________
4) ______________________________
5) ______________________________

2\.
1) Narong-san wa { a. mō ryō e kaerimashita. / b. mada ryō e kaette imasen. / c. mō heya de nete imasu. } Kyō wa zangyō ga aru node, nan-ji goro (　　　　) ka, wakarimasen.

2) Gogo no jisshū wa { a. itsu / b. dare / c. nani } ka, wakarimasen.
(　　　　) ni kiite mite kudasai.

3) Natsu-yasumi wa { a. hoteru ga komu / b. hoteru ga suku / c. hoteru ni denwa-suru } node,
yoyaku-(　　　　) ka dō ka, wakarimasen.

4) Koko de wa suitchi o irete, terebi ga (　　　　) ka dō ka, kensa-shimasu.
Moshi tsukanakattara, seisan-rain de { a. sutemasu. / b. kowashimasu. / c. naoshimasu. }

5) Zubon o (　　　　) mimashita ga, { a. chiisakatta / b. ōkikatta / c. nagakatta } desu.

3. Rei: Narong-san wa doko ni imasu ka, wakarimasen

……Narong-san wa doko ni iru ka, wakarimasen.

1) dōshite kikai ga koshō-shimashita ka, gen'in ga wakarimasen

……

2) paipu no nagasa ga nan-senchi arimasu ka, hakatte kudasai

……

3) buhin ga ikutsu nokotte imasu ka, kazoete kudasai

……

4) Tōkyō-tawā made dōyatte ittara ii desu ka, oshiete kudasai

……

4. Rei: 10-ji no shinkansen ni maniaimasu ka.

……Sā, michi ga konde iru node, maniau ka dō ka, wakarimasen.

1) Tōkyō-tawā kara Fujisan ga miemasu ka.

……Sā, kyō wa ______________ node, ______________, wakarimasen.

2) Kono tokei wa shūri-dekimasu ka.

……Sā, ______________ node, ______________, wakarimasen.

3) Ano mise no ryōri wa oishii desu ka.

……Sā, ______________ node, ______________, wakarimasen.

4) Tanaka-san wa o-genki desu ka.

……Sā, ______________ node, ______________, wakarimasen.

5. Rei: chotto kono ryōri o tabete kudasai

……Chotto kono ryōri o tabete mite kudasai.

1) jikan ga attara, Nihon no iroirona tokoro e ikitai desu

……

2) chotto kono fuku o kite mo ii desu ka

……

3) dō shitara ii ka, buchō ni iken o kikimasu

……

4) doko ga okashii ka, mō ichido yoku shirabete kudasai

……

6. 1) Migi no keisan ni wa machigai ga arimasu. →
Doko ga chigatte iru ka, mitsukete, naoshite kudasai.

$$\begin{array}{r} 375 \\ \times \quad 42 \\ \hline 750 \\ 1488 \\ \hline 15550 \end{array}$$

2) 1-mētoru no paipu kara 8-senchi no nagasa no buhin ga nan-ko tsukureru ka, kotaete kudasai.
Kotae ______________ -ko

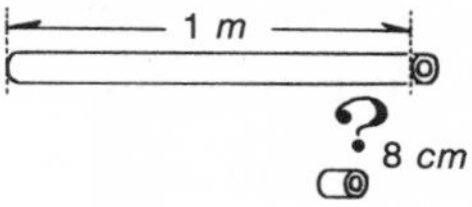

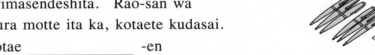

3) Onaji omosa no ringo 5-ko o omosa 300-guramu no hako ni irete hakattara, 1,700-guramu arimashita.
Ringo no omosa wa 1-ko nan-guramu desu ka.
Kotae ______________ -guramu

4) Rao-san wa 1-pon 150-en no bōrupen o 6-pon kaō to omoimashita. Demo, 100-en tarimasendeshita. Rao-san wa ikura motte ita ka, kotaete kudasai.
Kotae ______________ -en

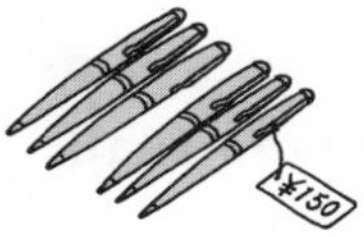

7. Shita no e wa atarashii kuruma o tsukuru mae ni suru iroirona shigoto desu. E no setsumei wa dore desu ka. Shita kara erande kudasai.

Rei (B) (   ) (   ) (   ) (   )

A: Tsukutta kuruma ga anzen ka dō ka, iroirona shiken o shite, chekku-shimasu.

B: O-kyaku-san wa donna kuruma ga ii to omotte iru ka, yoku shirabete, shiryō o tsukurimasu.

C: Kuruma no e o kaitari, konpyūtā o tsukattari shite, kuruma no dezain o kimemasu.

D: Atsumeta shiryō o minagara, kaigi de donna kuruma o tsukuttara ii ka, sōdan-shimasu.

E: Sonna kuruma ga hontō ni tsukureru ka dō ka, tsukutte mimasu.

Fukushū H

1. Rei: Buchō (ni) iken o kiite mimasu.
   1) Bangohan ( ) ato de, o-furo ( ) hairimasu.
   2) Kusuri o nonda node, netsu ( ) sagarimashita.
   3) Sōsa no junjo ( ) chigaimasu yo. Manyuaru ( ) tōri ni, yatte kudasai.
   4) Kōjō no naka ( ) hashiranai yō ni shite kudasai.
   5) Kono bideo ni wa rimokon ( ) tsuite imasu.
   6) Yatto Nihon no seikatsu ( ) naremashita.
   7) Nimotsu ( ) ochinai yō ni, kichinto nosete kudasai.
   8) Dorobō ( ) okane ( ) torarete shimaimashita.
   9) O-sake ( ) kome ( ) tsukuraremasu.
   10) Watashi no kodomo wa terebi o miru no ( ) daisuki desu.
   11) Mainichi densha de kaisha ( ) kayotte imasu.
   12) Kimura-san ( ) kekkon-shita no ( ) shitte imasu ka.
   13) Kaji ( ) uchi ga yakemashita.
   14) Kono michi wa kōjichū na node, kuruma ( ) tōremasen.
   15) Kono hon wa watashi no senmon ( ) kankei ( ) arimasen.

2. Rei: Tomodachi to o-sake o (nomimasu ··· nomu) no wa tanoshii desu.
   1) Konpyūtā no sōsa ga yatto (dekimasu ···) yō ni narimashita.
   2) Kazoku ga (shinpai-shimasu ···) yō ni, yoku tegami o kaite imasu.
   3) Kiken desu kara, zettai ni koko kara atama o (dashimasu ···) yō ni shite kudasai.
   4) Kesa no nyūsu o (kikimasu ···), bikkuri-shimashita.
   5) Kono mondai wa (muzukashii desu ···), zenzen wakarimasen.
   6) Narong-san wa doko e ikimashita ka.
      ···Sā, doko e (ikimasu ···) ka, wakarimasen.
   7) Saizu ga (aimasu ···) ka dō ka, chotto kite (mimasu ···) kudasai.
   8) Kinō wa atama ga (itai desu ···) node, kaisha o yasumimashita.

H

3. Tadashii mono o erande kudasai.

1) Hajimemashite. Narong desu. { a. Iroiro osewa ni narimashita. / b. Kyō kara osewa ni narimasu. / c. Shitsurei-shimasu. }

Dōzo yoroshiku onegai-shimasu.

…Watanabe desu. Kochira koso dōzo yoroshiku.

2) Kyō no jisshū wa zenbu owarimashita.

…Ja, kaette mo ii desu yo. { a. Gomen kudasai. / b. Gokurōsama deshita. / c. Sorosoro shitsurei-shimasu. }

3) Dō shita'n desu ka.

…Kaze o hiite shimatta'n desu.

Sō desu ka. { a. Otsukaresama deshita. / b. Dōzo o-genki de. / c. Odaiji ni. }

4) Natsu-yasumi wa inaka e kaeru yotei desu. Yokattara, issho ni ikimasen ka.

…Arigatō gozaimasu. { a. Tanoshimi ni shite imasu. / b. Mōshiwake arimasen. / c. Kamaimasen. }

5) Biiru, mō ippai dō desu ka.

…Iie, { a. dō itashimashite. / b. itadakimasu. / c. mō kekkō desu. }

6) Wāpuro o utsu no ga hayai desu ne.

…Iie, { a. sore hodo demo arimasen. / b. shikata ga arimasen. / c. mōshiwake arimasen. }

Dai 41 ka

Bunkei

1. Watashi wa Tanaka-san ni jisho o itadakimashita.
2. Watashi wa Suzuki-sensei ni Nihon-go o oshiete itadakimashita.
3. Okusan wa watashi ni Nihon-ryōri o tsukutte kudasaimashita.
4. Watashi wa musume ni tanjōbi no purezento o okutte yarimashita.

Reibun

1. Kireina Nihon-ningyō desu ne.

   …Ē. Konoaida Katō-san no okusan ga kudasaimashita.

2. Chūgoku de wa kodomo no tanjōbi ni nani o agemasu ka.

   …Nihon to daitai onaji desu. Omocha ya hon o yarimasu.

3. Yūbe wa osokatta desu ne. Takushii de kaetta'n desu ka.

   …Iie, kachō ni ryō made kuruma de okutte itadakimashita.

4. Hōmusutei wa dō deshita ka.

   …Tanoshikatta desu.

   Kazoku no minasan ga totemo shinsetsu ni shite kudasaimashita.

5. Okosan ni donna omiyage o katte agemasu ka.

   …Tokei ka rajikase o katte yaritai desu.

6. Tegami no kaki-kata ga wakaranai'n desu ga, chotto oshiete itadakemasen ka.

   …Ii desu yo.

Kaiwa

Tegami o mite morau

Narong: Anō, Nihon-go de tegami o kaita'n desu ga, chotto mite itadakemasen ka.

Takahashi: Ē, ii desu yo. Nan no tegami desu ka.

Narong: Hōmusutei no o-rei no tegami desu.

Takahashi: Konoaida no hōmusutei desu ne. Dō deshita ka.

Narong: Kazoku no minasan ga totemo shinsetsu ni shite kudasaimashita.

Takahashi: Sore wa yokatta desu ne.

Takahashi: Ēto, koko wa "shōtai-shite moratte" yori "shōtai-shite itadaite" no hō ga ii desu yo.
Teinei ni narimasu kara.

Narong: Sō desu ka. Arigatō gozaimashita.

Renshū A

1.

Watashi wa	shachō	ni tokei o itadakimashita.
	buchō	
	kachō	

2.

Shachō	wa watashi ni tokei o kudasaimashita.
Buchō	
Kachō	

3.

Watashi wa	otōto	ni saifu o yarimashita.
	imōto	
	kodomo	

4.

Watashi wa buchō ni	repōto o	naoshite	itadakimashita.
	kuruma de	okutte	
	kōjō o	annai-shite	

5.

Kachō no okusan wa	watashi ni ryōri o	tsukutte
	watashi ni ryokō no shashin o	misete
	watashi o Tōkyō-tawā e	tsurete itte

kudasaimashita.

6.

Watashi wa musuko ni	tokei o	katte	yarimashita.
	hon o	yonde	
	Fujisan no shashin o	okutte	

7.

Tegami no machigai o	naoshite	itadakemasen ka.
Wāpuro no tsukai-kata o	oshiete	
Mō ichido	setsumei-shite	

Renshū B

1. Rei 1: watashi wa tomodachi ni nekutai o moraimashita (buchō)

   ……Watashi wa buchō ni nekutai o itadakimashita.

   Rei 2: tomodachi wa watashi ni jisho o kuremashita (sensei)

   ……Sensei wa watashi ni jisho o kudasaimashita.

   1) watashi wa tomodachi ni tokei o moraimashita (buchō) ……
   2) watashi wa tomodachi ni terehon-kādo o moraimashita (kachō) ……
   3) tomodachi wa watashi ni mezurashii kitte o kuremashita (Katō-san) ……
   4) tomodachi wa watashi ni kabuki no kippu o kuremashita (shachō) ……

2. Rei: ……Watashi wa kodomo ni okashi o yarimashita.

   1) ……
   2) ……
   3) ……
   4) ……

3. Rei: Suzuki-sensei wa Nihon-go o oshiemashita

   ……Suzuki-sensei ni Nihon-go o oshiete itadakimashita.

   1) Nakamura-san wa honsha e tsurete ikimashita ……
   2) Takahashi-san wa tegami no machigai o naoshimashita ……
   3) Katō-san wa konpyūtā no hon o kashimashita ……
   4) buchō wa kōjō o annai-shimashita ……

4. Rei: okusan wa sukiyaki o tsukurimashita

   ……Okusan wa sukiyaki o tsukutte kudasaimashita.

   1) Katō-san wa tomodachi o shōkai-shimashita ……
   2) okusan wa Nihon no odori o misemashita ……
   3) Katō-san wa eki made kuruma de okurimashita ……
   4) okusan wa Nihon no uta o oshiemashita ……

5. Rei: jitensha o kaimasu (kodomo)
……Kodomo ni jitensha o katte yarimasu.
1) hon o yomimasu (kodomo) ……
2) kimono o kaimasu (imōto) ……
3) tanjōbi no purezento o okurimasu (musuko) ……
4) Nihon no shashin o misemasu (musume) ……

6. Rei: Dare ni Nihon-go o oshiete moraimashita ka. (Suzuki-sensei)
……Suzuki-sensei ni oshiete itadakimashita.
1) Itsu Katō-san no uchi e shōtai-shite moraimashita ka.
(senshū no nichi-yōbi) ……
2) Dare ga kuruma de okutte kuremashita ka. (Katō-san) ……
3) Katō-san ni doko e tsurete itte moraimashita ka.
(Kyōto no o-tera) ……
4) Okosan ni donna omiyage o katte agemasu ka. (omocha) ……

7. Rei: eki e ikitai desu, michi o oshiemasu
……Eki e ikitai'n desu ga, michi o oshiete itadakemasen ka.
1) Tōkyō-tawā e ikitai desu, chizu o kakimasu ……
2) wāpuro no tsukai-kata ga wakarimasen, oshiemasu ……
3) Nihon-go de tegami o kakimashita, mimasu ……
4) kono hon o yomitai desu, kashimasu ……

Renshū C

1. A: Ii sētā ① desu ne.

   B: Kore desu ka. Konoaida Katō-san no okusan ② ni itadakimashita.

   1) ① kireina terehon-kādo ② Katō-san

   2) ① ii jisho ② Tanaka-san

2. A: Hōmusutei wa dō deshita ka.

   B: Tanoshikatta desu.

   Okusan ga Nihon-ryōri o takusan tsukutte kudasaimashita.

   A: Sō desu ka. Yokatta desu ne.

   B: Ē. Kazoku no minasan ga totemo shinsetsu ni shite kudasaimashita.

   1) musume-san ga piano o hikimasu

   2) go-shujin ga Tōkyō-tawā e tsurete ikimasu

3. A: Hōmusutei ni itte, nani o shimashita ka.

B: Nihon no ryōri o narai①mashita.

A: Sō desu ka.

B: Kuni e kaettara, kodomo ni tsukutte② yaritai desu.

1) ① uta o utaimasu ② oshiemasu

2) ① odori o misete moraimasu ② shashin o misemasu

4. A: Anō, sumimasen.

B: Hai, nan desu ka.

A: Tegami no kaki-kata ga wakaranai①'n desu ga, oshiete② itadakemasen ka.

B: Ii desu yo.

1) ① Nihon-go de tegami o kakimashita ② mimasu

2) ① Tōkyō-tawā e ikitai desu ② chizu o kakimasu

Mondai

1. 1) ____________________

2) ____________________

3) ____________________

4) ____________________

5) ____________________

2.

1) Kono (   ) wa { a. Katō-san / b. Katō-san no okusan / c. Katō-san no okāsan } ni itadakimashita.

2) Kono (   ) wa Sentā o deru toki,

{ a. jibun de kaimashita. / b. Tanaka-san ga kudasaimashita. / c. Tanaka-san ni denwa-shimashita. }

3) Kinō wa { a. doko mo ikimasendeshita. / b. Nakamura-san no uchi e ikimashita. / c. kuruma de tomodachi to asobi ni ikimashita. }

Kaeri wa Nakamura-san ga kuruma de { a. okutte itadakimashita. / b. okutte kudasaimashita. / c. unten-shite yarimashita. }

4) Kuni e kaettara, (   ) ya (   ) ni

{ a. Nihon no odori o misete / b. Nihon no odori o oshiete / c. musume-san no odori no shashin o misete } yaritai desu.

5) (   ) no tegami no kaki-kata ga wakaranakatta node,

Takahashi-san ni oshiete { a. kudasaimashita. / b. itadakimashita. / c. agemashita. }

3. Tadashii hō o ○ de erande kudasai.

1) Watashi wa shachō ni tokei o (moraimashita, itadakimashita).

2) Mori-san wa watashi ni kabuki no kippu o (kudasaimashita, itadakimashita).

3) Netsu ga atta node, isha ni mite (agemashita, moraimashita).

4) Watashi wa Suzuki-sensei ni Nihon-go o oshiete (kudasaimashita, itadakimashita).

5) Takahashi-san wa watashi o Karuizawa e tsurete itte (kudasaimashita, itadakimashita).

6) Maiasa hana ni mizu o (kureta, yatta) node, kireina hana ga sakimashita.

7) Neru mae ni, itsumo kodomo ni hon o yonde (agemasu, yarimasu).

8) Kanai wa kuni kara kodomo no shashin o okutte (agemashita, kuremashita).

4. Rei: Watashi wa tomodachi (ni) hon o kashite moraimashita.

1) A: Ii shatsu desu ne.
B: Ē, Katō-san no okusan ( ) itadaita'n desu.

2) A: Wā, atarashii tokei desu ne.
B: Ē, tanjōbi ni buchō ( ) kudasatta'n desu.
A: Furui no wa dō shita'n desu ka.
B: Otōto ( ) yarimashita.

3) A: Yūbe wa osokatta desu ne. Takushii de kaetta'n desu ka.
B: Iie, Katō-san ( ) kuruma de okutte kudasatta'n desu.

4) A: Jōzu ni tegami ga kakemashita ne.
B: Jitsu wa Takahashi-san ( ) machigai ( ) naoshite itadaita'n desu.

5. Rei: Tegami no kaki-kata ga wakaranai'n desu ga, oshiete itadakemasen ka.

1) Nihon-go de tegami o kaita'n desu ga, ______________________

2) Konpyūtā no hon o yomitai'n desu ga, ______________________

3) Kanji no jisho ga hoshii'n desu ga, ______________________

4) Kikai no chōshi ga okashii'n desu ga, ______________________

6\.

Mainichi samui desu ga, Yamamoto-san o-genki desu ka. Konoaida wa musuko-san no tanjōbi no pātii ni shōtai-shite kudasatte, arigatō gozaimashita. Nihon-jin no uchi ni tomatta no wa hajimete deshita ga, kazoku no minasan ga shinsetsu ni shite kudasatte, hontō ni ureshikatta desu. Okusan ga tsukutte kudasatta Nihon-ryōri wa totemo oishikatta desu. Soreni musume-san no odori mo totemo kawaikute, kirei deshita. Musume-san o mite, kuni ni iru musume o omoidashimashita. Yamamoto-san no uchi de totta shashin o kazoku ni okutte yarimashita. Kitto ima goro shashin o mite iru deshō. Totemo tanoshikute, jikan o wasurete shimaimashita. Hontō ni arigatō gozaimashita. Jikan ga attara, zehi mata minasan ni aitai to omotte imasu. Mada mada samui node, kaze o hikanai yō ni ki o tsukete kudasai. Kazoku no minasan ni mo yoroshiku. O-genki de. Sayōnara. 1-gatsu 21-nichi Yamamoto Tarō-sama Lee

Rei 1: Lee-san wa Yamamoto-san no uchi e shōtai-shite moraimashita. (○)

Rei 2: Yamamoto-san wa kodomo ga hitori shika imasen. (×)

1) Okusan ni oishii Nihon-ryōri o tsukutte itadakimashita. ( )

2) Yamamoto-san no musume-san ga odori o misete kuremashita. ( )

3) Lee-san wa Yamamoto-san no uchi de totta shashin o ashita kazoku ni okutte ageyō to omotte imasu. ( )

4) Lee-san wa raigetsu mata Yamamoto-san no uchi e iku tsumori desu. ( )

Dai 42 ka

Bunkei

1. Uchi o kau tame ni, okane o tamete imasu.
2. Kono doraibā wa chiisai neji o shimeru no ni tsukaimasu.

Reibun

1. Nihon-go no shiryō ga yomemasu ka.
   …Ē. Muzukashii desu ga, atarashii gijutsu o narau tame ni, isshōkenmei yonde imasu.

2. Dōshite robotto o tsukatte iru'n desu ka.
   …Seisan no kosuto o sageru tame ni, tsukatte iru'n desu.

3. Konogoro kaeru no ga osoi desu ne.
   …Ē. Raishū no kaigi no tame ni, iroiro shiryō o tsukutte iru'n desu.

4. Kono kōgu wa nan ni tsukau'n desu ka.
   …Ana o akeru no ni tsukaimasu.

5. Kamera ga koshō-shita'n desu ga, sugu shūri-dekimasu ka.
   …Ima buhin ga nai node, shūri ni jikan ga kakarimasu.

6. Atarashii uchi wa dō desu ka.
   …Chikaku ni mise ga takusan atte, kaimono ni benri desu.

Kaiwa

Shain-ryokō ni sasowareru

Katō: Raigetsu Hakone e shain-ryokō ni iku'n desu ga, Rao-san mo sanka-shimasen ka.

Rao: Shain-ryokō?

Katō: Ē. Maitoshi aki ni minna de ryokō ni iku'n desu. Kono ryokō ni iku tame ni, maitsuki okane o tamete iru'n desu yo.

Rao: Sō desu ka.

Katō: Aki wa momiji ga kirei de, ryokō ni ii kisetsu desu. Soreni Hakone wa kireina mizuumi mo aru shi, Fujisan mo mieru shi, ii tokoro desu yo.

Rao: Sō desu ka. Itsu made ni mōshikondara ii desu ka.

Katō: Raishū no getsu-yōbi made ni onegai-shimasu. Kuwashii koto wa kakari no Satō-san ni kiite kudasai.

Renshū A

1.	Uchi o	kau	tame ni,	okane o tamemasu.
	Kanji o	benkyō-suru		jisho o kaimashita.
		Kazoku no		isshōkenmei hatarakimasu.
	Raishū no	kaigi no		junbi-shite imasu.

2.	Doriru wa ana o	akeru	no ni	tsukaimasu.
	Kono hon wa Nihon no koto o	shiru		yaku ni tachimasu.
	Kono tokei wa	naosu		1-shūkan kakarimasu.

3.	Bideo wa Nihon-go no	benkyō	ni	yaku ni tachimasu.
	Chikaku ni sūpā ga atte,	kaimono		benri desu.
	Aki wa suzushikute,	ryokō		ii desu.

Renshū B

1. Rei: kanji o benkyō-shimasu, jisho o kaimasu

   ……Kanji o benkyō-suru tame ni, jisho o kaimasu.

   1) ryokō ni ikimasu, sukoshi zutsu okane o tamemasu ……
   2) atarashii gijutsu o naraimasu, Nihon e kimashita ……
   3) dezain o kimemasu, kaigi o shimasu ……
   4) oishii ryōri o tsukurimasu, ii zairyō o erabimasu ……

2. Rei: isshōkenmei hatarakimasu (kazoku)

   ……Kazoku no tame ni, isshōkenmei hatarakimasu.

   1) tabako o yamemasu (kenkō) ……
   2) itsumo terebi o mite imasu (Nihon-go no benkyō) ……
   3) hon o karimashita (happyō no junbi) ……
   4) kaisha no hito ga pātii o shite kudasaimashita (watashi) ……

3. Rei: Dōshite Amerika e iku'n desu ka.

   (Eigo o benkyō-shimasu)

   ……Eigo o benkyō-suru tame ni, iku'n desu.

   1) Dōshite okane o tamete iru'n desu ka.
      (kekkon-shimasu) ……
   2) Dōshite robotto o tsukatte iru'n desu ka.
      (seisan no kosuto o sagemasu) ……
   3) Nan no tame ni, arubaito o shite iru'n desu ka.
      (ryokō ni ikimasu) ……
   4) Nan no tame ni, ano ranpu wa aru'n desu ka.
      (koshō o shirasemasu) ……

4. Rei: doraibā, chiisai neji o shimemasu
……Kono doraibā wa chiisai neji o shimeru no ni tsukaimasu.

1) mikisā, genryō o mazemasu ……
2) doriru, ita ni ana o akemasu ……
3) kikai, paipu o magemasu ……
4) kikai, ita o kezurimasu ……

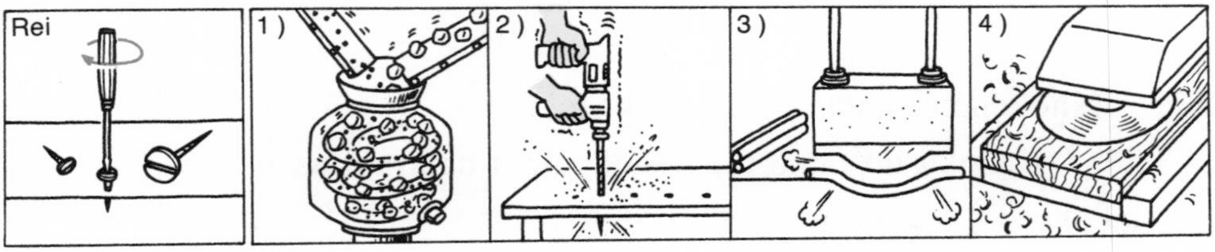

5. Rei 1: Koko wa shizuka de, ii mise desu ne. (yukkuri hanashimasu, ii desu) ……Ē, yukkuri hanasu no ni ii desu.
Rei 2: Chikaku ni mise ga atte, ii desu ne.
(kaimono-shimasu, benri desu) ……Ē, kaimono ni benri desu.

1) Eki kara chikakute, ii desu ne. (kaisha ni kayoimasu, benri desu) ……
2) Kono kasa wa karukute, ii desu ne.
(ryokō ni motte ikimasu, benri desu) ……
3) Chikaku ni kōen ga atte, ii desu ne. (sanpo-shimasu, ii desu) ……
4) Kono jisho wa senmon no kotoba ga ōkute, ii desu ne.
(jisshū-shimasu, yaku ni tachimasu) ……

6. Rei: Kyōto e ikimasu, nani ga ichiban benri desu ka
……Kyōto e iku no ni nani ga ichiban benri desu ka.

1) Nihon no shūkan o shirimasu, donna hon ga ii desu ka ……
2) uchi o tatemasu, donokurai okane ga hitsuyō desu ka ……
3) jidōsha o 1-dai tsukurimasu, donokurai jikan ga kakarimasu ka ……
4) kono kamera o naoshimasu, donokurai jikan ga kakarimasu ka ……

Renshū C

1. A: Nihon e ryokō ni kita'n desu ka.
   B: Iie, konpyūtā o benkyō-suru tame ni, kimashita.
   A: Sō desu ka. Ganbatte kudasai.

   1) kuruma no seibi o naraimasu
   2) Nihon no kaisha de jisshū-shimasu

2. A: Konogoro ryō e kaeru no ga osoi desu ne.
   B: Ē. Raishū no shutchō① no tame ni, iroiro junbi-shite② iru'n desu.
   A: Sō desu ka. Taihen desu ne.

   1) ① kaigi ② shiryō o tsukurimasu
   2) ① happyō ② repōto o matomemasu

3. A: Iroirona kōgu ga arimasu ne.

B: Ē, zenbu de 100-shurui gurai arimasu.

A: Kono kōgu wa nan ni tsukau'n desu ka.

B: Neji o shimeru no ni tsukaimasu.

1) boruto o hazushimasu

2) ana o akemasu

4. A: Atarashii uchi wa dō desu ka.

B: Chikaku ni sūpā ga atte①, kaimono② ni benri③ desu.

A: Sore wa ii desu ne.

1) ① chikaku ni kōen ga arimasu

② sanpo ③ ii desu

2) ① kūki ga kirei desu

② kenkō ③ ii desu

Mondai

1. 1) ______________________________

   2) ______________________________

   3) ______________________________

   4) ______________________________

   5) ______________________________

2. 1) { a. Kanji o benkyō-suru / b. Ryokō o suru / c. Hon-ya e iku } tame ni, (　　　　　) ga hoshii desu.

   2) (　　　　　) no tame ni, { a. kuruma ni notta / b. dekiru dake aruita / c. mainichi hashitta } hō ga ii desu.

   3) Kono kōgu wa (　　　　　) desu.
   { a. Paipu o kittari, magetari / b. Buhin o toritsuketari, hazushitari / c. Boruto o shimetari, yurumetari } suru no ni tsukaimasu.

   4) Koko wa { a. shizuka de, kireina / b. kūki mo kirei de, ii / c. eki kara chikakute, benrina } tokoro desu ga,
   (　　　　　) no ni chotto fuben desu.

   5) Kono wāpuro wa buhin ga oite nai node, (　　　　　) ni
   { a. 2, 3-nichi / b. 1-shūkan / c. 2-shūkan } gurai kakarimasu.

3. Rei 1: (Eigo o benkyō-suru) tame ni, Amerika e ikitai desu.

Rei 2: (Kazoku) no tame ni, isshōkenmei hatarakimasu.

1) ( ) tame ni, Nihon e kimashita.

2) ( ) tame ni, robotto ga takusan tsukawarete imasu.

3) ( ) no tame ni, maiasa jogingu o shite imasu.

4) ( ) no tame ni, shiryō o matomete imasu.

4.

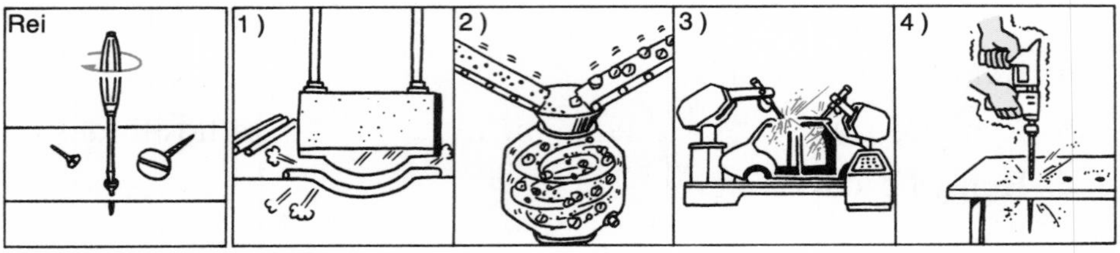

Rei: Kono doraibā wa chiisai neji o shimeru no ni tsukaimasu.

1) Kono kikai wa ______

2) Kono mikisā wa ______

3) Kono robotto wa ______

4) Kono doriru wa ______

5. Rei 1: Ōsaka e (iku) no ni, shinkansen ga ichiban benri desu.

Rei 2: Uchi no chikaku ni sūpā ga atte, (kaimono) ni benri desu.

1) Kono jisho wa gijutsu no kotoba o ( ) no ni ii desu.

2) Ippan-kenshū wa Nihon no koto o ( ) no ni totemo yaku ni tachimasu.

3) Aki wa momiji ga kirei de, ( ) ni ii kisetsu desu.

4) Supōtsu wa ( ) ni ii desu.

6. Rei: Kono biru o tsukuru no (ni) 2-nen kakarimashita.

1) Nihon-go o hanasu no ( ) muzukashii desu.

2) Watashi wa eiga o miru no ( ) suki desu.

3) Kinō no ban jishin ga atta no ( ) shitte imasu ka.

4) Kono hon wa Nihon no seikatsu ya shūkan o shiru no ( ) totemo ii hon desu.

7. “yō ni” ka “tame ni” ka “no ni” o irete kudasai.

Rei: Kanji ga kakeru (yō ni), mainichi benkyō-shite imasu.

1) Kono kasa wa karukute, ryokō ni motte iku ( ) benri desu.

2) Seisan no kosuto o sageru ( ), robotto o tsukatte imasu.

3) Kaisha ni okurenai ( ), hayaku okimasu.

4) Mori-san no musuko-san wa daigaku ni hairu ( ), isshōkenmei benkyō-shite imasu.

8.

Nakamura-san wa Narita-kūkō no chikaku ni sunde imasu. Kaisha ga aru Tōkyō kara uchi made 2-jikan gurai kakarimasu.

Nakamura-san wa dekiru dake kaisha kara chikai tokoro ni uchi o kaitai to omotte imashita. Demo, Tōkyō wa takakute, kaemasendeshita. Sorede, ima sunde iru tokoro ni kimemashita. Koko kara mainichi kaisha ni kayou no wa taihen desu ga, eki kara chikai shi, uchi no soba ni kireina kōen mo atte, sumu no ni totemo ii tokoro da to omotte imasu.

Nakamura-san no uchi ni wa Nakamura-san no otōto-san mo issho ni sunde imasu. Kotoshi 21-sai de, Tōkyō no daigaku de benkyō-shite imasu. Otōto-san wa rainen daigaku o detara, ginkō de hatarakitai to omotte imasu. Ima wa yoru chikaku no sūpā de arubaito o shite imasu.

Otōto-san wa sono okane de, natsu-yasumi ni tomodachi to Tai e ikō to omotte imasu.

Tadashii mono ni wa ○, tadashikunai mono ni wa × o irete kudasai.

1) Nakamura-san no uchi wa kaisha kara tōi node, kaisha ni kayou no wa taihen desu. ( )

2) Kaisha kara tōi desu ga, ii tokoro na node, Nakamura-san wa kono uchi o katte yokatta to omotte imasu. ( )

3) Nakamura-san no otōto-san wa ginkōin ni naru tame ni, sūpā de hataraite imasu. ( )

4) Nakamura-san no otōto-san wa Tai e ryokō ni iku tame ni, arubaito o shite imasu. ( )

Dai 43 ka

Bunkei

1. Imanimo ame ga furisō desu.
2. Chotto tabako o katte kimasu.

Reibun

1. Tana kara nimotsu ga ochisō desu yo.
   …A, dōmo.　Sugu oroshimasu.

2. Okashi wa ikaga desu ka.
   …Oishisō desu ne.　Hitotsu itadakimasu.

3. Kono mise de omiyage o kaimasen ka.　Shinamono mo ōi shi, yosasō desu yo.
   …Sō desu ne.　Koko ni shimashō.

4. Kuni ni nimotsu o okuritai'n desu ga, hako wa arimasen ka.
   …Kono danbōru wa dō desu ka.
   Kore wa jōbusō desu ne.　Arigatō gozaimasu.

5. Sā, ikimashō.
   …Sumimasen.　Kamera o wasuremashita.
   Chotto totte kimasu kara, matte ite kudasai.

6. Chotto dekakete kimasu.
   …Konban ryō de pātii ga arimasu yo.
   Ē.　Yūgata made ni kaette kimasu.

Kaiwa

Shain-ryokō

Satō: Minasan, Fujisan o bakku ni shite, shashin o torimashō.

Rao: Katō-san-tachi wa omiyage-ya no hō e ikimashita yo.
Chotto yonde kimasu.

Satō: Ii tokoro deshō?

Rao: Ē. Bōto ni notte iru hito mo imasu ne.

Satō: Minna tanoshisō desu ne.

Rao: Fujisan mo subarashii shi, momiji mo kirei da shi, hontō ni kite yokatta desu. Ii omoide ni narimasu.

Renshū A

1\.

Imanimo	ame ga	furi	sō desu.
	hi ga	kie	
	nimotsu ga	ochi	

2\.

Kono ryōri wa	oishi	sō desu.
Kono jisho wa	yosa	
Kono hako wa	jōbu	

3\.

Chotto	nomimono o	katte	kimasu.
	denwa o	kakete	
	kaimono ni	itte	

Renshū B

1. Rei: ame ga furimasu ……Ame ga furisō desu.
   1) nimotsu ga ochimasu ……
   2) ki ga taoremasu ……
   3) himo ga kiremasu ……
   4) hi ga kiemasu ……

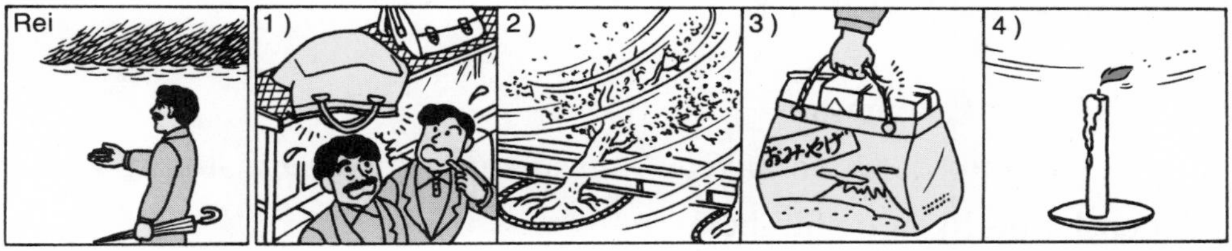

2. Rei: ame ga furimasu, kasa o motte ikimashō
   ……Ame ga furisō desu kara, kasa o motte ikimashō.
   1) himo ga kiremasu, kaemasu ……
   2) fukuro ga yaburemasu, atarashii no o kaimasu ……
   3) tana kara nimotsu ga ochimasu, oroshimashō ……
   4) gasorin ga nakunarimasu, irete okimasu ……

3. Rei: tegami o moratte, ureshii desu
   ……Lee-san wa tegami o moratte, ureshisō desu.
   1) tegami ga konakute, sabishii desu ……
   2) shigoto ga takusan atte, isogashii desu ……
   3) kaze o hiite, kibun ga warui desu ……
   4) byōki ga naotte, genki desu ……

4. Rei: sono nimotsu wa omoi desu, motte agemashō
   ⋯⋯Sono nimotsu wa omosō desu ne. Motte agemashō.
   1) kono zasshi wa omoshiroi desu, chotto misete kudasai ⋯⋯
   2) kono mise wa shinamono ga ii desu, koko de kaimashō ⋯⋯
   3) sono hako wa jōbu desu, sore ni hon o iremashō ⋯⋯
   4) kono ryōri wa oishii desu, kore ni shimashō ⋯⋯

5. Rei: denwa o kakemasu
   ⋯⋯Chotto denwa o kakete kimasu kara, koko de matte ite kudasai.
   1) densha no jikan o shirabemasu ⋯⋯
   2) michi o kikimasu ⋯⋯
   3) otearai e ikimasu ⋯⋯
   4) koin-rokkā ni nimotsu o azukemasu ⋯⋯

6. Rei: Doko e iku'n desu ka. (ii tenki na node, chotto sanpo-shimasu)
   ⋯⋯Ii tenki na node, chotto sanpo-shite kimasu.
   1) Doko e iku'n desu ka.
   (nodo ga kawaita node, chotto jūsu o kaimasu) ⋯⋯
   2) Doko e iku'n desu ka.
   (heya ni kamera o wasureta node, torimasu) ⋯⋯
   3) Doko e iku'n desu ka.
   (tomodachi ga kuru node, eki e mukae ni ikimasu) ⋯⋯
   4) Doko e itta'n desu ka.
   (Hakone e ryokō ni ikimashita) ⋯⋯

Renshū C

1. A: A, fukuro ga yaburesō① desu yo.
   B: Hontō da. Ja, ano mise de atarashii② no o kaimasu.

   1) ① fukuro kara mono ga ochimasu ② motto ōkii desu
   2) ① fukuro no himo ga kiremasu ② motto jōbu desu

2. A: Isogashisō① desu ne.
   B: Ē, pātii no junbi o shite iru'n② desu.
   A: Ja, tetsudatte③ agemashō.
   B: Sumimasen.

   1) ① sono hako wa omoi desu ② hon ga haitte imasu
   ③ mochimasu
   2) ① kibun ga warui desu ② atama ga itai desu
   ③ kusuri o motte kimasu

3. A: A, ikenai.

B: Dō shita'n desu ka.

A: Kagi o kakeru no o wasuremashita.

Chotto kakete kimasu kara, matte ite kudasai.

B: Hai.

1) mado o shimemasu

2) hiitā o keshimasu

4. A: Doko e iku'n desu ka.

B: Denchi ga nakunatta① node, chotto katte② kimasu.

A: Sō desu ka. Itte irasshai.

1) ① ii tenki desu ② sanpo-shimasu

2) ① tomodachi ga kimasu ② eki e mukae ni ikimasu

Mondai

1\. 1) ______________________________

2) ______________________________

3) ______________________________

4) ______________________________

5) ______________________________

2\.

1) Nimotsu ga (　　　　　)sō desu kara, { a. kabā o kakete / b. kagi o kakete / c. tana kara oroshite } okimasu.

2) Fukuro ga (　　　　　)sō desu kara, ano mise de motto { a. ōkii / b. takai / c. jōbuna } no o kaimasu.

3) Rao-san wa konogoro { a. mainichi zangyō de / b. jisshū no naiyō ga muzukashikute, / c. jisshū no happyō no junbi de } (　　　　　)sō desu.

4) Hiitā o { a. tsukeru / b. kesu / c. shimeru } no o wasurete shimatta node, chotto (　　　　　) kimasu.

5) Rao-san wa sakki { a. mizuumi / b. omiyage-ya / c. otearai } no hō e itta node, watashi ga (　　　　　) kimasu.

3. 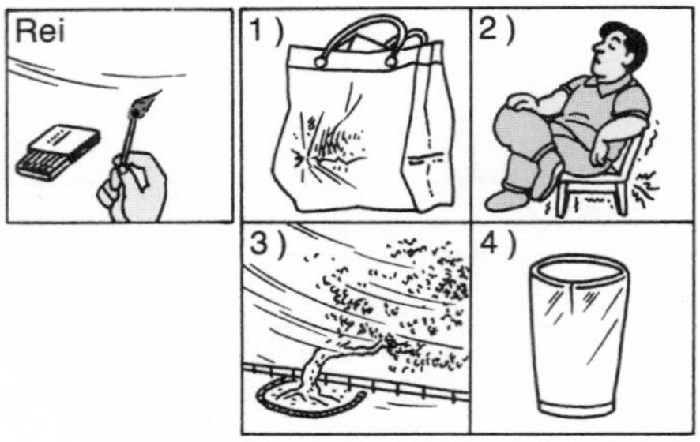

Rei: Matchi no hi ga kiesō desu.

1) ______________________

2) ______________________

3) ______________________

4) ______________________

4. Rei: Ame ga yamisō desu kara, sorosoro dekakemasu.

1) Imanimo ame ga furisō desu kara, ______________________

2) Kyō wa ii tenki ni narisō desu kara, ______________________

3) Tana kara nimotsu ga ochisō desu kara, ______________________

4) Omokute, fukuro no himo ga kiresō desu kara, ______________________

43

5. Rei: A: Sono nimotsu wa (omo)sō desu ne.
Watashi ga (motte) agemashō ka.
B: Sumimasen. Onegai-shimasu.

1) A: Dono okashi ni shimasu ka.
B: Kore ga ichiban (   )sō desu kara, kore ni shimasu.
A: Aji wa dō desu ka.
B: Un, hontō ni (   ) desu ne.

2) A: Yuki wa mō yamimashita ka.
B: Iie, mada futte imasu. Totemo (   )sō desu.
A: Ja, kōto o (   ) dekakemashō.

3) A: Doko de omiyage o kaimashō ka.
B: Kono mise wa dō desu ka.
Nedan mo (   )sō da shi, shinamono mo (   )sō desu yo.

4) A: Danbōru ga hoshii'n desu ga・・・
Kuni ni nimotsu o (   ) no ni iru'n desu.
B: Ja, kore wa dō desu ka.
A: Kore wa (   )sō desu ne.
Kore o kudasai.

6. Rei: A: Doko e iku'n desu ka.

B: Tabako ga nakunatta node, katte kimasu.

1) A: Doko e iku'n desu ka.

B: Nodo ga kawaita node, ______________________________

2) A: Kagi o kakeru no o wasurete shimatta node, ______________

B: Ja, koko de matte imasu.

3) A: Eki e iku michi ga yoku wakarimasen ne.

B: Sō desu ne. Chotto ano hito ni ______________________

4) A: Doko e iku'n desu ka.

B: Kyō wa ii tenki na node, ___________________________

A: Nan-ji goro ryō e kaerimasu ka.

B: ____

7. 42, 43 ka no kaiwa o yonde, shitsumon ni kotaete kudasai.

1) Rao-san wa doko e shain-ryokō ni ikimashita ka.

____

2) Dōshite maitoshi aki ni shain-ryokō ni iku'n desu ka.

____

3) Ryokō no kakari wa dare desu ka.

____

4) Rao-san wa shain-ryokō ni sanka-shite, dō omotte imasu ka.

____

Dai 44 ka

Bunkei

1. Yūbe o-sake o nomi-sugimashita.
2. Kono jisho wa ji ga ōkikute, miyasui desu.
3. Heya o kirei ni shimasu.

Reibun

1. Dō shita'n desu ka.

   ···Yūbe tabe-sugite, onaka no chōshi ga warui'n desu.

2. Kochira no sētā wa ikaga desu ka.

   ···Kore wa ōki-sugimasu ne.　Motto chiisai no o misete kudasai.

3. Atarashii wāpuro wa dō desu ka.

   ···Sōsa ga kantan de, tsukaiyasui desu.

4. Kono tēburu ni wa atarashii zairyō ga tsukawarete imasu.

   ···Ima made no to dō chigau'n desu ka.

   Netsu ni tsuyokute, iro ga kawarinikui'n desu.

5. Zubon no nagasa wa kore de ii desu ka.

   ···Naga-sugimasu kara, mō sukoshi mijikaku shite kudasai.

Kaiwa

Kopii o toru

Narong: Anō, kopii no tori-kata o oshiete itadakemasen ka.

Ikeda: Ii desu yo. Nani o kopii-suru'n desu ka.

Narong: Kono shiryō desu.
Ji ga chiisa-sugite, yominikui node, motto ōkiku shitai'n desu.

Ikeda: Ja, 2-bai ni shitara ii desu yo.

Narong: Hai.

Ikeda: Kono botan de kami no saizu o erande, sorekara sutāto-botan o oseba, kopii ga demasu・・・
Hora, kore de dō desu ka.

Narong: Ōkiku narimashita ne. Kore nara, yomiyasui desu.
Dōmo arigatō gozaimashita.

44

Renshū A

1.

O-sake o	nomi	-sugimashita.
Gohan o	tabe	
Okane o	tsukai	

2.

Kono kutsu wa	chiisa	-sugimasu.
Kono ryōri wa	kara	
Kono mondai wa	fukuzatsu	

3.

Kono himo	wa	kire	yasui desu.
Kono setsumeisho		wakari	
Kono bōrupen		kaki	

4.

Kono koppu	wa	ware	nikui desu.
Kono kusuri		nomi	
Nihon-jin no namae		oboe	

5.

Oto	o	ōki	ku	shimasu.
Nedan		yasu	ku	
Heya		kirei	ni	
Kaigi		raishū	ni	

Renshū B

1. Rei: gohan o tabemashita ······Gohan o tabe-sugimashita.
   1) tabako o suimashita ······
   2) yūbe o-sake o nomimashita ······
   3) satō o iremashita ······
   4) nimotsu o nosemashita ······

2. Rei: kono kamera wa takai desu ······Kono kamera wa taka-sugimasu.
   1) kono uwagi wa ōkii desu ······
   2) kono zubon wa nagai desu ······
   3) kono himo wa hosoi desu ······
   4) kono mondai wa kantan desu ······

3. Rei 1: o-sake o nomimashita, atama ga itai desu
   ······O-sake o nomi-sugite, atama ga itai desu.
   Rei 2: kono kaban wa omoi desu, motemasen
   ······Kono kaban wa omo-sugite, motemasen.
   1) terebi o mimashita, me ga itai desu ······
   2) omiyage o kaimashita, okane ga nakunarimashita ······
   3) kono ryōri wa karai desu, taberaremasen ······
   4) kono mondai wa fukuzatsu desu, wakarimasen ······

4. Rei 1: kono koppu wa sugu waremasu
……Kono koppu wa wareyasui desu.
Rei 2: kono garasu wa nakanaka waremasen
……Kono garasu wa warenikui desu.
1) yasui tokei wa sugu kowaremasu ……
2) shiroi shatsu wa sugu yogoremasu ……
3) ATM no kuruma wa nakanaka koshō-shimasen ……
4) kono tēburu wa nakanaka kizu ga tsukimasen ……

5. Rei 1: Lee-san no ji wa yomiyasui desu ka. (hai, kirei desu)
……Hai, kirei de, yomiyasui desu.
Rei 2: Kono kusuri wa nomiyasui desu ka. (iie, nigai desu)
……Iie, nigakute, nominikui desu.
1) Kono wāpuro wa tsukaiyasui desu ka. (hai, sōsa ga kantan desu) ……
2) Kono kutsu wa hakiyasui desu ka. (hai, karui desu) ……
3) Nihon wa sumiyasui desu ka. (iie, mono ga takai desu) ……
4) Kono setsumeisho wa wakariyasui desu ka. (iie, katakana no kotoba ga ōi desu) ……

6. Rei 1: oto ga chiisai desu, ōkii desu
……Oto ga chiisai desu kara, ōkiku shite kudasai.
Rei 2: heya ga kitanai desu, kirei desu
……Heya ga kitanai desu kara, kirei ni shite kudasai.
1) kopii no iro ga usui desu, koi desu ……
2) ushiro no kami ga nagai desu, mijikai desu ……
3) setsumei ga fukuzatsu desu, kantan desu ……
4) gohan no ryō ga ōi desu, hanbun desu ……

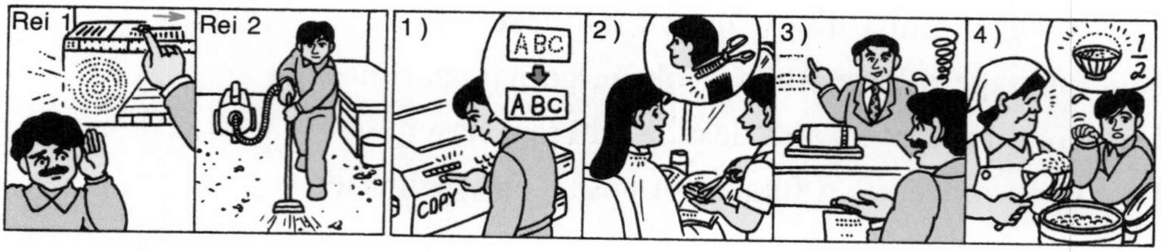

Renshū C

1. A: Dō shita'n desu ka.

   B: O-sake o nomi① -sugite, atama ga itai② 'n desu.

   A: Sore wa ikemasen ne.

   1) ① tabemasu　② kibun ga warui desu

   2) ① tabako o suimasu　② nodo no chōshi ga okashii desu

44

2. A: Kochira no bideo-kamera① wa ikaga desu ka.

   B: Ā, kore wa sōsa ga kantan de②, tsukai③ yasui desu ne.

   A: Ē. Ima ichiban yoku urete imasu yo.

   B: Ja, kore o kudasai.

   1) ① terebi　② ōkii desu　③ mimasu

   2) ① wāpuro　② ji ga kirei desu　③ yomimasu

3. A: Kono tēburu ni wa atarashii zairyō ga tsukawarete imasu.
B: Ima made no to dō chigau'n desu ka.
A: Jōbu de,① kizu ga tsukinikui'n desu.②
B: Ja, itsu made mo kirei desu ne.

1) ① netsu ni tsuyoi desu ② iro ga kawarimasu
2) ① jōbu desu ② yogoremasu

4. A: Kono ita ni ana o akete① kudasai.
B: Hai・・・ Kore de ii desu ka.
A: Chiisa②-sugimasu ne. Motto ōkiku③ shite kudasai.
B: Wakarimashita. Yarinaoshimasu.

1) ① ita o kirimasu ② nagai desu ③ mijikai desu
2) ① ita o kezurimasu ② atsui desu ③ usui desu

Mondai

1\.
1) ______________________________
2) ______________________________
3) ______________________________
4) ______________________________
5) ______________________________

2\.

1) Kinō no pātii de o-sake o (   ),
- a. onaka ga itai desu.
- b. atama ga itai desu.
- c. nodo ga itai desu.

2) Kono (   ) wa
- a. pittari desu.
- b. chiisa-sugimasu.
- c. ōki-sugimasu.

3) Kono wāpuro wa
- a. ji ga kirei de,
- b. sōsa ga fukuzatsu de,
- c. sōsa ga kantan de,

(   )yasui desu.

4) Kono kuruma no (   ) wa
- a. warenikukute,
- b. wareyasukute,
- c. yogorenikukute,

anzen desu.

5) Kono paipu wa (   )-sugimasu kara, motto
- a. nagaku
- b. mijikaku
- c. usuku

shite kudasai.

3.

Rei 1: Gohan o tabe-sugimashita.

Rei 2: Kono kamera wa taka-sugimasu.

1) ______________________________

2) ______________________________

3) ______________________________

4) ______________________________

4. Rei: O-sake o nomi-sugite, atama ga itai desu.

1) Hataraki-sugite, ______________________________

2) Depāto de kaimono-shi-sugite, ______________________________

3) Kono ryōri wa kara-sugite, ______________________________

4) Kono nimotsu wa omo-sugite, ______________________________

5. Rei 1: Sono kutsu wa hakiyasui desu ka. (hai, karui desu)

……Hai, karukute, hakiyasui desu.

Rei 2: Sono hon wa yomiyasui desu ka. (iie, ji ga chiisai desu)

……Iie, ji ga chiisakute, yominikui desu.

1) Sono kusuri wa nomiyasui desu ka. (hai, amai desu)

……

2) Kanji wa oboeyasui desu ka. (iie, fukuzatsu desu)

……

3) Sono kamera wa tsukaiyasui desu ka. (hai, kantan desu)

……

4) Sono jisho wa wakariyasui desu ka. (iie, rei ga sukunai desu)

……

6. Rei: Kono himo wa hosokute, (c)
1) Kono kopii wa usukute, ( )
2) Kono kusuri wa nigakute, ( )
3) Kono enpitsu wa mijika-sugite, ( )
4) Nihon wa mono ga taka-sugite, ( )

a. nominikui desu.
b. suminikui desu.
c. kireyasui desu.
d. kakinikui desu.
e. yominikui desu.

7. Rei: Rajio no oto ga ōkii desu kara, (chiisaku) shite kudasai.
1) Heya ga kitanai desu kara, ( ) shite kudasai.
2) Shukudai no ryō ga ōi desu kara, motto ( ) shite kudasai.
3) Gasu no hi ga tsuyo-sugimasu kara, motto ( ) shite kudasai.
4) Ashita wa tsugō ga warui desu kara, ( ) shite kudasai.

8. Rei: Nihon de wa fuyu ni naru to, samuku (narimasu, shimasu).

1) Kaze wa dō desu ka.
……Okagesama de, netsu mo sagatte, yoku (narimashita, shimashita).

2) Nomimono wa nani ga ii desu ka.
……Kyō wa atsui node, biiru ni (narimasu, shimasu).

3) Ano michi wa kōjichū desu ne.
……Ē, michi ga semai node, hiroku (natte, shite) iru'n desu.

4) Sukoshi kanji ga kakeru yō ni (narimashita, shimashita).
……Ja, dekiru dake kanji o tsukatte repōto o kaku yō ni (natte, shite) kudasai.

Dai 45 ka

Bunkei

1. Jishin ga okita baai wa, sugu hi o keshite kudasai.
2. Kusuri o nonda noni, mada netsu ga sagarimasen.

Reibun

1. Konogoro kaji ga ōi node, ki o tsukete kudasai.

   ···Hai. Man'ichi kaji ga okita baai wa, dō shitara ii desu ka.

   Sugu 119-ban ni denwa-shite kudasai.

2. Kopii-ki no shūri ga owarimashita.

   Mata chōshi ga okashii baai wa, renraku-shite kudasai.

   ···Hai. Arigatō gozaimashita.

3. Nichi-yōbi ame de mo, pikunikku ni ikimasu ka.

   ···Iie. Ame no baai wa, raishū ni shimasu.

4. Sumimasen.

   ···Hai, nan desu ka.

   Jidō-hanbaiki no chōshi ga okashii'n desu. Okane o ireta noni, tabako ga denai'n desu.

5. Kyō wa nichi-yōbi na noni, kaisha e iku'n desu ka.

   ···Ē. Shigoto ga isogashii'n desu.

Kaiwa

Miitingu

Nakamura:	Kyō 1-nichi jisshū-shite mite, dō deshita ka.
Lee:	Hitotsu mondai ga aru'n desu ga· · ·
Nakamura:	Nan deshō ka.
Lee:	Onaji hōhō de shirindā o tsukutte iru noni, tama ni uchigawa ni hibi ga hairu'n desu.
Nakamura:	Ā, sore desu ka. Reikyaku-ondo ni mondai ga atta baai wa, sō narimasu.
Lee:	Ja, ondo-kanri o shikkari yaranakereba narimasen ne.
Nakamura:	Sono tōri desu. Ashita kara kono ten ni ki o tsukete, sagyō no yari-kata o kaete mimashō.

Renshū A

1.

Rain ga	tomatta	baai wa, watashi o yonde kudasai.
Tsukai-kata ga	wakaranai	
Enjin no chōshi ga	warui	
Shūri ga	hitsuyōna	
Kikai ga	koshō no	

2.

Okane o	ireta	noni,	kippu ga demasen.
1-nen Nihon ni	sunde iru		Nihon-go ga heta desu.
Kono mise wa	mazui		nedan ga takai desu.
Kare wa Nihon-go ga	jōzuna		amari hanashimasen.
Kyō wa	yasumi na		shigoto o shinakereba narimasen.

Renshū B

1. Rei: jishin ga okimasu, sugu hi o keshite kudasai

    ……Jishin ga okita baai wa, sugu hi o keshite kudasai.

    1) man'ichi kaji ga okimasu, sugu 119-ban ni denwa-shimasu ……
    2) kōtsū-jiko ga okimasu, sugu keisatsu ni shirasemasu ……
    3) akai ranpu ga tsukimasu, sugu suitchi o kitte kudasai ……
    4) rain ga tomarimasu, sugu gen'in o shirabete kudasai ……
    5) denwa-bangō ga wakarimasen, 104-ban ni denwa-shimasu ……

2. Rei: kikai no chōshi ga warui desu, watashi o yonde kudasai

    ……Kikai no chōshi ga warui baai wa, watashi o yonde kudasai.

    1) kopii no iro ga usui desu, kono botan de chōsetsu-shimasu ……
    2) tsugō ga warui desu, denwa de shirasete kudasai ……
    3) shūri ga hitsuyō desu, kakari no hito ni renraku-shite kudasai ……
    4) kaji desu, ano hijōguchi kara nigete kudasai ……
    5) ame desu, pikunikku o raishū ni shimasu ……

3. Rei: takushii o yobimashita, mada kimasen

    ……Takushii o yonda noni, mada kimasen.

    1) okane o iremashita, kippu ga demasen ……
    2) tegami o dashimashita, mada henji ga kimasen ……
    3) yakusoku o shimashita, tomodachi wa kimasendeshita ……
    4) dare mo imasen, denki ga tsuite imasu ……
    5) kamera o motte ikimashita, kōjō de shashin ga toremasendeshita ……

4. Rei: Netsu wa sagarimashita ka.
(kusuri o nomimashita, mada sagarimasen)
……Iie, kusuri o nonda noni, mada sagarimasen.

1) Narong-san wa mō kaette kimashita ka.
(12-ji o sugimashita, mada kaette kimasen) ……

2) Lee-san wa mō kimashita ka.
(kaigi ga hajimarimashita, mada kimasen) ……

3) Pātii no nomimono wa tarimashita ka.
(takusan kaimashita, tarimasendeshita) ……

4) Supōtsu-sentā wa sugu wakarimashita ka.
(chizu o motte ikimashita, michi ni mayotte shimaimashita) ……

5) Shiken wa dekimashita ka.
(isshōkenmei benkyō-shimashita, amari dekimasendeshita) ……

5. Rei 1: suzushii desu, kūrā o tsukete imasu
……Suzushii noni, kūrā o tsukete imasu.

Rei 2: kin'en desu, tabako o sutte imasu
……Kin'en na noni, tabako o sutte imasu.

1) karada no chōshi ga warui desu, o-sake o nonde imasu ……
2) kono kami wa usui desu, yaburenikui desu ……
3) yasashii shiken desu, dekimasendeshita ……
4) nichi-yōbi desu, kaisha e ikanakereba narimasen ……
5) shingō ga aka desu, michi o watatte imasu ……

Renshū C

1. A: Konogoro kaji① ga ōi desu kara, ki o tsukete kudasai.
   B: Hai. Kaji① ga okita baai wa, dō shitara ii desu ka.
   A: Awatenai de, 119-ban ni denwa-shite② kudasai.
   B: Wakarimashita.

   1) ① jishin ② hi o keshimasu
   2) ① kōtsū-jiko ② keisatsu ni shirasemasu

2. A: Rain ni mondai ga okita baai wa, ranpu ga aka ni kawarimasu kara, sugu suitchi o kitte kudasai.
   B: Hai, wakarimashita.

   1) rain no chōshi ga warui desu
   2) kikai ga koshō desu

3. A: Kaze① wa dō desu ka.

   B: Mainichi kusuri o nonde iru② noni, mada naoranai'n desu.

   A: Sore wa ikemasen ne.

   Isha ni mite moratta hō ga ii desu yo.

   B: Hai, sō shimasu.

   1) ① kega ② mainichi kusuri o tsukete imasu

   2) ① onaka no chōshi ② kesa mo kusuri o nomimashita

4. A: Sumimasen.

   B: Hai, nan desu ka.

   A: Jidō-hanbaiki no chōshi ga okashii'n desu.

   Sen-en satsu o ireta① noni, otsuri② ga denai'n desu.

   B: Sō desu ka. Sugu shirabemasu.

   1) ① botan o oshimashita ② tabako

   2) ① rebā o mawashimashita ② otsuri

Mondai

1\. 1) ______________________________

2) ______________________________

3) ______________________________

4) ______________________________

5) ______________________________

2\. 1) { a. Jishin / b. Kaji / c. Jiko } ga okita baai wa, sugu (   ) kudasai.

2) Rain ni { a. koshō ga nai / b. mondai ga nai / c. mondai ga atta } baai wa, sugu (   ), watashi o yonde kudasai.

3) Ototoi kara (   ) noni,
{ a. onaka no chōshi ga warui desu. / b. mada kaze ga naorimasen. / c. netsu ga sagarimasen. }

4) Okane o (   ) noni, { a. tabako / b. otsuri / c. tabako to otsuri } ga demasen.

5) Onaji hōhō de (   ) o tsukutte iru noni,
{ a. tama ni hibi ga hairimasu. / b. yoku hibi ga hairimasu. / c. sukoshi warete imasu. }

3. Rei: jishin ga okimasu

……Jishin ga okita baai wa, sugu hi o keshite kudasai.

1) man'ichi kaji ga okimasu

……

2) kōtsū-jiko ga okimasu

……

3) rain ni mondai ga arimasu

……

4) denwa-bangō ga wakarimasen

……

4. Rei: (Jishin) no baai wa, erebētā o tsukawanai de kudasai.

1) ( ) no baai wa, sugu 119-ban ni denwa-shite kudasai.

2) ( ) no baai wa, pikunikku ni ikimasen.

3) Rain ga ( ) no baai wa, akai ranpu ga tsukimasu.

4) Shingō ga ( ) no baai wa, kuruma wa tomaranakereba narimasen.

5. Rei 1: Kaze wa naorimashita ka.

……Hai, kusuri o nonda node, naorimashita.

Rei 2: Kaze wa naorimashita ka.

……Iie, mainichi kusuri o nonde iru noni, mada naorimasen.

1) Shiken wa dekimashita ka.

……Iie, ____________ noni, ____________

2) Fakkusu no okuri-kata ga wakarimasu ka.

……Hai, ____________ node, ____________

3) Tōkyō-tawā e iku michi wa sugu wakarimashita ka.

……Iie, ____________ noni, ____________

4) Pātii no nomimono wa tarimashita ka.

……Iie, ____________ noni, ____________

6. Rei: Moshi okane ga attara, (b) a. eki no hito ni shirasemasu.

1) Shinjuku e itta toki, (   )

2) Bideo-kamera nara, (   )

3) Okane o irete, kono botan o osu to, (   )

4) Kippu ga denai baai wa, (   )

a. eki no hito ni shirasemasu.
b. Yōroppa o ryokō-shitai desu.
c. Tōkyō-denki ga yasukute, ii desu.
d. kono kamera o kaimashita.
e. kippu to otsuri ga demasu.

7.

> Kaji wa hito ga takusan sunde iru Tōkyō ya Ōsaka nado ōkii machi ni ōi desu. Hokkaidō nado samui tokoro mo ōi desu. Nihon no fuyu wa samukute, yoku hi o tsukau node, kaji wa fuyu ni ōi desu.
>
> Jishin ga okita toki mo, yoku kaji ni narimasu. 1923-nen 9-gatsu tsuitachi ni Tōkyō de ōkina jishin ga arimashita. Sono toki kowareta uchi wa 128,266-ken de, yaketa uchi wa 447,128-ken desu. Chōdo hirugohan no junbi de hi o tsukatte ita node, kaji ga okimashita. Kono jishin de 100,000-nin ijō no hito ga shinimashita.
>
> Jishin wa kowai, shikashi, kaji no hō ga motto kowai to Nihon-jin wa omotte imasu.

* -ken: uchi o kazoeru ii-kata

1) 1-nen de itsu ga ichiban kaji ga ōi desu ka. Sore wa dōshite desu ka.

____

2) 1923-nen no jishin de dōshite ōkina kaji ga okimashita ka.

____

3) Kono jishin de kowareta uchi to yaketa uchi to, dochira ga ōi desu ka.

____

4) Jishin ga okita baai wa, mazu nani o shinakereba naranai to omoimasu ka.

____

Fukushū I

1.

Rei: akimasu	(b)	a. tomarimasu
1) tsukimasu	( )	b. shimarimasu
2) ugokimasu	( )	c. oroshimasu
3) agarimasu	( )	d. yunyū-shimasu
4) komimasu	( )	e. kiemasu
5) maniaimasu	( )	f. bunkai-shimasu
6) nosemasu	( )	g. hazushimasu
7) toritsukemasu	( )	h. sagarimasu
8) shimemasu	( )	i. sukimasu
9) kumitatemasu	( )	j. yurumemasu
10) yushutsu-shimasu	( )	k. okuremasu

Rei: benri	(g)	a. fukuzatsu
1) kirei	( )	b. usui
2) kantan	( )	c. hosoi
3) daisuki	( )	d. daikirai
4) urusai	( )	e. yawarakai
5) katai	( )	f. yowai
6) tsuyoi	( )	g. fuben
7) futoi	( )	h. kitanai
8) atsui	( )	i. mazui
9) omoshiroi	( )	j. shizuka
10) umai	( )	k. tsumaranai

2. Rei: Buchō ni kōjō o (annai-shimasu ···annai-shite) itadakimashita.

1) Katō-san no okusan ga Nihon-ryōri o (tsukurimasu ···   ) kudasaimashita.

2) Nihon-go de tegami o kaita'n desu ga, chotto (mimasu ···   ) itadakemasen ka.

3) Eki kara chikakute, kaisha ni (kayoimasu ···   ) no ni benri desu.

4) Fukuro no himo ga (kiremasu ···   )sō desu kara, atarashii no o kaimasu.

5) (Isogashii desu ···   )sō desu ne. Tetsudatte agemashō.

6) Chotto uketsuke ni nimotsu o (azukemasu ···   ) kimasu.

7) Rajio no oto ga (ōkii desu ···   )-sugimasu kara, motto (chiisai desu ···   ) shite kudasai.

8) Kono terebi wa ōkikute, (mimasu ···   )yasui desu.

9) Koko wa (kin'en desu ···   ) noni, ano hito wa tabako o sutte imasu.

10) Yūbe isshōkenmei (benkyō-shimasu ···   ) noni, shiken ga dekimasendeshita.

3. Tadashii mono o erande kudasai.

1) Repōto ni jisshū no kansō o dekiru dake { a. kuwashiku / b. daitai / c. pittari } kaite kudasai.

2) Abunai desu kara, kikai no shita ni { a. kanarazu / b. zettai ni / c. kichinto } te o irenai yō ni shite kudasai.

3) { a. Moshi / b. Ikura / c. Imanimo } ame ga furisō desu kara, hayaku kaerimashō.

4) Ryokō ni iku tame ni, { a. sukoshi shika / b. sukoshi zutsu / c. nakanaka } okane o tamete imasu.

5) Kono tēburu wa katakute, kizu ga tsukinikui node,
{ a. konogoro / b. tama ni / c. itsu made mo } kirei desu.

6) Narong-san wa doko e ikimashita ka.
… { a. Soreja, / b. Yā, / c. Sā, } doko e itta ka, wakarimasen.

7) Kinō o-sake o nomi-sugimashita. { a. Sorede, / b. Soreni, / c. Korekara, } atama ga itai desu.

8) Hiragana ya katakana wa hotondo yomemasu. { a. Desukara, / b. Shikashi, / c. Soshite, } kanji wa zenzen yomemasen.

9) { a. Man'ichi / b. Ikura / c. Konogoro } kaji ga okita baai wa, sugu hijōguchi kara nigete kudasai.

10) Musume-san ni donna omiyage o katte agemasu ka.
…Kimono { a. ka / b. nado / c. shika } ningyō o katte yaritai desu.

Dai 46 ka

Bunkei

1. Chōdo ima kara eiga ga hajimaru tokoro desu.
2. Kare wa senshū Nihon e kita bakari desu.

Reibun

1. Hirugohan wa mō tabemashita ka.

   …Iie, korekara taberu tokoro desu.

   Ja, issho ni tabemashō.

2. Kaigi no shiryō wa mō dekimashita ka.

   …Sumimasen. Ima kopii-shite iru tokoro desu.

   Mō sukoshi matte kudasai.

3. Osoku natte, sumimasen.

   Shigoto ga nakanaka owaranakatta'n desu.

   …Watashi mo tattaima kita tokoro desu.

4. Kono kabe wa sakki penki o nutta bakari desu kara,

   sawaranai yō ni shite kudasai.

   …Hai, wakarimashita.

5. Kono kamera wa katta bakari na noni, furasshu ga tsukanai'n desu.

   …Sugu katta mise e motte itta hō ga ii desu yo.

Kaiwa

Happyō no junbi

Rao: Kono hon, arigatō gozaimashita.

Katō: Iie. Yaku ni tachimashita ka.

Rao: Ē. Shiritai koto ga kuwashiku kaite atta node, totemo tasukarimashita.

Katō: Happyō made ato 1-shūkan shika arimasen ne. Junbi wa susunde imasu ka.

Rao: Ē, happyō no naiyō wa daitai matomemashita. Korekara zu ya hyō o kaku tokoro desu.

Katō: Jā, mō sukoshi desu ne. Taihen datta deshō?

Rao: Ē, Nihon-go de matomeru no ni kurō-shimashita.

Katō: Sō desu ka. Ii happyō ga dekiru yō ni, ganbatte kudasai.

Rao: Hai, arigatō gozaimasu.

Renshū A

1\. Chōdo ima kara

		dekakeru	tokoro desu.
	eiga ga	hajimaru	
	minna de	shokuji-suru	

2\. Ima

ryōri o	tsukutte iru	tokoro desu.
repōto o	kaite iru	
nimotsu o	matomete iru	

3\. Tattaima

shigoto ga	owatta	tokoro desu.
densha ga	deta	
uchi e	kaetta	

4\.

Sakki	okita	bakari desu.
Kono kamera wa kinō	katta	
Kimura-san wa sengetsu	kekkon-shita	

Renshū B

1. Rei: ocha o nomimasu

   ……Chōdo ima kara ocha o nomu tokoro desu.
   Issho ni ikaga desu ka.

   1) shokuji-shimasu ……
   2) tenisu o shimasu ……
   3) pātii ga hajimarimasu ……
   4) shain-ryokō no bideo o mimasu ……

2. Rei: Kaigi no shiryō wa mō dekimashita ka. (kopii-shimasu)

   ……Sumimasen. Ima kopii-shite iru tokoro desu kara,
   mō sukoshi matte kudasai.

   1) Repōto wa mō dekimashita ka. (kakimasu) ……
   2) Shorui wa mō dekimashita ka. (chekku-shimasu) ……
   3) Sentakuki wa mō shūri-dekimashita ka. (shūri-shimasu) ……
   4) Kaigi no junbi wa mō dekimashita ka. (yarimasu) ……

3. Rei: Lee-san wa mō dekakemashita ka.

   ……Hai, tattaima dekaketa tokoro desu.

   1) 8-ji no basu wa mō demashita ka. ……
   2) Takahashi-san wa mō kaerimashita ka. ……
   3) Shigoto wa mō owarimashita ka. ……
   4) Hikōki wa mō tsukimashita ka. ……

4. Rei: Katō-san wa imasu ka. (tattaima uchi e kaerimashita)
……Iie, tattaima uchi e kaetta tokoro desu.

1) Koshō no gen'in ga wakarimashita ka. (ima shirabete imasu) ……
2) Kesa Ōsaka ni tsuita'n desu ka. (tattaima tsukimashita) ……
3) Kagi wa mitsukarimashita ka. (ima sagashite imasu) ……
4) Happyō ni tsukau zu wa mō dekimashita ka. (korekara kakimasu) ……

5. Rei: sakki okimashita, mada asagohan o tabete imasen
……Sakki okita bakari desu kara, mada asagohan o tabete imasen.

1) sakki shokuji-shimashita, mada onaka ga ippai desu ……
2) sakki shawā o abimashita, mada kami ga nurete imasu ……
3) kesa penki o nurimashita, mada kawaite imasen ……
4) sengetsu kaisha ni hairimashita, mada shigoto ni narete imasen ……

6. Rei: kono kamera wa sengetsu kaimashita, kowaremashita
……Kono kamera wa sengetsu katta bakari na noni,
mō kowarete shimaimashita.

1) sakki denwa-bangō o kikimashita, wasuremashita ……
2) senshū okane o moraimashita, nakunarimashita ……
3) sakki sōji-shimashita, yogoremashita ……
4) kono kuruma wa senshū shūri-shimashita, koshō-shimashita ……

Renshū C

1. A: A, Narong-san.
   Chōdo ima kara ocha o nomu tokoro desu.
   Issho ni ikaga desu ka.
   B: Hai, arigatō gozaimasu.

   1) bideo o mimasu
   2) pātii o hajimemasu

2. A: Kaigi no junbi wa mō dekimashita ka.
   B: Sumimasen. Ima shiryō o kopii-shite iru tokoro desu.
   A: Sorosoro jikan desu kara, isoide kudasai.
   B: Hai, wakarimashita.

   1) shiryō o chekku-shimasu
   2) tsukue o narabemasu

3. A: Kudamono wa ikaga desu ka.
①

B: Arigatō gozaimasu.

Demo, ima shokuji-shita bakari desu kara, kekkō desu.
②

1) ① okashi ② gohan o tabemasu

2) ① nomimono ② kōhii o nomimasu

4. A: Irasshaimase.

B: Anō, kono kamera wa senshū katta bakari na noni,
① ②
furasshu ga tsukanai'n desu.
③

A: Okashii desu ne. Ja, sugu shirabete mimashō.

1) ① tēpu-rekōdā ② shūri-shimasu

③ oto ga demasen

2) ① tokei ② denchi o kaemasu

③ ugokimasen

Mondai

1.

1) Narong-san wa korekara { a. hitori de / b. minna de / c. okāsan to } (   ) tokoro desu.

2) Futari wa tattaima { a. kuru / b. itta / c. kita } tokoro desu.

Eiga wa mōsugu (   ).

3) Happyō no (   ) wa ima { a. hajimeru / b. yatte iru / c. owatta } tokoro desu.

4) Sakki penki o (   ) bakari desu kara,

{ a. mada kawaite imasen.
b. mō kawakimashita.
c. kawaita tokoro desu. }

5) Kono tēpu-rekōdā wa senshū (   ) bakari na noni,

{ a. mō tsukai-kata o wasurete shimaimashita.
b. totemo chōshi ga ii desu.
c. chōshi ga waruku narimashita. }

2. Rei: A: Hirugohan wa mō tabemashita ka.
B: Iie, ima kara (taberu) tokoro desu.

1) A: Kōgi wa owarimashita ka.
B: Hai, tattaima ( ) tokoro desu.

2) A: Eiga wa mō hajimarimashita ka.
B: Iie, chōdo ima kara ( ) tokoro desu.

3) A: Kagi wa mitsukarimashita ka.
B: Iie, ima isshōkenmei ( ) tokoro desu.

4) A: Koshō no gen'in wa wakarimashita ka.
B: Iie, mada desu. Ima ( ) tokoro desu.

3. Rei: Sakki gohan o (tabeta) bakari desu kara, mada onaka ga ippai desu.

1) Sakki ( ) bakari desu kara, mada nemui desu.

2) Sakki shawā o ( ) bakari desu kara, mada kami ga nurete imasu.

3) Sengetsu kaisha ni ( ) bakari desu kara, mada shigoto ni narete imasen.

4) Ano kenshūsei wa senshū Nihon e ( ) bakari desu kara, Nihon no koto ga yoku wakaranai to omoimasu.

4. Rei: kono kamera wa senshū kaimashita
……Kono kamera wa senshū katta bakari na noni, mō kowarete shimaimashita.

1) senshū okane o moraimashita
……

2) sakki setsumei o kikimashita
……

3) kono tokei wa senshū shūri-shimashita
……

4) kono tsukue wa sakki fukimashita
……

46

5. Shita no [   ] kara kotoba o erande, (   ) ni irete kudasai.
(Onaji kotoba o 2-kai ijō tsukatte mo ii desu.)

Rei: Watashi wa hon o yomu (no) ga suki desu.

1) Kazoku no (   ) ni, isshōkenmei hatarakimasu.
2) Sugu byōin e itta (   ) ga ii desu.
3) Watashi wa rainen kanojo to kekkon-suru (   ) desu.
4) Watashi wa ichido mo shinkansen ni notta (   ) ga arimasen.
5) Kono shatsu wa sentaku-shita (   ) na noni, mō yogorete shimaimashita.
6) Sakki watashi ga yatta (   ) ni, enjin o kumitatete kudasai.
7) Chōdo ima kara ocha o nomu (   ) desu. Issho ni ikaga desu ka.
8) Watashi no shumi wa eiga o miru (   ) desu.
9) Watashi wa kanji o yomu (   ) ga dekimasen.
10) Ryokō ni iku (   ) ni, okane o tamete imasu.

tokoro, bakari, tame, no, koto, tsumori, tōri, hō

6. 46 ka no kaiwa o yonde, tadashii mono ni wa ○, tadashikunai mono ni wa × o tsukete kudasai.

1) Rao-san wa Katō-san ni karita hon o yonde iru tokoro desu. (   )
2) Kono hon wa shiritai koto ga kuwashiku kaite atta node, yaku ni tachimashita. (   )
3) Happyō no junbi wa zenbu owarimashita. (   )
4) Nihon-go de happyō no naiyō o matomeru no wa taihen deshita. (   )

Dai 47 ka

Bunkei

1. Tenki-yohō ni yoru to, ashita wa ame ga furu sō desu.
2. Dareka kita yō desu.

Reibun

1. Kinō Ōsaka no hoteru de kaji ga atta sō desu ne.
   …Ē, watashi mo shinbun o yonde, bikkuri-shimashita.

2. Eki no mae ni dekita resutoran wa yasukute, oishii sō desu yo.
   …Sō desu ka. Ja, kondo issho ni itte mimashō.

3. Shingapōru e itta koto ga arimasu ka.
   …Iie, arimasen ga, totemo kirei da sō desu ne.
   Ē, zehi asobi ni kite kudasai.

4. Genkan de oto ga shimashita yo. Dareka kita yō desu.
   …Sō desu ka. Ja, chotto mite kimasu.

5. Michi ga konde imasu ne.
   …Mukō ni patokā ga tomatte imasu yo.
   Dōmo jiko no yō desu ne.

Kaiwa

Jishin no nyūsu o kiite

Rao: Kesa San Francisco de jishin ga atta sō desu ne.

Mori: Ē. Watashi mo terebi no nyūsu o mite, bikkuri-shimashita.

Satō: Biru ga taoretari, kōsoku-dōro ga kowaretari shite, zuibun ōkina jishin datta yō desu ne.

Rao: Katō-san wa ima San Francisco deshō?
Daijōbu deshō ka.

Mori: Ē. Sorede nan-do mo denwa-shite iru'n desu ga, kakaranai'n desu.

Rao: Shinpai desu ne.

Satō: Daijōbu desu yo. Kitto renraku ga arimasu yo.

Renshū A

1. Tegami ni yoru to,

Rao-san wa	mōsugu kuni e	kaeru	sō desu.
	konoaida Hakone e	itta	
	Nihon de motto	jisshū-shitai	
	mainichi	isogashii	
	totemo	genki da	

2.

Lee-san wa	nanika yōji ga	aru	yō desu.
	dokoka	dekaketa	
	ima	isogashii	
	kyō wa	himana	
	dōmo	byōki no	

Renshū B

1. Rei: ii tenki ni narimasu

   ……Tenki-yohō ni yoru to, ashita wa ii tenki ni naru sō desu.

   1) taifū ga kimasu ……

   2) tsuyoi kaze ga fukimasu ……

   3) mushiatsui desu ……

   4) ame desu ……

2. Rei: Amerika de ōkina jishin ga arimashita

   ……Nyūsu ni yoru to, Amerika de ōkina jishin ga atta sō desu.

   1) jishin de biru ga kowaremashita ……

   2) Hokkaidō de hikōki ga ochimashita ……

   3) kaji de depāto ga yakemashita ……

   4) kotoshi wa kōtsū-jiko ga ōkatta desu ……

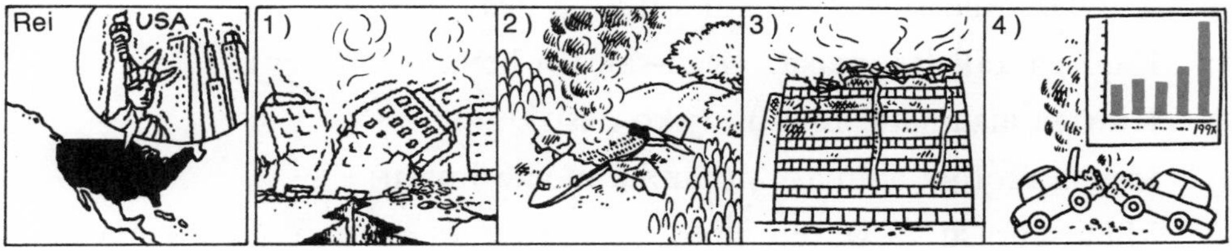

3. Rei: Doko de jiko ga atta'n desu ka. (eki no chikaku)

   ……Eki no chikaku de atta sō desu.

   1) Jiko de nan-nin shinda'n desu ka. (3-nin) ……

   2) Kaji no gen'in wa nan datta'n desu ka. (tabako no hi) ……

   3) Rao-san wa itsu kuni e kaeru'n desu ka. (raigetsu no hajime ni) ……

   4) Han-san no jisshū wa donokurai nobiru'n desu ka. (hantoshi) ……

4. Rei: dareka kimashita

……Dareka kita yō desu.

1) rōka ni dareka imasu ……

2) dokoka ni kagi o otoshimashita ……

3) Lee-san wa nanika komatte imasu ……

4) heya ni dorobō ga hairimashita ……

5. Rei: Nokku-shite mo, henji ga arimasen. (Rao-san wa dokoka ikimashita)

……Ē, Rao-san wa dokoka itta yō desu ne.

1) Kagi ga kakatte imasu. (Rao-san wa heya ni imasen) ……

2) Hito ga atsumatte imasu. (jiko desu) ……

3) Henna nioi ga shimasu. (nanika moete imasu) ……

4) Mado-garasu ga warete imasu. (koko kara dorobō ga hairimashita) ……

6. Rei: dareka kimashita, chotto mite kimasu

……Dareka kita yō desu kara, chotto mite kimasu.

1) nanika moete imasu, shirabete kimasu ……

2) Lee-san wa genki desu, shinpai-shinai de kudasai ……

3) mōtā ga koshō desu, shirabete mimasu ……

4) Watanabe-san wa rusu desu, mata ato de kimashō ……

Renshū C

1. A: Rao-san wa mōsugu kuni e kaeru① sō desu yo.
   B: Hontō desu ka. Itsu desu ka.
   A: Raigetsu no hajime da② sō desu.

   1) ① Lee-san wa nyūin-shimashita
      ② 1-shūkan gurai mae desu
   2) ① Ikeda-san wa mōsugu kekkon-shimasu
      ② 10-gatsu desu

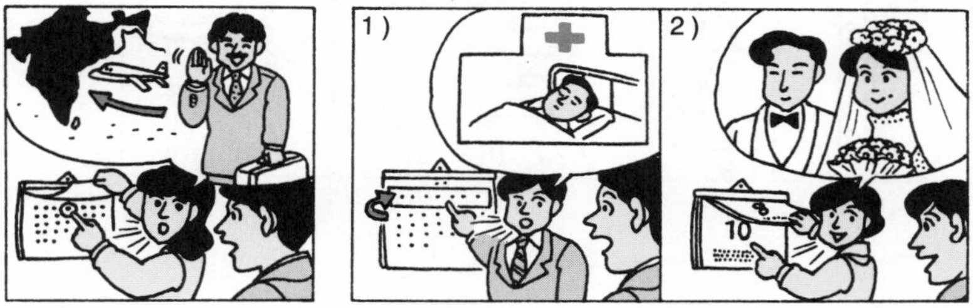

2. A: Kesa no nyūsu o kikimashita ka.
   B: Iie, nanika atta'n desu ka.
   A: San Francisco de ōkina jishin ga atta sō desu yo.
   B: Hontō desu ka. Kowai desu ne.

   1) Hokkaidō de hikōki ga ochimashita
   2) Tōkyō no hoteru de kaji ga arimashita

3. A: Kagi ga kakatte imasu yo.

B: Sō desu ne. Watanabe-san wa inai yō desu ne.

A: Ja, mata ato de kimashō.

1) dokoka dekakemashita

2) rusu desu

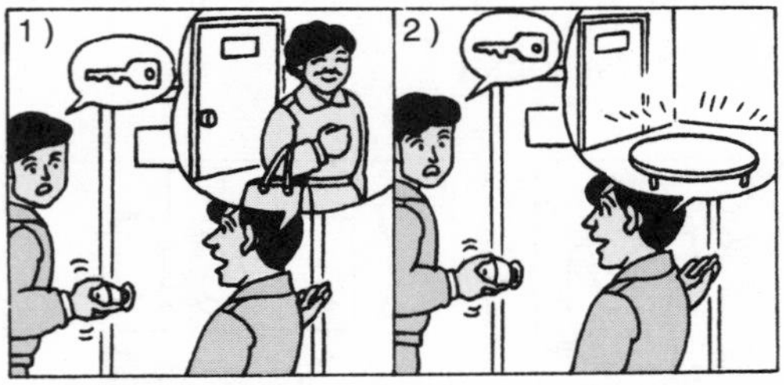

4. A: Genkan de oto ga shimashita yo. Dareka kita ① yō desu.

B: Sō desu ka. Ja, chotto mite kimasu.

A: Dare deshita ka.

B: Yūbin-ya ② deshita.

1) ① imasu ② kodomo

2) ① kimashita ② shinbun-ya

Mondai

1. 1) (　　　　) ni yoru to, ashita wa

- a. tenki ga shinpai da
- b. ii tenki ni naru
- c. tenki ga waruku naru

} sō desu.

2) Kesa no (　　　　) ni yoru to,

- a. hikōki-jiko de hito ga takusan shinda
- b. kōtsū-jiko de hito ga takusan kega o shita
- c. jishin de hito ga takusan shinda

} sō desu.

3) Rao-san wa {

- a. kongetsu no hajime
- b. kongetsu no owari
- c. raigetsu no owari

} ni (　　　　) sō desu.

4) Narong-san no heya wa {

- a. denki ga kiete
- b. mado ga shimatte
- c. kagi ga kakatte

} imasu.

Narong-san wa dokoka (　　　　) yō desu.

5) Gomi ga (　　　　) kara, henna {

- a. oto ga shimashita.
- b. nioi ga shimashita.
- c. aji deshita.

}

2. ( ) no naka ni kotoba o irete kudasai.

1) A: Tanaka-san no hanashi ni yoru to, Lee-san wa senshū byōki de Tōkyō-byōin ni ( ) sō desu yo.
B: Sore wa shinpai desu ne.

2) A: Ikeda-san, mōsugu ( ) sō desu ne.
Omedetō gozaimasu.
B: Arigatō gozaimasu.

3) A: Kinō kono chikaku de kōtsū-jiko ga ( ) sō desu.
B: Hontō desu ka. Kowai desu ne.

4) A: Tai e itta koto ga arimasen ga, ( ) sō desu ne.
B: Ē, hontō ni kirei desu yo. Zehi kite kudasai.

3. Rei: A: Kono shashin o miru to, Bangkok wa kuruma ga (ō)sō desu ne.
B: Ē, Narong-san no hanashi ni yoru to, hontō ni (ōi) sō desu ne.

1) A: Kyō wa tenki ga warukute, imanimo ame ga ( )sō desu ne.
B: Ē, tenki-yohō ni yoru to, kyō wa ame ga ( ) sō desu.

2) A: Atatakaku natte, mōsugu sakura ga ( )sō desu ne.
B: Sō desu ne. Nyūsu ni yoru to, Kyūshū de wa mō ( ) sō desu yo.

3) A: Soto wa yuki ga futte ite, ( )sō desu ne.
B: Ē, tenki-yohō ni yoru to, ashita mo ( ) sō desu.

4) A: Rao-san wa itsumo ( )sō desu ne.
B: Ē, okagesama de.
A: Kazoku no minasan mo o-genki desu ka.
B: Ē, tegami ni yoru to, minna ( ) sō desu.

4. Rei: Genkan no hō de oto ga shimashita. Dareka kita ________ yō desu.

1) Narong-san no heya o nokku-shite mo, henji ga arimasen.
________________ yō desu.

2) Mukō ni hito ga takusan atsumatte imasu.
________________ yō desu.

3) Henna nioi ga shimasu. ________________ yō desu.

4) Michi ga nurete imasu. ________________ yō desu.

5. Rei: Dokoka ni saifu o otoshita yō desu kara, chotto sagashite kimasu.

1) Rōka ni dareka iru yō desu kara, ____________________________

2) Mōtā ga koshō no yō desu kara, ____________________________

3) Tanaka-san wa rusu no yō desu kara, ________________________

4) Dōmo kaze o hiita yō desu kara, ____________________________

6.

Kinō watashi no uchi ni dorobō ga hairimashita. Watashi ga yūgata chotto kaimono ni itta toki, hairaremashita. Doa no kagi o kakete oita noni, dorobō wa kagi o kowashite haitta yō desu. Kagi ga kowarete imashita. Tsukue no hikidashi ni okane ga haitte imashita ga, dorobō wa wakaranakatta yō desu. Keredomo, tsukue no ue ni oite atta kamera o torarete shimaimashita. Katta bakari na noni, totemo zannen deshita.

Tadashii mono ni wa ○, tadashikunai mono ni wa × o irete kudasai.

1) Yūbe watashi ga nete iru toki, dorobō ni hairaremashita. (   )

2) Dorobō ni okane to kamera o torarete shimaimashita. (   )

3) Dorobō wa doa no kagi o kowashite, haitta yō desu. (   )

4) Watashi wa dekakeru toki, doa no kagi o kakeru no o wasurete shimaimashita. (   )

Dai 48 ka

Bunkei

1. Buchō wa Katō-san o Ōsaka e shutchō-sasemashita.
2. Watashi wa musume ni piano o narawasemasu.

Reibun

1. Kopii-ki ga koshō-shita node, shūri o onegai-shimasu.
   …Wakarimashita. Kakari no mono o sugu sochira e ikasemasu.

2. Nakamura-san, Lee-san wa mō kaetta'n desu ka.
   …Ē, netsu ga atta node, ryō e kaerasemashita.

3. Mō osoi desu kara, musuko ni kuruma de okurasemasu.
   …Sumimasen. Onegai-shimasu.

4. Kono kōjō no koto o motto shiritai'n desu ga…
   …Ja, kakari no mono ni panfuretto o motte kosasemasu.

5. Sumimasen. Kaze o hiita node, kyō 1-nichi yasumasete itadakemasen ka.
   …Wakarimashita. Odaiji ni.

Kaiwa

O-shōgatsu

Takahashi-san no okusan: O-matase shimashita.
Kochira e dōzo.

Narong: Wā, sugoi gochisō desu ne.

Okusan: Ē. O-shōgatsu-ryōri na'n desu yo.

Narong: Zenbu okusan ga tsukutta'n desu ka.

Okusan: Iie, musume ni iroiro tetsudawasemashita.

Takahashi: Akemashite omedetō gozaimasu.

Minna: Akemashite omedetō gozaimasu.

Okusan: Sā, Narong-san, enryo naku dōzo.

Narong: Itadakimasu.

Okusan: A, yuki desu yo.

Narong: Wā, kirei desu ne. Nihon no o-shōgatsu wa ii desu ne.

Renshū A

1.

				shieki		
I	ka	ki	masu	ka	ka	semasu
	iso	gi	masu	iso	ga	semasu
	no	mi	masu	no	ma	semasu
	yo	bi	masu	yo	ba	semasu
	tsuku	ri	masu	tsuku	ra	semasu
	tetsuda	i	masu	tetsuda	wa	semasu
	mo	chi	masu	mo	ta	semasu
	nao	shi	masu	nao	sa	semasu

			shieki	
II	tabe	masu	tabe	sasemasu
	shirabe	masu	shirabe	sasemasu
	oboe	masu	oboe	sasemasu

			shieki	
III	ki	masu	ko	sasemasu
	shi	masu	sa	semasu

2. Buchō wa | Katō-san / Takahashi-san / Ishikawa-san | o | Amerika e / kaigi ni / Ōsaka e | ikasemashita. / shusseki-sasemashita. / shutchō-sasemashita.

3. Watashi wa | musuko / musume / otōto | ni | shigoto / heya / kuruma | o | tetsudawasemasu. / katazukesasemasu. / arawasemasu.

4. Sumimasen ga, | ashita / hayaku / denwa o | yasumasete / kaerasete / tsukawasete | itadakemasen ka.

Renshū B

1. Rei: musume wa ginkō e ikimasu
   ······Musume o ginkō e ikasemasu.
   1) kodomo wa kōen de asobimasu ······
   2) kodomo wa uchi e kaerimasu ······
   3) kodomo wa juku ni kayoimasu ······
   4) musuko wa eki e mukae ni kimasu ······
   5) musume wa kaimono ni ikimasu ······

2. Rei: musume wa suiei o naraimasu
   ······Musume ni suiei o narawasemasu.
   1) otōto wa shigoto o tetsudaimasu ······
   2) musuko wa kuruma o unten-shimasu ······
   3) kodomo wa jibun no nimotsu o mochimasu ······
   4) imōto wa ocha o motte kimasu ······
   5) kodomo wa rekishi no hon o yomimasu ······

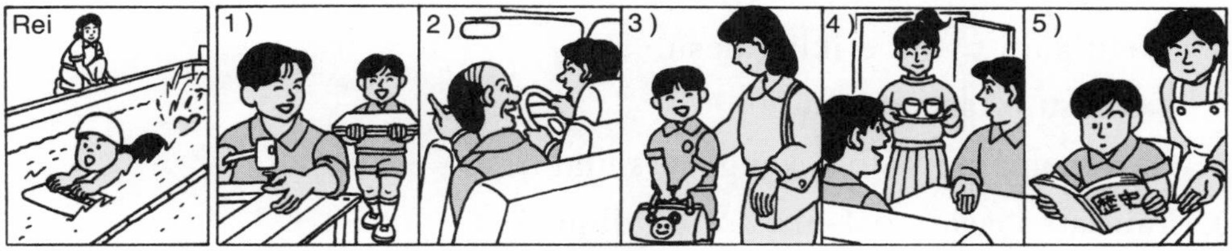

3. Rei 1: netsu ga arimasu, kodomo wa yasumimasu
   ······Netsu ga aru node, kodomo o yasumasemasu.
   Rei 2: karada ni ii desu, kodomo wa mainichi gyūnyū o nomimasu
   ······Karada ni ii node, kodomo ni mainichi gyūnyū o nomasemasu.
   1) taifū ga kimasu, kodomo wa hayaku uchi e kaerimasu ······
   2) watashi wa tsugō ga warui desu, musuko wa kawari ni ikimasu ······
   3) michi ga wakarinikui desu, musuko wa eki made mukae ni ikimasu ······
   4) heya ga kitanai desu, kodomo wa heya o sōji-shimasu ······
   5) mō osoi desu, musuko wa eki made okurimasu ······

4. Rei: Kōjō no naka o mitai'n desu ga· · ·
(annai-shimasu) ······ Ja, kakari no mono ni annai-sasemasu.

1) Kono kōjō no seisan-kanri ni tsuite shiritai'n desu ga· · ·
(setsumei-shimasu) ······

2) Kōjō no panfuretto o moraitai'n desu ga· · ·
(motte kimasu) ······

3) Kikai no chōshi ga okashii'n desu ga· · ·
(shirabemasu) ······

4) Terebi o naoshite moraitai'n desu ga· · ·
(sugu shūri-shimasu) ······

5) Hayaku terebi o todokete moraitai'n desu ga· · ·
(sugu haitatsu-shimasu) ······

5. Rei: 4-ji ni kaeritai desu
······ Sumimasen ga, 4-ji ni kaerasete itadakemasen ka.

1) kyō 1-nichi yasumitai desu ······
2) gogo kara byōin e ikitai desu ······
3) fakkusu o tsukaimasu ······
4) Yokohama no kōjō o kengaku-shitai desu ······
5) rain no shashin o 1-mai toritai desu ······

Renshū C

1. A: Lee-san wa ①kyō yasumi na'n desu ka.

   B: Ē, netsu ga atta node, ②gogo kara jisshū o yasumasemashita.

   Ato de yōsu o mi ni iku tsumori desu.

   1) ① mō kaerimashita ② ryō e kaerimasu

   2) ① imasen ② byōin e ikimasu

2. A: Wā, sugoi gochisō desu ne.

   Junbi ga taihen datta deshō?

   B: Iie, musume ni tetsudawasemashita kara.

   1) zairyō o katte kimasu

   2) sukoshi tsukurimasu

3.　A: Kuni e kaeru junbi wa mō dekimashita ka.

B: Ē, dekimashita.

A: Ja, nimotsu o matomete oite kudasai.

Kaisha no mono ni kūkō made <u>hakobase</u>masu kara.

1)　motte ikimasu

2)　okurimasu

4.　A: Sumimasen ga, kyō <u>1-nichi yasumasete</u>① itadakemasen ka.

B: Dō shita'n desu ka.

A: <u>Yūbe kara sukoshi netsu ga aru</u>②'n desu.

B: Wakarimashita.　Odaiji ni.

1)　① 4-ji ni kaerimasu

② byōin e kusuri o morai ni ikitai desu

2)　① gogo kara yasumimasu

② onaka no chōshi ga warui desu

Mondai

1. 1) ______________________________

2) ______________________________

3) ______________________________

2\.

1) Lee-san wa { a. kibun ga warui / b. netsu ga aru / c. tsugō ga warui } yō na node, Nakamura-san wa Lee-san o ryō e (   ).

2) Michi ga (   ) node, Nakamura-san wa eki made
{ a. mukae ni ikimasu. / b. musuko-san o mukae ni ikasemasu. / c. musuko-san to issho ni mukae ni ikimasu. }

3) Katō-san wa musume-san ni (   ) o { a. narawasete imasu. / b. oshiete imasu. / c. utawasete imasu. }

4) Shinamono wa (   ) made ni
{ a. watashi ga uchi e todokemasu. / b. mise e motte ikasemasu. / c. mise no mono ni uchi e todokesasemasu. }

5) (   ) node, kyō wa { a. hayaku kaerimasu. / b. kaisha o yasumimasu. / c. kaisha ni okuremasu. }

3.

Rei: ikimasu	ikasemasu	kaerimasu	
kakimasu		araimasu	
isogimasu		katazukemasu	
hanashimasu		shirabemasu	
mochimasu		kakemasu	
asobimasu		shimasu	
yasumimasu		(Nihon e) kimasu	

4. Rei 1: Kyō wa ii tenki na node, kodomo (o) soto de (asobimasu … asobasemasu).

Rei 2: Nimotsu ga omoi node, musuko (ni) nimotsu o (mochimasu … motasemasu).

1) Heya ga kitanai node, musume ( ) heya o (sōji-shimasu …).

2) Taifū ga kuru node, kodomo ( ) hayaku uchi e (kaerimasu …).

3) Isogashii toki, kodomo ( ) uchi no shigoto o (tetsudaimasu …).

4) Buchō wa tsugō ga warui node, kawari ni Katō-san ( ) kaigi ni (shusseki-shimasu …).

5. Rei: Sumimasen ga, chotto denwa o tsukawasete itadakemasen ka.

1) Karada no chōshi ga warui node, ＿＿＿＿＿＿＿＿ itadakemasen ka.

2) Konban taishikan de pātii ga aru node, ＿＿＿＿＿＿＿＿ itadakemasen ka.

3) Kono hon wa watashi no senmon to kankei ga aru node, chotto ＿＿＿＿＿＿＿＿ itadakemasen ka.

4) Sumimasen ga, ano robotto no shashin o 1-mai ＿＿＿＿＿＿＿＿ itadakemasen ka.

6. Rei: Sentakuki o shūri-shite moraitai'n desu ga・・・

……Ja, mise no mono o sugu (ikimasu, (ikasemasu), itte moraimasu).

1) Hitori de kono nimotsu o motte kita'n desu ka.

……Iie, tomodachi ni (tetsudawasemashita, tetsudatte kuremashita, tetsudatte moraimashita).

2) Mō osoi desu kara, sorosoro shitsurei-shimasu.

……Ja, musuko ni eki made (okurimasu, okurasemasu, okutte agemasu).

3) Honsha e iku michi ga wakarimasu ka.

……Ē, Katō-san ni chizu o (kakasemashita, kaite itadakimashita, kaite kudasaimashita) kara.

4) Kuruma no seisan-rain o kengaku-sasete itadakemasen ka.

……Ja, kōjō no mono ni (annai-shimasu, annai-sasemasu, annai-shite itadakimasu).

7.

12-gatsu no owari wa Nihon de wa o-shōgatsu no junbi de minna isogashiku narimasu. Uchi no naka o zenbu sōji-shinakereba naranai shi, o-shōgatsu no gochisō mo tsukuranakereba narimasen kara. Takahashi-san no uchi de mo, okusan hitori de wa murina node, uchi no hito minna ga tetsudaimasu. Gakkō wa 25-nichi goro kara, kaisha wa 29-nichi goro kara yasumi ni narimasu. Sorede okusan wa kodomo ni wa heya o katazukesasetari, mado o fukasetari shimasu. Go-shujin ni wa kuruma de issho ni kaimono ni itte moraimasu. Soshite okusan wa kazoku no tame ni, isshōkenmei oishii o-shōgatsu-ryōri o tsukurimasu.

12-gatsu 31-nichi no yoru wa 12-ji goro ni naru to, chikaku no o-tera kara kane no oto ga kikoemasu. Sono oto o kikinagara kazoku minna de oiwai o shimasu.

kane

Tadashii mono ni wa ○, tadashikunai mono ni wa × o irete kudasai.

1) O-shōgatsu no junbi wa taihenna node, kodomo ni uchi no naka no iroirona shigoto o tetsudawasemasu. (   )

2) Kodomo ni o-shōgatsu-ryōri o tsukurasemasu. (   )

3) Go-shujin ni kaimono o tetsudatte moraimasu. (   )

4) 12-gatsu 31-nichi no yoru wa o-shōgatsu no junbi de totemo tsukareru node, nani mo shinai de, hayaku nemasu. (   )

Dai 49 ka

Bunkei

1. Shachō wa 3-ji ni kochira e koraremasu.
2. Buchō wa mō o-kaeri ni narimashita.
3. O-kyaku-sama wa robii ni irasshaimasu.

Reibun

1. Itsu o-kuni e kaeraremasu ka.
   ··· Asatte kaerimasu.

2. Sumimasen. Kono zasshi o o-yomi ni narimasu ka.
   ··· Iie, yomimasen. Dōzo.

3. Pātii no shashin o goran ni narimashita ka.
   ··· Iie, mada desu. Zehi misete kudasai.

4. Nihon-go ga o-jōzu desu ne. Donokurai benkyō-nasaimashita ka.
   ··· 3-kagetsu gurai desu.

5. Ano kata o go-zonji desu ka.
   ··· Ē. AOTS no Tanaka-san desu.

6. Nani o meshiagarimasu ka.
   ··· Sō desu ne. Ja, tenpura o onegai-shimasu.

Kaiwa

Denwa o kakeru

Rao:	Moshi moshi, Tanaka-san no otaku desu ka.
Tanaka-san no okusan:	Hai, sō desu.　Dochira-sama desu ka.
Rao:	Indo no Rao desu ga, go-shujin wa irasshaimasu ka.
Okusan:	Chotto dekakete imasu.
Rao:	Sō desu ka.　Nan-ji goro o-kaeri ni narimasu ka.
Okusan:	Sugu kaeru to omoimasu ga・・・
	A, chotto o-machi kudasai.　Ima kaette kimashita.
	--
Tanaka:	Ā, Rao-san, o-matase shimashita.
	O-kawari arimasen ka.
Rao:	Ē, okagesama de genki desu.
	Tanaka-san, ashita no pātii ni kite kudasaru sō desu ne.
Tanaka:	Ē, ikimasu yo.　Rao-san ni aitai desu kara.
Rao:	Arigatō gozaimasu.　Tanoshimi ni shite imasu.
	Ja, shitsurei-shimasu.

Renshū A

1.

				sonkei		
I	ka	ki	masu	ka	ka	remasu
	i	ki	masu	i	ka	remasu
	yasu	mi	masu	yasu	ma	remasu
	yo	bi	masu	yo	ba	remasu
	kae	ri	masu	kae	ra	remasu
	a	i	masu	a	wa	remasu
	hana	shi	masu	hana	sa	remasu

			sonkei	
II	kake	masu	kake	raremasu
	de	masu	de	raremasu
	oki	masu	oki	raremasu
	ori	masu	ori	raremasu

			sonkei	
III	ki	masu	ko	raremasu
	shi	masu	sa	remasu

2. Shachō wa

sakki	dekakeraremashita.
10-ji ni	koraremasu.
ashita Ōsaka e	shutchō-saremasu.

3. Buchō wa

kono repōto	o o-	yomi	ni narimashita.
honsha ni denwa		kake	
Katō-san		yobi	

4. Shachō wa

achira ni	irasshaimasu.
sō	osshaimashita.
kono hanashi o	go-zonji desu.

Renshū B

1. Rei: chotto dekakemashita (buchō)

   ……Buchō wa chotto dekakeraremashita.

   1) atarashii kōjō ni tsuite hanashimasu (shachō) ……

   2) pātii ni shusseki-shimasu (Tanaka-san) ……

   3) tattaima kaerimashita (o-kyaku-sama) ……

   4) kono hon o kakimashita (Suzuki-sensei) ……

2. Rei: Donna omiyage o kawaremashita ka. (Nihon-ningyō)

   ……Nihon-ningyō o kaimashita.

   1) Dochira de Nihon-go o narawaremashita ka. (Kenshū Sentā) ……

   2) Itsu nimotsu o okuraremashita ka. (ototoi) ……

   3) Itsu o-kuni e kaeraremasu ka. (asatte) ……

   4) Nan-ji no hikōki ni noraremasu ka. (yūgata 6-ji no hikōki) ……

3. Rei: kono shinbun o yomimasu ka

   ……Kono shinbun o o-yomi ni narimasu ka.

   1) tabako o suimasu ka ……

   2) tsukai-kata ga wakarimasu ka ……

   3) buchō wa sugu modorimasu ka ……

   4) Tanaka-san ni aimashita ka ……

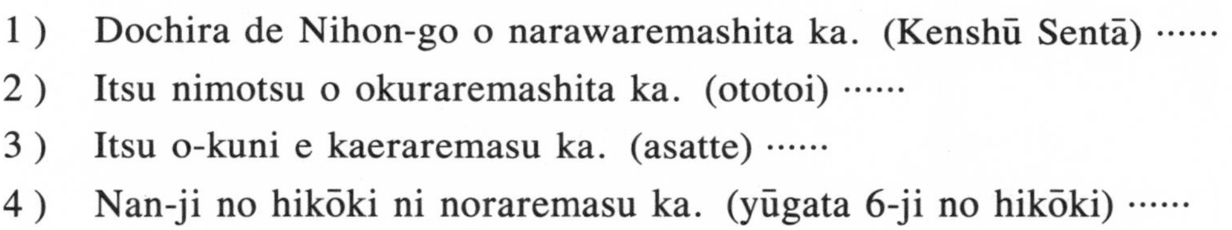

4. Rei: Itsu kono kamera o o-kai ni narimashita ka. (ototoi)
……Ototoi kaimashita.

1) Donokurai o-machi ni narimashita ka. (10-pun gurai) ……
2) Go-shujin wa nan-ji goro o-dekake ni narimashita ka. (12-ji mae ni) ……
3) Nan-ji goro otaku e o-kaeri ni narimasu ka. (yoru 10-ji goro) ……
4) Maiban nan-ji goro o-yasumi ni narimasu ka. (11-ji sugi ni) ……

5. Rei: ashita Tōkyō e ikimasu ka
……Ashita Tōkyō e irasshaimasu ka.

1) hirugohan wa mō tabemashita ka ……
2) saisho ni shachō ga aisatsu-shimasu ka ……
3) ano eiga wa mō mimashita ka ……
4) Tanaka-san o shitte imasu ka ……

6. Rei: Nihon de nani o shimasu ka
……Nihon de nani o nasaimasu ka.

1) itsu Nihon e kimashita ka ……
2) namae wa nan to iimasu ka ……
3) kazoku wa doko ni sunde imasu ka ……
4) itsu kekkon-shimashita ka ……

Renshū C

1. A: Itsu o-kuni e kaeraremasu ka.

   B: Asatte kaerimasu.

   A: Nimotsu① wa mō matomerare②mashita ka.

   B: Hai, mō matome②mashita.

   1) ① omiyage ② kaimasu

   2) ① nimotsu ② okurimasu

2. A: Sumimasen. Kono zasshi o o-yomi ni narimasu ka.

   B: Iie, yomimasen. Dōzo.

   1) koko ni kakemasu

   2) kono haizara o tsukaimasu

3. A: Dochira kara irasshaimashita ka.

B: Indo no Delhi desu.

A: Sō desu ka. Nihon-go ga o-jōzu desu ne.

Ima made donokurai benkyō-nasaimashita ka.
①

B: 3-kagetsu gurai desu.
②

1) ① Nihon ni imasu ② 1-nen

2) ① jisshū-shimashita ② 6-kagetsu

4. A: Shitsurei desu ga, o-namae wa nan to osshaimasu ka.

B: AOTS no Tanaka desu.

A: Tanaka-sama desu ne.

Ja, dōzo kochira de o-machi ni natte kudasai.

1) kochira ni o-kake ni narimasu

2) kaijō no hō e irasshaimasu

Mondai

1. 1) ______________________________
   2) ______________________________
   3) ______________________________
   4) ______________________________
   5) ______________________________

2. 1) Buchō wa Rao-san no jisshū no happyō o (   )mashita.

   Happyō no naiyō wa { a. totemo yokatta desu. / b. totemo kantan deshita. / c. totemo muzukashikatta desu. }

   2) Lee-san ga okureta node, Tanaka-san wa (   ) gurai

   { a. norimashita. / b. machimashita. / c. tachimashita. }

   3) Rao-san wa Indo no Delhi kara { a. ikimashita. / b. kimashita. / c. imashita. }

   4) Kore wa (   ) no shashin desu.

   Rao-san no tonari ni { a. tatte iru / b. suwatte iru / c. yasunde iru } hito wa buchō no

   Mori-san desu.

   5) Tanaka-san ga Katō-san ni denwa-shita toki,

   Katō-san wa { a. imashita. / b. imasendeshita. / c. uchi e kaerimashita. }

   Katō-san wa (   ) goro kaisha e modorimasu.

3.

Rei: kakimasu	kakaremasu	dekakemasu	
hanashimasu		okimasu	
kaerimasu		orimasu	
ikimasu		(Nihon e) kimasu	
yasumimasu		sanka-shimasu	
naraimasu		shusseki-shimasu	

4. Rei: pātii ni shusseki-shimasu ka (shachō)
……Shachō wa pātii ni shusseki-saremasu ka.
1) itsu kochira e kimashita ka (shachō)
……
2) mō dekakemashita ka (buchō)
……
3) donna koto o hanashimashita ka (kachō)
……
4) nan-ji goro kaisha e modorimasu ka (Katō-san)
……

5. Rei: Kono hon wa dare ga kakimashita ka. (Suzuki-sensei)
……Suzuki-sensei ga o-kaki ni narimashita.
1) Pātii no toki, dare ga saisho ni hanashimasu ka. (shachō)
……
2) Rao-san no omiyage wa dare ga kaimashita ka. (Katō-san)
……
3) Kono kuruma ni wa dare ga norimasu ka. (o-kyaku-sama)
……
4) Jisshū no sukejūru wa dare ga kimemasu ka. (buchō)
……

6. Rei: Itsu Nihon e kimashita ka. ……Itsu Nihon e irasshaimashita ka.
1) Nani o tabemasu ka. ……
2) Ano eiga wa mō mimashita ka. ……
3) Itsu kekkon-shimashita ka. ……
4) Ima nani o shite imasu ka. ……

7. Rei: Ashita doko e ikimasu ka.

……Ashita dochira e irasshaimasu ka.

1) Namae wa nan to iimasu ka.

……

2) Kyaku wa doko ni imasu ka.

……

3) Ano hito no uchi o shitte imasu ka.

……

4) Nihon-go ga jōzu desu ne. Donokurai benkyō-shimashita ka.

……

8. Rei: A: Rao-san wa kekkon-shite imasu ka.

(kekkon-shite irasshaimasu ka)

B: Iie, dokushin desu.

1) A: Sensei wa imasu ka.

(　　　　　)

B: Iie, chotto dekakemashita. Sugu modoru to omoimasu.

(　　　　　) (　　　　　)

2) A: Buchō wa itsu Ōsaka e shutchō-shimasu ka.

(　　　　　)

B: Asatte da to itte imashita.

(　　　　　)

A: Itsu kaerimasu ka.

(　　　　　)

B: Kin-yōbi desu.

3) A: Buchō, ashita pātii ga aru no o shitte imasu ka.

(　　　　　)

B: Ē, kinō kikimashita.

4) A: Tsukaremashita ka.

(　　　　　)

B: Ē, sukoshi.

A: Ja, kochira de sukoshi yasunde kudasai.

(　　　　　)

B: Hai, arigatō gozaimasu.

Dai 50 ka

Bunkei

1. Watashi ga shachō no nimotsu o o-mochi shimasu.
2. Watashi wa Nihon de 1-nen jisshū-itashimashita.

Reibun

1. O-isogashisō desu ne.　O-tetsudai shimashō ka.
   ··· Sumimasen.　Onegai-shimasu.

2. Bangkok e zehi irasshatte kudasai.
   Iroirona tokoro o go-annai shimasu.
   ··· Hai, arigatō gozaimasu.

3. O-namae wa nan to osshaimasu ka.
   ··· Lee to mōshimasu.　Chūgoku kara mairimashita.

4. Konban otaku ni irasshaimasu ka.
   ··· Hai, orimasu.

5. Tanaka-san no jūsho o go-zonji desu ka.
   ··· Denwa-bangō wa zonjite orimasu ga, jūsho wa zonjimasen.

6. Shachō ga kakareta e o goran ni narimashita ka.
   ··· Hai, haiken-shimashita.

7. Ashita no yotei o o-kiki ni narimashita ka.
   ··· Hai, Katō-san kara ukagaimashita.

8. Nani mo gozaimasen ga, dōzo meshiagatte kudasai.
   ··· Hai.　Itadakimasu.

Kaiwa

Sōbetsukai

Katō: Soredewa, korekara Rao-san no sōbetsukai o hajimetai to omoimasu.
Minasama, o-isogashii tokoro, go-shusseki kudasaimashite, arigatō gozaimasu.
Dewa, mazu hajime ni Rao-san ni go-aisatsu o onegai-shimasu.

Rao: Minasan, konbanwa.
Watakushi wa kyonen no 4-gatsu ni Nihon e mairimashita ga, okagesama de buji ni jisshū ga owarimashita.
Totemo ii benkyō ni narimashita.
Kuni e kaette mo, kono keiken o ikashite, ganbaritai to omoimasu.
Minasama no go-shinsetsu wa wasuremasen.
Hontō ni arigatō gozaimashita.

Renshū A

1.	Watashi ga	nimotsu takushii denwa-bangō	o o-	mochi yobi shirabe	shimasu.
2.	Watashi ga	Bangkok yotei tsukai-kata	o go-	annai renraku setsumei	shimasu.

3.	Watashi wa	Indo kara 1-nen Nihon ni Tōkyō-denki de	mairimashita. orimashita. jisshū-itashimashita.

Renshū B

1. Rei: shachō no nimotsu o mochimasu

    ······Watashi ga shachō no nimotsu o o-mochi shimasu.

    1) takushii o yobimasu ······

    2) kūkō made okurimasu ······

    3) eki de buchō o machimasu ······

    4) buchō ni raishū no yotei o kikimasu ······

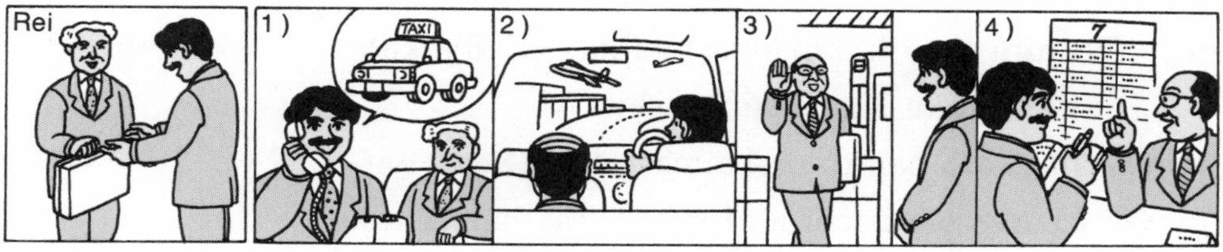

2. Rei: machi o annai-shimasu

    ······Watashi ga machi o go-annai shimasu.

    1) minasama ni aisatsu-shimasu ······

    2) o-kyaku-sama ni tsukai-kata o setsumei-shimasu ······

    3) buchō ni yotei o renraku-shimasu ······

    4) buchō ni Tanaka-san o shōkai-shimasu ······

3. Rei: Sanpuru o misete kudasai.

    ······Hai. Sugu o-mise shimasu.

    1) Katarogu o okutte kudasai. ······

    2) Hayaku nimotsu o todokete kudasai. ······

    3) Takushii o yonde kudasai. ······

    4) Ashita no yotei o shirasete kudasai. ······

4. Rei: ashita Tōkyō e ikimasu

……Ashita Tōkyō e mairimasu.

1) ashita uchi ni imasu ……

2) sensei no o-tegami o mimashita ……

3) kachō kara o-hanashi o kikimashita ……

4) buchō ni omiyage o moraimashita ……

5. Rei: Dochira kara irasshaimashita ka. (Chūgoku)

……Chūgoku kara mairimashita.

1) O-namae wa nan to osshaimasu ka. (Lee) ……

2) Go-kazoku wa dochira ni sunde irasshaimasu ka.
(Tai no Bangkok) ……

3) Shachō ga kakareta e o goran ni narimashita ka. (hai, mō) ……

4) Takahashi-san no okusan o go-zonji desu ka. (hai) ……

6. Rei: 6-ji made ni irasshatte kudasai. (hai, kanarazu ikimasu)

……Hai, kanarazu mairimasu.

1) Pātii ni zehi shusseki-nasatte kudasai. (hai, shusseki-shimasu) ……

2) Dōzo enryo naku meshiagatte kudasai. (hai, tabemasu) ……

3) Mō sukoshi o-machi ni natte kudasai. (ja, robii ni imasu) ……

4) Mō ichido o-namae o osshatte kudasaimasen ka.
(Tōkyō-denki no Katō to iimasu) ……

Renshū C

1. A: A, ame ga futte imasu ne.
   B: Kasa o o-kashi shimashō ka.
   A: Sumimasen. Onegai-shimasu.

   1) eki made okurimasu
   2) takushii o yobimasu

2. A: Ōsakajō e irasshatta (①) koto ga arimasu ka.
   B: Iie.
   A: Dewa, kondo watashi ga go-annai (②) shimasu.

   1) ① kabuki o goran ni narimasu ② shōtai-shimasu
   2) ① Yoshida-san ni o-ai ni narimasu ② shōkai-shimasu

3. A: Hai, Tōkyō-denki de gozaimasu.

B: Tanaka to mōshimasu ga, Katō-san wa irasshaimasu ka.

A: Katō wa ima dekakete orimasu ga· · ·

B: Sō desu ka. Ja, mata o-kake shimasu.

1) Ōsaka e shutchō-shite imasu

2) kyō wa yasunde imasu

4. A: Tanaka-san ① o go-zonji desu ka.

B: Hai, zonjite orimasu.

Konoaida Sentā de o-ai shimashita. ②

1) ① Tanaka-san no okusan

② pātii de o-hanashi shimashita

2) ① Tanaka-san no otaku

② otaku e ukagaimashita

Mondai

1. 1) ______________________
   2) ______________________
   3) ______________________
   4) ______________________
   5) ______________________

2. 1) Ame ga futte imasu kara, watashi no (   ) o
   { a. mochimasu. / b. kashimasu. / c. karimasu. }

   2) Tanaka-san ga (   ) e kitara,
   watashi ga { a. annai-shimasu. / b. shōkai-shimasu. / c. shōtai-shimasu. }

   3) Narong-san wa (   ) Tai e kaerimasu ga,
   kaeru mae ni, { a. Sentā ni denwa-shitai / b. Sentā e ikitai / c. Sentā ni tomaritai } to omotte imasu.

   4) Mori-san wa (   ) o { a. shitte imasu. / b. shirimasen. / c. zonjite orimasu. }

   5) Tanaka-san wa ima uchi ni { a. imasu / b. imasen / c. kaerimashita } kara,
   mata ato de (   ).

3. Rei: Dareka sensei no kaban o motte kudasai.
……Watashi ga o-mochi shimasu.

1) Dareka pātii no junbi o tetsudatte kudasai.
……

2) Dareka shachō o eki made kuruma de okutte kudasai.
……

3) Dareka kono shorui o buchō ni watashite kudasai.
……

4) O-kyaku-sama ga o-kaeri ni naru node, dareka takushii o yonde kudasai.
……

4. Rei: Pātii de saisho ni watashi ga (go-aisatsu shimasu).

1) Watashi ga kono kikai no tsukai-kata o (   ).

2) Chotto (   ). Kochira wa Tōkyō-denki no Katō-san desu.

3) Katō-san ga Indo e irasshattara, watashi ga machi o (   ).

4) Watashi ga kekkon-suru toki wa, sensei o kekkonshiki ni (   ).

50

5. Rei: Raishū Tōkyō e ikimasu. ……Raishū Tōkyō e mairimasu.

1) Watashi wa Lee to iimasu. ……

2) Buchō ni Nihon-ningyō o moraimashita. ……

3) Ashita no gogo Nihon o shuppatsu-shimasu. ……

4) Suzuki-sensei o yoku shitte imasu. ……

6. Rei: Bangohan wa mō meshiagarimashita ka. (hai)
……Hai, itadakimashita.

1) Pasupōto o motte irasshaimasu ka. (hai)
……

2) Ano kata o go-zonji desu ka. (iie)
……

3) Hakone de totta shashin o goran ni narimashita ka. (hai)
……

4) Ashita no yotei o o-kiki ni narimashita ka. (hai)
……

7. Rei: Moshi moshi, Tanaka-san no (otaku) desu ka.

1) A: Moshi moshi, Tōkyō-denki de ( ).

B: Tanaka to ( ) ga, Katō-san wa ( ) ka.

A: Mōshiwake arimasen. Katō wa ima Ōsaka e shutchō-shite ( ).

B: Itsu ( ) ka.

A: Ashita modorimasu.

B: Ja, mata ashita ( ).

2) A: Ā, Tanaka-san, shibaraku desu. Rao desu.

B: Ā, Rao-san, o-genki desu ka.

A: Ē, okagesama de, genki desu.
Tanaka-san wa ashita no pātii ni ( ) ka.

B: Ē, ( ).

A: Ja, 5-ji ni robii de ( ) shite imasu.

B: Wakarimashita.

A: Dewa, shitsurei-shimasu.

50

8. Rei: Minasan, <u>konbanwa</u>.

Watashi wa Rao to ________________. Indo kara ________________.
Watashi wa Sentā de 5-shūkan Nihon-go o benkyō-________________.
Sorekara Tōkyō-denki de 6-kagetsu konpyūtā o jisshū-________________.
Jisshū wa totemo ________________ ni narimashita. Kuni e kaette mo,
kono ________________, ganbaritai to omoimasu. Minasan no
________________ wa wasuremasen. Hontō ni arigatō gozaimashita.

Fukushū J

1. Rei: Suzuki-sensei (ni) Nihon-go o oshiete itadakimashita.
   1) Musume ( ) ningyō o katte yarimashita.
   2) Tōkyō-tawā e ikitai'n desu ( ), michi o oshiete itadakemasen ka.
   3) Raishū no happyō ( ) tame ni, iroiro junbi-shite imasu.
   4) Chikaku ni sūpā ga atte, kaimono ( ) benri desu.
   5) Kono doriru wa ita ( ) ana o akeru no ( ) tsukaimasu.
   6) Tana kara nimotsu ( ) ochisō desu.
   7) Kopii no ōkisa o 2-bai ( ) shimasu.
   8) Rain ( ) mondai ga okita baai wa, ranpu ga aka ( ) kawarimasu.
   9) Ame ( ) baai wa, pikunikku o raishū ( ) shimasu.
   10) Chizu o motte itta noni, michi ( ) mayotte shimaimashita.
   11) Kono kuruma ( ) shūri-shita bakari na noni, mō koshō-shite shimaimashita.
   12) Buchō wa Katō-san ( ) Ōsaka e shutchō-sasemashita.
   13) Watashi wa musume ( ) ryōri o tetsudawasemasu.
   14) Watashi wa Tanaka ( ) mōshimasu.
   15) Sensei ga Bangkok e irasshattara, watashi ( ) go-annai shimasu.

2.

	sonkei	**kenjō**
Rei: imasu	irasshaimasu	orimasu
ikimasu, kimasu		
	osshaimasu	
tabemasu, nomimasu		itadakimasu
	nasaimasu	
mimasu	goran ni narimasu	
shitte imasu		zonjite orimasu
	o-kiki ni narimasu	

3. Tadashii mono o erande kudasai.

1) Kono bideo no haitatsu o onegai-dekimasu ka.

…Hai, { a. kashikomarimashita. / b. sono tōri desu. / c. gokurōsama deshita. }

2) Kusuri o nonde iru noni, mada kaze ga naoranai'n desu.

… { a. Sore wa ikemasen ne. / b. Sore hodo demo arimasen. / c. Shikata ga arimasen ne. } Dōzo odaiji ni.

3) Kono hon, dōmo arigatō gozaimashita. Watashi no senmon to kankei ga atta node, { a. totemo kurō-shimashita. / b. totemo tasukarimashita. / c. o-matase shimashita. }

…Sore wa yokatta desu ne.

4) Shibaraku desu ne. O-kawari arimasen ka.

…Ē, { a. otsukaresama / b. okagesama de / c. kochira koso }, genki desu.

5) Jisshū wa dō deshita ka.

… { a. Otsukaresama deshita. / b. Tanoshimi ni shite imasu. / c. Totemo ii benkyō ni narimashita. }

Kono keiken o ikashite, korekara mo ganbaritai to omoimasu.

Fukushū K

1. (   ) no naka ni "yomu" o iroirona katachi ni kaete, irete kudasai.

   Rei: Watashi wa rekishi no hon o (yomi)tai desu.

   1) Himana toki, ongaku o kiitari, hon o (   )ri shite imasu.
   2) Shinbun o (   )nagara gohan o tabemasu.
   3) Kaigi no mae ni, kono shiryō o yoku (   ) oite kudasai.
   4) Kono zasshi wa mada (   ) imasen.
   Konban (   ) to omotte imasu.
   5) Hiragana wa yomemasu ga, katakana wa sukoshi shika (   ).
   6) Nihon no shinbun ga sukoshi (   ) yō ni narimashita.
   7) Kono kanji wa nan to (   )'n desu ka.
   8) Kono hon wa iroirona kuni de (   ) imasu.
   9) Watashi wa hon o (   ) no ga suki desu.
   10) Tegami o (   ), anshin-shimashita.
   11) Kono jisho wa ji ga chiisakute, (   )nikui desu.
   12) Hon o (   )-sugite, me ga itaku narimashita.
   13) Kesa no shinbun wa mō yomimashita ka.
   …Iie, korekara (   ) tokoro desu.
   14) Kodomo ni ii hon o takusan (   )semasu.
   15) Sono hon o (   )ra, watashi ni mo (   )sete itadakemasen ka.
   16) Setsumeisho o (   )ba, tsukai-kata ga wakarimasu.
   17) Muzukashikute, ikura (   ) mo, imi ga wakarimasen.
   18) Neru mae ni, itsumo kodomo ni hon o (   ) yarimasu.
   19) Kinō (   ) hon wa totemo omoshirokatta desu.
   20) Buchō wa Rao-san no repōto o (   )remashita ka.
   21) Sensei wa mō kono hon o o-(   ) ni narimashita ka.

2. Rei: Ashita wa tabun (ame desu … ame) deshō.

   1) Watashi wa karaoke ga suki dewa arimasen.
   Uta ga (heta desu …   )'n desu.
   2) Kare wa kinō kara kaisha o yasunde imasu.
   (Byōki desu …   ) kamo shiremasen.

K

3) Nedan ga (yasui desu ···)ba, kono terebi o kaimasu.

4) Sōsa ga (kantan desu ···) nara, kono bideo-kamera o kaimasu.

5) Kono nimotsu wa (omoi desu ···), motemasen.

6) (Takai desu ···) ga donokurai aru ka, hakatte mite kudasai.

7) A, kotchi no ringo no hō ga akakute, (oishii desu ···)sō desu yo.

8) Kochira no bideo-kamera wa ikaga desu ka.
···Ā, sōsa ga (kantan desu ···)sō desu ne. Kore o kudasai.

9) Kono zubon wa (nagai desu ···)-sugimasu kara, motto (mijikai desu ···) shite kudasai.

10) Urusai desu kara, (shizuka desu ···) shite kudasai.

11) Narong-san no hanashi ni yoru to, Tai wa kireina (kuni desu ···) sō desu.

12) Lee-san wa konogoro shigoto ga (hima desu ···) yō desu.

13) Ashita wa (nichi-yōbi desu ···) noni, kaisha e ikanakereba narimasen.

14) Kono mise wa shurui mo (ōi desu ···) shi, shinamono mo (kirei desu ···) shi, koko de kaimashō.

3. Tadashii mono o erande kudasai.

1) Kaisha ni renraku-shitai node,
chotto denwa o { a. tsukatte kudasaimasen ka. / b. tsukatte itadakemasen ka. / c. tsukawasete itadakemasen ka. }

2) Kono ryōri wa kara-sugite, { a. tabemasen. / b. taberaremasen. / c. tabe-sugimashita. }

3) Tenki-yohō ni yoru to, ashita wa ame ga { a. furisō desu. / b. furu sō desu. / c. furu to omoimasu. }

K

4) Mukō ni patokā ga tomatte imasu.

Dōmo
- a. jiko da sō desu.
- b. jiko no yō desu.
- c. jiko deshō.

5) Basu ga nakanaka konakatta node,
- a. kaisha ni okurete shimaimashita.
- b. takushii de itta hō ga ii desu.
- c. itsu kuru ka, wakarimasen.

6) Jishin ga okita baai wa,
- a. uchi ga kowaremashita.
- b. bikkuri-shimashita.
- c. sugu hi o keshite kudasai.

7) Kono isu wa penki o nutta bakari desu kara,
- a. suwatte mo ii desu.
- b. suwaru yō ni shite kudasai.
- c. suwaranai yō ni shite kudasai.

8) Jidō-hanbaiki ni okane o ireta noni, tabako ga
- a. demasu.
- b. demasen.
- c. dete shimaimashita.

9) Osoku narimashita kara, sorosoro shitsurei-shimasu.

…Sō desu ka. Ja, musuko ni eki made
- a. okuraremasu.
- b. okurasemasu.
- c. okutte yarimasu.

10) Sensei, sono nimotsu wa omosō desu ne.

Watashi ga
- a. o-mochi shimasu.
- b. o-mochi ni narimasu.
- c. motasemasu.

4. a to b ga daitai onaji imi ni naru yō ni, ( ) ni kotoba o irete kudasai.

Rei: a: Ashita wa tabun ii tenki da to omoimasu.

b: Ashita wa tabun (ii tenki deshō).

1) a: Natsu-yasumi wa Karuizawa e iku tsumori desu.

b: Natsu-yasumi wa Karuizawa e ( ) to omotte imasu.

2) a: Watashi wa mada jōzu ni Nihon-go o hanasu koto ga dekimasen.

b: Watashi wa mada jōzu ni ( ).

3) a: Kono resutoran wa nedan ga yasukute, mise no hito ga shinsetsuna node, itsumo koko de tabete imasu.

b: Kono resutoran wa ( ) shi,
( ) shi, itsumo koko de tabete imasu.

4) a: Mōtā no oto ga okashii desu. Koshō kamo shiremasen.

b: Mōtā no oto ga okashii desu. ( ) yō desu.

5) a: Shigoto ga owatte kara, tomodachi to shokuji ni ikimasu.

b: Shigoto ga ( ) ato de, tomodachi to shokuji ni ikimasu.

6) a: Tenki ga yokattara, koko kara Fujisan ga miemasu.

b: Tenki ga ( )ba, koko kara Fujisan ga miemasu.

7) a: Kaisha ni okureru toki wa, kanarazu renraku-shite kudasai.

b: Kaisha ni okureru toki wa, kanarazu ( ) yō ni shite kudasai.

8) a: Watashi wa buchō ni ryō made kuruma de okutte itadakimashita.

b: Buchō wa watashi o ryō made kuruma de ( ).

9) a: Netsu ga arimasu kara, hayaku kaette mo ii desu ka.

b: Netsu ga ( ) node, hayaku ( ) itadakemasen ka.

10) a: Shachō wa mō otaku e kaeraremashita.

b: Shachō wa mō otaku e o-( ) ni narimashita.

Joshi

1. **[wa]**

   1) Kono isu wa kowarete imasu. (Dai 29 ka)

   2) Repōto wa mō kakimashita ka.
   …Iie, mada kaite imasen. (31)

   3) Kōjō no naka de wa arukinagara tabako o suwanai de kudasai. (28)

   4) Hiragana wa kakemasu ga, katakana wa kakemasen. (27)

2. **[mo]**

   Nimotsu mo ōi shi, ame mo futte iru shi, takushii de kaerimasu. (28)

3. **[no]**

   1) Shutchō wa 1-shūkan gurai no yotei desu. (31)

   2) Manyuaru no tōri ni, kikai o sōsa-shite kudasai. (34)

   3) Mainichi sagyō no ato de, miitingu o shite imasu. (34)

   4) Kazoku no tame ni, isshōkenmei hatarakimasu. (42)

   5) Ame no baai wa, pikunikku o raishū ni shimasu. (45)

   6) Mukō ni patokā ga tomatte imasu. Dōmo jiko no yō desu. (47)

4. **[o]**

   1) Katō-san wa watashi o uchi e shōtai-shite kudasaimashita. (41)

   2) Buchō wa Katō-san o Ōsaka e shutchō-sasemashita. (48)

   3) Terebi no oto o ōkiku shite kudasai. (44)

   4) 12-ji o sugita noni, Narong-san wa mada kaette kimasen. (45)

5. **[ga]**

   1) Watashi wa Nihon-go ga sukoshi hanasemasu. (27)

   2) Shigoto ga isogashikute, doko mo ikemasen. (39)

   3) Ikeda-san wa wāpuro o utsu no ga hayai desu. (38)

   4) Heya kara umi ga miemasu. (27)

   5) Eki no chikaku ni sūpā ga dekimashita. (27)

6) Denki ga tsuite imasu. (29)

7) Ashita kanai ga Nihon e kimasu. (31)

8) Asoko ni posutā ga hatte arimasu. (30)

9) Koko de kuruma no bodii ga yōsetsu-saremasu. (37)

10) Watashi ga yarimasu kara, sono mama ni shite oite kudasai. (30)

11) Michi ga wakaranai'n desu ga, oshiete kudasaimasen ka. (26)

6. **[ni]**

1) Kare ni kono shigoto o tanomimasu. (28)

2) Watashi wa otōto ni kamera o kowasaremashita. (37)

3) Watashi wa musume ni piano o narawasemasu. (48)

4) Ishikawa-san ni otoko no ko ga umaremashita. (38)

5) Hikōki wa 6-ji ni Nihon ni tsukimasu. (27)

6) Takushii ni kamera o wasurete shimaimashita. (29)

7) Kabe ni e ga kakete arimasu. (30)

8) Koin-rokkā ni nimotsu o azukete kimasu. (43)

9) Kono kikai wa ita ni ana o akeru no ni tsukaimasu. (42)

10) Rain ni mondai ga okita baai wa, sugu suitchi o kitte kudasai. (45)

11) Kaigi no jikan ni okuremashita. (26)

12) Ame no baai wa, pikunikku o raishū ni shimasu. (45)

13) Karada ni warui desu kara, tabako o yameta hō ga ii desu. (32)

14) Watashi no uchi wa chikaku ni mise ga atte, kaimono ni benri desu. (42)

15) Yatto Nihon no seikatsu ni naremashita. (36)

16) Nihon-go de shitsumon ni kotaeru no wa muzukashii desu. (38)

17) Mainichi densha de kaisha ni kayoimasu. (38)

18) Chizu o motte itta noni, michi ni mayotte shimaimashita. (46)

19) Kono kōjō de wa 1-nichi ni 1,500-dai kuruma ga seisan-sarete imasu. (37)

20) Kono tēburu ni wa atarashii zairyō ga tsukawarete imasu. (44)

7. **[de]**

1) Supōtsu-sentā made 5, 6-pun de ikemasu. (27)
2) Kyō no jisshū wa kore de owarimasu. (30)
3) Enjin o kumitatemashita. Kore de ii desu ka. (34)
4) Sumimasen ga, mō sukoshi ōkii koe de itte kudasai. (27)
5) Byōki de kaisha o yasumimashita. (39)

8. **[to]**

1) Ashita Ōsakajō e ikō to omotte imasu. (31)
2) Asoko ni "Tomare" to kaite arimasu. (33)
3) Kono jisshū wa watashi no senmon to kankei ga arimasen. (40)

9. **[kara]**

1) O-sake wa kome kara tsukuraremasu. (37)
2) Sakki honsha no Yoshida-san kara denwa ga arimashita. (33)

10. **[ka]**

1) Kaigi wa nan-ji ni owaru ka, wakarimasen. (40)
2) Pātii ni korareru ka dō ka, shirasete kudasai. (40)
3) Kodomo ni tokei ka rajikase o katte yaritai desu. (41)

Fōmu no tsukai-kata

1. **[masu-kei]**

masu-kei + nagara ~	Ongaku o kikinagara kōhii o nomimasu. (Dai 28 ka)
masu-kei + yasui desu	Kono jisho wa ji ga ōkikute, miyasui desu. (44)
masu-kei + nikui desu	Netsu ni tsuyokute, iro ga kawarinikui desu. (44)
o + **masu-kei** + ni narimasu	Buchō wa mō o-kaeri ni narimashita. (49)
o + **masu-kei** + shimasu	Watashi ga sensei no nimotsu o o-mochi shimasu. (50)

2. **[te-kei]**

te-kei + imasu	Himana toki, itsumo terebi o mite imasu. (28)
	Denki ga tsuite imasu. (29)
te-kei + imasen	Repōto wa mada matomete imasen. (31)
te-kei + shimaimashita	Takushii ni kamera o wasurete shimaimashita. (29)
te-kei + arimasu	Kabe ni e ga kakete arimasu. (30)
te-kei + okimasu	Ryokō ni iku mae ni, kippu o katte okimasu. (30)
te-kei + kure	Kono nimotsu wa jama da kara, katazukete kure. (33)
te-kei + mimasu	Nihon no o-sake o nonde mimasu. (40)
te-kei + itadakimasu	Watashi wa Suzuki-sensei ni Nihon-go o oshiete itadakimashita. (41)
te-kei + kudasaimasu	Okusan wa watashi ni Nihon-ryōri o tsukutte kudasaimashita. (41)
te-kei + yarimasu	Watashi wa musume ni tanjōbi no purezento o okutte yarimashita. (41)
te-kei + kudasaimasen ka	Michi ga wakaranai'n desu ga, oshiete kudasaimasen ka. (26)
te-kei + itadakemasen ka	Tegami no kaki-kata o oshiete itadakemasen ka. (41)
te-kei + kimasu	Chotto tabako o katte kimasu. (43)

3. **[nai-kei]**

nai-kei + nai de, ~	Eigo o tsukawanai de, Nihon-go dake de jisshū-shimasu.	(34)

4. **[jisho-kei]**

jisho-kei + tsumori desu	Rainen kekkon-suru tsumori desu.	(31)
jisho-kei + na	Suitchi ni sawaru na.	(33)
jisho-kei + yō ni narimashita	Nihon-go ga hanaseru yō ni narimashita.	(36)
jisho-kei + no wa ~	Minna de shokuji-suru no wa tanoshii desu.	(38)
jisho-kei + no ga ~	Watashi wa hon o yomu no ga suki desu.	(38)
jisho-kei + tame ni, ~	Uchi o kau tame ni, okane o tamete imasu.	(42)
jisho-kei + no ni ~	Kono doraibā wa chiisai neji o shimeru no ni tsukaimasu.	(42)

5. **[ta-kei]**

ta-kei + tōri ni, ~	Ima watashi ga yatta tōri ni, enjin o kumitatete kudasai.	(34)
ta-kei + ato de, ~	Shigoto ga owatta ato de, kaisha no hito to shokuji ni ikimasu.	(34)
ta-kei + bakari desu	Kare wa senshū Nihon e kita bakari desu.	(46)

6. **[ikō-kei]**

ikō-kei + to omotte imasu	Ashita ōsakajō e ikō to omotte imasu.	(31)

7.

{**jisho-kei** / **nai-kei** ~nai} + yō ni, ~	Nihon-go ga jōzu ni naru yō ni, isshōkenmei benkyō-shimasu.	(36)
	Wasurenai yō ni, memo o totte kudasai.	(36)
{**jisho-kei** / **nai-kei** ~nai} + yō ni shite kudasai	Kanarazu jikan o mamoru yō ni shite kudasai.	(36)
	Jikan ni okurenai yō ni shite kudasai.	(36)

8. **jisho-kei** / **te-kei** + iru / **ta-kei** } + tokoro desu	Chōdo ima kara eiga ga hajimaru tokoro desu. (46)
	Ima ryōri o tsukutte iru tokoro desu. (46)
	Tattaima shigoto ga owatta tokoro desu. (46)
9. **ta-kei** / **nai-kei** ~nai } + hō ga ii desu	Sugu byōin e itta hō ga ii desu. (32)
	Kyō wa o-furo ni hairanai hō ga ii desu. (32)
10. **te-kei** / **nai-kei** ~nai de } + ~	Manyuaru o mite sōsa-shimasu. (34)
	Saifu o motanai de dekakete shimaimashita. (34)
11. **[futsū-kei]**	
futsū-kei + shi, ~	Nimotsu mo ōi shi, ame mo futte iru shi, takushii de kaerimasu. (28)
futsū-kei + to itte imashita	Yoshida-san wa kaigi no shiryō o okutte kure to itte imashita. (33)
futsū-kei + sō desu	Tenki-yohō ni yoru to, ashita wa ame ga furu sō desu. (47)
dōshi futsū-kei + no o ~	Kimura-san ga kekkon-shita no o shitte imasu ka. (38)
dōshi / **i-keiyōshi** } **futsū-kei**; **na-keiyōshi** / **meishi** } **futsū-kei** ~ ~~da~~ } + deshō	Zutto ii tenki na node, ashita mo hareru deshō. (32)
	Ashita no asa wa samui deshō. (32)
	Ashita wa tabun ii tenki deshō. (32)
dōshi / **i-keiyōshi** } **futsū-kei**; **na-keiyōshi** / **meishi** } **futsū-kei** ~ ~~da~~ } + kamo shiremasen	Gogo kara yuki ga furu kamo shiremasen. (32)
	Ashita no shiken wa muzukashii kamo shiremasen. (32)
	Kare wa byōki kamo shiremasen. (32)

dōshi, **i-keiyōshi** — **futsū-kei**
na-keiyōshi — **futsū-kei**
meishi — ~ ~~da~~
+ ka, ~

Kaigi wa nan-ji ni owaru ka, wakarimasen. (40)
Koshō no toki, dō shitara ii ka, oshiete kudasai. (40)
Kōbe wa donna machi ka, shirimasen. (40)

dōshi, **i-keiyōshi** — **futsū-kei**
na-keiyōshi — **futsū-kei**
meishi — ~ ~~da~~
+ ka dō ka, ~

Pātii ni korareru ka dō ka, shirasete kudasai. (40)
Kotae ga tadashii ka dō ka, tashikamete kudasai. (40)
Sono hanashi wa hontō ka dō ka, wakarimasen. (40)

dōshi, **i-keiyōshi** — **futsū-kei**
na-keiyōshi — **futsū-kei**
meishi — ~ da→ ~na
+ n desu

Kaze o hiita'n desu. (26)
Kinō wa isogashikatta'n desu. (26)
Kanai ga byōki na'n desu. (26)

dōshi, **i-keiyōshi** — **futsū-kei**
na-keiyōshi — **futsū-kei**
meishi — ~ da→ ~na
+ node, ~

Yōji ga aru node, hayaku kaerimasu. (39)
Kibun ga warui node, kaette mo ii desu ka. (39)
Kyō wa nichi-yōbi na node, kuruma ga sukunai desu. (39)

dōshi, **i-keiyōshi** — **futsū-kei**
na-keiyōshi — **futsū-kei**
meishi — ~ da→ ~na
+ noni, ~

Kusuri o nonda noni, mada netsu ga sagarimasen. (45)
Kono kami wa usui noni, yaburenikui desu. (45)
Kyō wa nichi-yōbi na noni, kaisha e ikanakereba narimasen. (45)

dōshi, **i-keiyōshi** — **futsū-kei**
na-keiyōshi **futsū-kei**
~ da→ ~na
meishi **futsū-kei**
~ da→ ~ no
+ yō desu

Dareka kita yō desu. (47)
Lee-san wa kyō wa himana yō desu. (47)
Lee-san wa dōmo byōki no yō desu. (47)

12. **dōshi masu-kei** **i-keiyōshi** ~i̸ **na-keiyōshi** } + sō desu	Imanimo ame ga furisō desu. Kono ryōri wa oishisō desu. Kono hako wa jōbusō desu.	(43) (43) (43)
dōshi masu-kei **i-keiyōshi** ~i̸ **na-keiyōshi** } + sugimasu	Yūbe o-sake o nomi-sugimashita. Kono kutsu wa chiisa-sugimasu. Kono mondai wa fukuzatsu-sugimasu.	(44) (44) (44)
13. **dōshi te-kei,** **i-keiyōshi** ~i̸ kute, **na-keiyōshi**, **meishi** } ~ de, } + ~	Tegami o yonde, anshin-shimashita. Tsugō ga warukute, ikemasen. Sōsa ga fukuzatsu de, mada oboeraremasen.	(39) (39) (39)
14. **dōshi ta-kei**, **nai-kei** ~nai **i-keiyōshi** ~i **na-keiyōshi** ~na **meishi** ~ no } + baai wa, ~	Jishin ga okita baai wa, sugu hi o keshite kudasai. Tsukai-kata ga wakaranai baai wa, watashi o yonde kudasai. Ame no baai wa, pikunikku o raishū ni shimasu.	(45) (45) (45)

Dōshi, keiyōshi no iroirona tsukai-kata

1. **hayai** (i-keiyōshi) ⟶ **hayaku** (fukushi)

hayai	Maiasa hayaku okimasu.	(Dai 14 ka)
hayai	Nihon-jin wa hayaku hanashimasu.	(14)
ii	Nihon-go ga yoku wakarimasu.	(9)
	Gakusei no toki, yoku sukii ni ikimashita.	(23)
umai	Shigoto ga umaku ikimashita.	(34)
kuwashii	Jisshū no naiyō o kuwashiku kakimasu.	(36)

2. **jōzu[na]** (na-keiyōshi) ⟶ **jōzu ni** (fukushi)

jōzu[na]	Nihon-go ga mada jōzu ni hanasemasen.	(27)
kirei[na]	Heya o kirei ni sōji-shimasu.	(30)
buji[na]	Buji ni jisshū ga owarimashita.	(50)

3. **ōkii** (i-keiyōshi) ⟶ **Ōkiku narimasu.**
jōzu[na] (na-keiyōshi) ⟶ **Jōzu ni narimasu.**
tenki (meishi) ⟶ **Tenki ni narimasu.**

Kore o mawasu to, oto ga ōkiku narimasu.	(19)
Nihon-go ga jōzu ni narimashita.	(19)
Kyō wa ii tenki ni narimashita.	(19)

4. **mijikai** (i-keiyōshi) ⟶ **Mijikaku shimasu.**
kirei[na] (na-keiyōshi) ⟶ **Kirei ni shimasu.**
hanbun (meishi) ⟶ **Hanbun ni shimasu.**

Naga-sugimasu kara, mijikaku shite kudasai.	(44)
Heya o kirei ni shite kudasai.	(44)
Nihon-jin wa jikan o muda ni shimasen.	(38)
Kazoku no minasan ga shinsetsu ni shite kudasaimashita.	(41)
Gohan no ryō o hanbun ni shimasu.	(44)

5. **nagai** (i-keiyōshi) ⟶ **nagasa** (meishi)

nagai	Paipu no nagasa o hakatte kudasai.	(40)
omoi	Kono nimotsu wa omosa ga 5-kiro arimasu.	(40)
takai	Tōkyō-tawā no takasa wa 333-mētoru desu.	(40)
ōkii	Ji no ōkisa o 2-bai ni shimasu.	(40)

6. **yasumimasu** (dōshi) ⟶ **yasumi** (meishi)

yasumimasu	Ashita wa yasumi desu.	(12)
hajimemasu	Raigetsu no hajime ni Tai e ikimasu.	(31)
owarimasu	8-gatsu no owari ni kuni e kaerimasu.	(31)
hanashimasu	Nihon-jin no hanashi ga wakaru yō ni narimashita.	(36)
kumitatemasu	Koko wa kumitate-rain desu.	(37)
kaerimasu	Kaisha no kaeri ni yoku nomi-ya e ikimasu.	(38)
ikimasu	Iki mo kaeri mo densha ga konde imasu.	(38)

7. **tsukaimasu** (dōshi) ⟶ **tsukai-kata** (meishi)

tsukaimasu	Wāpuro no tsukai-kata o oshiete kudasai.	(14)
kakimasu	Tegami no kaki-kata o oshiete kudasai.	(14)
yomimasu	Kanji no yomi-kata ga wakarimasen.	(14)
shimasu	Kikai no sōsa no shi-kata ga wakarimasen.	(26)

Jidōshi to tadōshi

{ tadōshi { jidōshi	ka	te-kei	reibun
tsukemasu **tsukimasu**	15 26	tsukete tsuite	Denki o tsukete kudasai. Denki ga tsuite imasu.
keshimasu **kiemasu**	15 26	keshite kiete	Denki o keshite kudasai. Denki ga kiete imasu.
akemasu **akimasu**	15 26	akete aite	Mado o akete kudasai. Mado ga aite imasu.
shimemasu **shimarimasu**	15 26	shimete shimatte	Mado o shimete kudasai. Mado ga shimatte imasu.
kowashimasu **kowaremasu**	37 29	kowashite kowarete	Kodomo wa tokei o kowashimashita. Kono isu wa kowarete imasu.
kirimasu **kiremasu**	7 29	kitte kirete	Hasami de kami o kitte kudasai. Himo ga kirete imasu.
kakemasu **kakarimasu**	38 29	kakete kakatte	Kagi o kakete oite kudasai. Kagi ga kakatte imasu.
kakemasu **kakarimasu**	7 47	kakete kakatte	Kaisha ni denwa o kakemasu. Denwa ga nakanaka kakarimasen.
iremasu **hairimasu**	17 13	irete haitte	Kōhii ni satō o irete kudasai. Kaban ni hon ga haitte imasu.
dashimasu **demasu**	17 23	dashite dete	Kaban kara hon o dashite kudasai. Botan o osu to, kippu ga demasu.

tadōshi / jidōshi	ka	te-kei	reibun
agemasu **agarimasu**	33 32	agete agatte	Kurēn de nimotsu o agemasu. Netsu ga agarimasu.
sagemasu **sagarimasu**	33 32	sagete sagatte	Kurēn de nimotsu o sagemasu. Netsu ga sagarimasu.
naoshimasu **naorimasu**	18 32	naoshite naotte	Isu o naoshite kudasai. Byōki ga naorimashita.
otoshimasu **ochimasu**	29 36	otoshite ochite	Koppu o otoshite shimaimashita. Tana kara nimotsu ga ochimasu.
urimasu **uremasu**	15 35	utte urete	Depāto de iroirona mono o utte imasu. Kono bideo ga ichiban yoku urete imasu.
atsumemasu **atsumarimasu**	38 47	atsumete atsumatte	Watashi wa sekai no kitte o atsumete imasu. Mukō ni hito ga atsumatte imasu.
mitsukemasu **mitsukarimasu**	40 46	mitsukete mitsukatte	Bin no kizu o mitsukemashita. Kagi ga mitsukarimasen.
nakushimasu **nakunarimasu**	17 43	nakushite nakunatte	Pasupōto o nakushite shimaimashita. Gasorin ga nakunatte shimaimashita.
kaemasu **kawarimasu**	13 44	kaete kawatte	Jisshū no yotei o kaemasu. Jisshū no yotei ga kawarimashita.
hajimemasu **hajimarimasu**	18 45	hajimete hajimatte	9-ji kara benkyō o hajimemasu. Mōsugu kaigi ga hajimarimasu.

Fukushi, fukushi-teki hyōgen

1.	**sakki**	Sakki honsha no Yoshida-san kara denwa ga arimashita.	(Dai 33 ka)
	tattaima	Tattaima densha ga deta tokoro desu.	(46)
	chōdo	Chōdo ima kara eiga ga hajimaru tokoro desu.	(46)
	mōsugu	Mōsugu natsu-yasumi desu.	(31)
	konogoro	Konogoro kaji ga ōi node, ki o tsukete kudasai.	(45)
	itsu made mo	Itsu made mo Nihon no koto o wasuremasen.	(44)
2.	**zenbu**	Kono botan o osu to, kikai ga zenbu tomarimasu.	(36)
	hotondo	Katakana ga hotondo kakeru yō ni narimashita.	(36)
	kanari	Nihon-go ga kanari hanaseru yō ni narimashita.	(36)
	zuibun	Kyō wa zuibun hito ga ōi desu ne.	(28)
	sukoshi zutsu	Ryokō ni iku tame ni, sukoshi zutsu okane o tamemasu.	(42)
	tama ni	Itsumo Nihon no eiga o mimasu ga, tama ni Amerika no eiga o mimasu.	(45)
3.	**mazu**	Mazu koko ni kono buhin o toritsukemasu.	(34)
	tsugi ni	Tsugi ni pakkingu o hamemasu.	(34)
	saki ni	Saki ni heya e ikimashō. Sorekara ryō no naka o annai-shimasu.	(26)
	saisho ni	Saisho ni shachō ga aisatsu-nasaimasu.	(49)
	saigo ni	Saigo ni watashi ga aisatsu-itashimasu.	(49)
4.	**nakanaka**	Kotoba ga nakanaka oboeraremasen.	(27)
	zettai ni	Kono kikai ni zettai ni sawaranai yō ni shite kudasai.	(36)
	kanarazu	Kaisha o yasumu toki wa, kanarazu denwa de renraku-suru yō ni shite kudasai.	(33)
	man'ichi	Man'ichi kaji ga okita baai wa, sugu 119-ban ni denwa-shite kudasai.	(45)
	dōmo	Hito ga atsumatte imasu. Dōmo jiko no yō desu.	(47)
	imanimo	Imanimo ame ga furisō desu.	(43)

5. **jōzu ni**	Nihon-go ga mada jōzu ni hanasemasen.	(27)
kirei ni	Heya o kirei ni sōji-shite oite kudasai.	(30)
buji ni	Okagesama de buji ni jisshū ga owarimashita.	(50)
umaku	Shigoto ga umaku ikimashita.	(34)
kuwashiku	Repōto ni jisshū no kansō o kuwashiku kaite kudasai.	(36)
6. **hakkiri**	Tenki ga warukute, Fujisan ga hakkiri miemasen.	(27)
yukkuri	Natsu-yasumi wa inaka de yukkuri yasumu tsumori desu.	(31)
pittari	Kono fuku wa saizu ga pittari aimasu.	(40)
shikkari	Boruto o shikkari shimete kudasai.	(34)
kichinto	Dōgu o kichinto shimatte oite kudasai.	(30)
isshōkenmei	Isshōkenmei gijutsu o narau tsumori desu.	(31)
mada	Mada kōgu o tsukatte imasu kara, sono mama ni shite oite kudasai.	(30)
zutto	Zutto ii tenki desu kara, ashita mo hareru deshō.	(32)
yatto	Sakura ga nakanaka sakimasendeshita ga, yatto sakimashita.	(28)

Setsuzoku no iroiro

1. **~nagara**	Terebi o minagara gohan o tabemasu.	(Dai 28 ka)
~ shi	Kirei da shi, nioi mo ii shi, kono hana o kaimashō.	(28)
soreni	Dōshite itsumo kono mise de kaimono-suru'n desu ka.	
	…Nedan mo yasui shi, soreni shinamono mo ōi desu kara.	(28)
~ toka	Repōto ni donna koto o kaitara ii desu ka.	
	…Tatoeba koko ga yokatta toka, muzukashikatta toka, jibun no kansō o kaite kudasai.	(36)
2. **sorede**	Kono resutoran wa oishii shi, nedan mo yasui desu.	
	…Sorede hito ga ōi'n desu ne.	(28)
~te	Kesa no nyūsu o kiite, bikkuri-shimashita.	(39)
~kute	Shigoto ga isogashikute, doko mo ikemasen.	(39)
~ de	Sōsa ga fukuzatsu de, yoku wakarimasen.	(39)
	Jishin de uchi ga kowaremashita.	(39)
~ node	Yōji ga aru node, hayaku kaerimasu.	(39)
	Ashita wa yasumi na node, tomodachi to dekakemasu.	(39)
3. **shikashi**	Kono kōjō wa chiisai desu. Shikashi, ii seihin o tsukutte imasu.	(40)
~ noni	Kusuri o nonda noni, mada netsu ga sagarimasen.	(45)
	Nichi-yōbi na noni, kaisha e ikanakereba narimasen.	(45)
4. **~ba**	Kono setsumeisho o yomeba, tsukai-kata ga wakarimasu.	(35)
	Nedan ga yasukereba, kaimasu.	(35)
~ nara	Kamera nara, Shinjuku ga yasui desu.	(35)
~ baai wa	Man'ichi kaji ga okita baai wa, 119-ban ni denwa-shite kudasai.	(45)
	Ame no baai wa, pikunikku o raishū ni shimasu.	(45)

5. **soreja**	Tomodachi no kekkonshiki ga aru node, hayaku kaette mo ii desu ka.	
	…Kekkonshiki desu ka. Soreja shikata ga arimasen ne.	(39)
soredewa	Soredewa, korekara Rao-san no sōbetsukai o hajimemasu.	(50)
dewa	Dewa, mazu hajime ni Rao-san ni go-aisatsu o onegai-shimasu.	(50)
6. **tokorode**	Konpyūtā no sōsa ni naremashita ka.	
	…Ē, okagesama de.	
	Yokatta desu ne. Tokorode, repōto no koto desu ga, kansō ga kaite arimasen ne.	(36)

Sakuin

— E —

— F —

— G —

— H —

— I —

— J —

— K —

— M —

— O —

— P —

— R —

— S —

— T —

— U —

— W —

新日本語の基礎Ⅱ
本冊　ローマ字版

1993年7月21日　初版第1刷発行
1995年9月22日　第 2 刷 発 行

編　集　財団法人 海外技術者研修協会
発　行　株式会社 スリーエーネットワーク
〒101 東京都千代田区猿楽町2-6-3(松栄ビル)
電話　営業 03(3292)5751
編集 03(3292)6521
印　刷　高山グラフィックス株式会社

 ISBN4-906224-86-5